DANGEROUS INTIMACIES

# DANGEROUS INTIMACIES

*Toward a Sapphic History of the British Novel*

Ⓖ LISA L. MOORE

Duke University Press   Durham & London   1997

820.
9
M78

© 1997 Duke University Press
All rights reserved
Printed in the United States of America on acid-free paper ∞
Typeset in Monotype Garamond by Keystone Typesetting, Inc.
Library of Congress Cataloging-in-Publication Data appear on the
last printed page of this book.

⑥ CONTENTS

# ⑥ ACKNOWLEDGMENTS

Many people have contributed to the labor of putting this book together, and I am grateful to all of them. But a few deserve special mention. Ann Cvetkovich tirelessly and on short notice read draft after draft of the manuscript and always offered just the right professional and personal perspective to help me get to the next stage of the project. She's a superb colleague and friend, as is Laura Mandell, who read Chapter 3 and the Conclusion cheerfully and at the last minute, making it possible to complete the book. Elizabeth Butler Cullingford's generous and exhaustive comments on a near final draft were most helpful. Ken Wissoker's intelligent and compassionate guidance through the editorial process has been invaluable. My students in a 1992 graduate seminar at the University of Texas, "Inventing Sexuality in Eighteenth-Century Prose," will recognize many of their own insights on these pages. Many other teachers, friends, and colleagues read portions of this manuscript along the way, and I thank them; they include Sabrina Barton, Phillip Barrish, Lance Bertelson, Scarlett Bowen, Laura Brown, Zofia Burr, Walter Cohen, Andrew Cooper, Mary Jacobus, Leah Marcus, Biddy Martin, Terry Rowden, Harry Shaw, Charlotte Sussman, Keith Walters, Helena Woodard, Alok Yadav, and Tim Young.

I am also grateful to those friends who never read the manuscript but who nonetheless were made aware of its every move by a frazzled author; for keeping me sane and even cheerful, I thank Paige Warren, Denise Mayorga; Ann Webb; Katie Kane; Geraldine Heng and Shaan Heng Devan; Bill and Pat

Warren; my aunts Dianne Schultz and Diana Davidson Dick; my sister, Carolyn Moore; and my brother, David Moore. I also appreciate the work of my parents, Joyce and Don Moore, in reading the dissertation that formed the germ of this project.

The astonishing bibliographic and critical resources of my research assistant, George Boulukos, have enriched this project on nearly every page. I also appreciate the research assistance of Janet Hayes and Virginia Woodruff.

Revisions to this manuscript were supported in the summer of 1992 by a Summer Research Award from the University of Texas at Austin.

# Toward a Sapphic History of the British Novel

Female Friends, Female Fiends

In April 1789, as Louis XVI and his family retreated to the National Assembly buildings following the sack of the Tuileries, the English diarist Hester Lynch Thrale reflected on the sexual politics of the situation. In the volumes she later published as *Thraliana,* she mused: "Nature does get strangely out of Fashion sure enough: One hears of Things now, fit for the Pens of Petronius only, or Juvenal to record and satyrize: The Queen of France is at the Head of a Set of Monsters called by each other *Sapphists,* who boast her Example; and deserve to be thrown with the *He* Demons that haunt each other likewise, into Mount Vesuvius." And later Thrale observes, "Mrs. Siddons has told me that her Sister was in personal Danger once from a female Fiend of this Sort; & I have no Reason to disbelieve the Assertion."[1] The equation of homosexuality with foreign, especially French, manners had, of course, a long history in English xenophobia. But the political argument being made here—that the "sapphism" of the queen of France signified a historical moment comparable with the decadence of the Roman Empire as recorded by the Silver Age satirists—suggests that female homosexuality was being pressed epistemologically to explain not only the moral superiority but also the national distinctiveness of the English at a time when the nation was undergoing precipitous political, economic, and cultural threats from within and without.[2] And questions of literary genre—here, satire—are equally called on to explain this overdetermined rumor.

Despite her horror of "female Fiends," Hester Thrale greatly admired the rural retreat of perhaps the most famous female couple of the century, the so-called Ladies of Llangollen, Lady Eleanor Butler and Sarah Ponsonby. Thrale met the couple in 1796 and confessed herself delighted both with their "most heavenly Retreat—a Convent in Miniature" and with the society of the ladies themselves, who by this time were the favored correspondents of many of the leading literary figures of their day, including Edmund Burke, Wordsworth, and Anna Seward, herself the devoted companion of Honora Sneyd.[3] Thrale even composed five stanzas of verse celebrating the relationship and household maintained by Butler and Ponsonby. Perhaps taking Butler and Ponsonby's relationship as a model, Thrale for years pursued the novelist Frances Burney, wheedling and begging her in letters and in person to move into the household as Thrale's companion, confiding to her diary, "If I dye abroad I shall leave all my Papers in Charge with Fanny Burney; I have at length conquered all her Scruples, & won her Confidence & her Heart: 'tis the most valuable Conquest I ever *did* make, and dearly, very dearly, do I love my little *Tayo*, so the People at Otaheite call a *Bosom Friend*."[4] Yet, as I document in Chapter 3, contemporary observers other than Thrale wondered whether Butler and Ponsonby were actually sexually intimate.

How can contemporary critics of eighteenth-century culture understand this paradox? What was it about Marie Antoinette's "sapphism" that allowed Hester Thrale to condemn it so vituperatively, even while she celebrated, admired, and may have sought to emulate Butler and Ponsonby?[5] What are the political and literary consequences of such a distinction? In this book I seek to understand the role played by a particular literary genre—the novel—in the emergence of a post-Enlightenment understanding of sexual identity. I contend that the task of distinguishing "female fiends" such as Marie Antoinette from "female friends" such as Butler and Ponsonby was one of the cultural labors that the novel was called on to perform. The ways in which the novel shaped the self-understanding of its bourgeois readers helped those readers make sense of the public violences being done in the name of Englishness in increasingly private, ultimately psychic terms, allowing for the simultaneous emergence of putative freedoms as well as repressive institutions.

I argue that the late-eighteenth-century English novel is engaged in the complex process of producing identity *per se* as a quintessentially modern category. The modernity of this race-, class-, sex-, gender-, and nation-marked category lies in the characteristic movement by which all these indexes of particularity are erased, so that identity is naturalized and violently imposed hierarchies of difference are universalized out of sight. The category of sexuality, as a discourse of naturalness, is an effective vehicle for "disappearing" external differences, recoding them as differences within, differences of desire. The readings that follow demonstrate the ways in which the Enlightenment fiction of the coherent, unified subject placed enormous pressure on the domestic space to reflect and support this coherence. Yet novels of courtship and marriage must also contend with desire and hence with the body itself; the fiction of unique and knowable selfhood must therefore battle its shadow, the inevitably disruptive, unconscious, and incoherent status of sexuality. Sexual identity thus bears much of the burden for legitimating bourgeois ascension, in that the domestic novel offers powerful stories of the importance of creating and consolidating the domestic space and female virtue within it.

The four novels examined here, when read together, help demonstrate how female homosocial spaces operated a guarantee of English moral purity. Hence the category of female friendship is the principal syntax through which the complicated grammar of gender, sexuality, race, and nation is parsed in this study. Powerful, recent commentators have made it possible to understand how central female sexuality has been to the notion of self articulated out of these collisions. Michel Foucault demonstrates how sexuality came to be considered "the truth of the self," so that what we would now call sexual identity—that complex matrix of practices, desires, disavowals, and fantasized identifications—worked as the ur-text of any identity story.[6] Expanding on Foucault's insight, Nancy Armstrong argues in *Desire and Domestic Fiction* that the feminine "self" emerged by the end of the eighteenth century as the paradigm for modern selfhood, whether masculine or feminine: "The modern individual was first and foremost a woman."[7]

These insights—Foucault's about sexuality and Armstrong's about the gender of identity—suggest the importance of giving priority to female sexuality as an analytic category. If the modern subject was "first and foremost a woman," in Armstrong's terms, and the founding category of modern subjectivity was sexuality, as Foucault argues, then the sexuality of the bourgeois woman came under intense cultural pressure in the late eighteenth century, bearing the weight of cultural explanation that extended far beyond the domestic purview of the middle-class lady.[8] The prominence of "desire" in Armstrong's title seems to promise an exploration of sexuality, but the book's critical lens is that of gender. With increasing urgency, feminist theorists have attempted to disarticulate the categories of sexuality and gender, pointing to the ways in which we repeat the strategy of patriarchal culture by collapsing the two and thus obscure specifically sexual differences among women.[9] I will return to this issue in an examination of lesbian historiography; for the moment, however, I want to note how the work of Foucault has provided a lever with which to pry apart the ideologically embedded category of "female sexuality" by speaking of "sexuality" as a term distinct from gender, perhaps the privileged term through which modern power relations operate. Rather than a natural emanation of gender role or identity, sexuality can be understood as a category that culture must insistently gender (just as gender must be sexualized), a laborious process rendered even more burdensome by the necessity of naturalizing the process itself out of sight. Of course, Foucault's texts themselves fail to pursue these questions; indeed, his supreme disinterest in the sedimentation of power relations into culturally sanctioned institutions such as gender has been the object of much feminist critique of these texts.[10] The possibilities for a feminist reading of pre-, un-, or disgendered sexualities, then, remain open.

The urgency of such a project, however, is brought into relief by the materials I consider in this book. Sexual practices, desires, and identifications—as distinct from gendered ones—are frequently, though differentially, linked with the emerging categories of race and nation in the novels under discussion here. While valuable work is beginning to emerge on the connections between gender and race in the early modern period,[11] sexuality for the most part remains appended to gender in these studies; a distinct argument for the relation between female sexuality and colonial ideology is hampered by a failure to attend to sexuality's specificity. Yet the sexual imagination of early modern Europe insistently pillaged from travel accounts, museum collections, and other textual and material representations of colonial worlds. The process traced in this book is the emergence not only of notions of sexually aberrant racial and national Others but also of a properly "white" (a ubiquitously unmarked term) and "English" (a term insistently and proudly marked) sexuality that depended on the virtue of the bourgeois woman for its moral purity. The presence of a racial Other—such as the African slave Juba in

Maria Edgeworth's *Belinda* or the half-Indian schoolgirl Jane Cumming in the Scottish court case that I discuss in Chapter 3—can offer a conduit for recognizing and identifying otherwise unspeakable sexual improprieties, improprieties that must nonetheless be represented in the text in order to mark the limits of bourgeois feminine sexuality.

The cultural changes for which I argue take place against a backdrop of almost unprecedented disruption in England's legislative and economic systems. Thus, although social mobility had been an increasingly visible phenomenon in English society since the Renaissance, its speed increased so much during the eighteenth and early nineteenth centuries that it was experienced by many who lived through it as an almost millenarian shift in the organization of society. New wealth was pouring into the British economy as a result of the slave trade and the appropriation of raw materials through colonialism. While this newly available capital offered opportunities for personal self-enrichment, it also introduced new risks, the result of the definitionally unstable cash and credit economy now rapidly emerging to displace a feudal economy based on land ownership and land tenure. In the context of such economic and political upheaval, it is not surprising that seemingly nonpolitical ideas such as virtue and femininity should be placed under enormous pressure to offer a respite from the vertiginous speed of social change. Ironically, the way such representations could offer the ideal of respite was by changing: by adapting to fit the ideological needs of the newly powerful British professional class, needs generated by its rise to prominence and the aristocratic and popular threats to its authority.

The period 1748–1816 was framed by the threat of violence both abroad and at home. Yet this was also the period when, according to Foucault, the rule of force and hierarchy was being supplanted in cultural history by the rule of discourse and hegemony. How to explain this seeming paradox? I contend that a specific definition of female sexuality—that of the domestic woman—as produced by the new bourgeois genre of the novel, played a crucial role in reconciling public violence with private virtue.

## Arguing Lesbian History

The "domestic woman" is, of course, a class-specific construct, an ideal of the bourgeois matron that emerged at the end of the eighteenth century after a long history of contestation over the value, status, and even identity of women. The eighteenth century is thus of particular interest to historians of both feminism and female sexuality. Its debates are distinct from, on the one hand, the medieval and Renaissance *querelle des femmes,* primarily a religious dispute about the consequences of the fall of Eve for the status of European women, and its concomitant ribald assumption of women's sexual voraciousness and, on the other, the familiar nineteenth-century doctrine of female sexual passivity that gave rise to maternalist arguments for the political value and recognition of women's special role as social nurturers and moral guardians. The eighteenth century in England represents not just the transition between these two worldviews but also a series of contestations and reformulations of which the outcome was often in doubt. Representations of relations between women are frequent and important sites of such contestations.

In drawing attention to the sexual reading of intimacy between women that is offered in these texts, my argument appears to oppose much of the received wisdom about lesbian history and eighteenth-century sexuality. Louis Crompton, for example, in his splendid study of Georgian, Romantic-era, and Victorian homophobia, justifies his very slight attention to lesbianism by claiming that the person on whom he focused his study "would have to be a man since lesbians in England (unlike their sisters in Europe) were not criminals under the law."[12] The absence of any mention of female homosexuality in English criminal statutes has become an axiomatic justification, in both lesbian and gay studies and eighteenth-century studies of sexuality,[13] for a failure to explore other resources that might help construct historical and literary accounts of nonheterosexual practices and identities among women in the period. For example, Peter Wagner, whose *Eros Revived: Erotica of the Enlightenment in England and America* is rich with examples of female homosexual desires and activities in eighteenth-century erotic writing, frustratingly hinders research by categorizing activities such as sex between women using dildos and clitoral stimulation of one woman by another as "masturbation" rather than female homosexuality.[14] Such a content for such a category merely explicates the assumption, on the part of Wagner and others, that sex between women isn't really sex at all and therefore cannot sustain the interest of either eighteenth-century lawmakers or present-day historians and critics. In fact, the legal case that I discuss in Chapter 3 reveals that the period saw plenty of legal discussion of female homosexuality not limited to the criminal statutes:

*Pirie and Woods v. Cumming Gordon* offers a clear example of a fully engaged account of the relation between lesbianism and the law in the eighteenth and early nineteenth centuries.

Only very recently has this assumption—that the eighteenth century holds nothing of interest to the critic or historian of lesbian culture—been challenged.[15] Historian Randolph Trumbach has carefully described the emergence, "after 1770," of "a role for women . . . attracted to women," sometimes called "tommies," according to Trumbach. But he notes that "the more usual term was sapphist—with sapphist and tommy being the high and low terms for women, as sodomite and molly were for men." Literary historian Martha Vicinus draws links between modern lesbian identity and what she calls "four dominant ways" in which "lesbian desire appears to have been defined" in the seventeenth and eighteenth centuries.[16] Vicinus's four categories—the transvestite, the cross-dressed actress, the occasional lover of women, and the romantic friend—powerfully inform the representations of female friendship available in the novel.[17] In this book I focus on the last category—romantic friendship—because its putative chastity gave it such a powerful explanatory role in articulating the legitimacy of bourgeois culture. Concerned as she is with the history of ideas and identities, Vicinus has little to say about the specific work of literary representation in developing or challenging these categories. In "The Apparitional Lesbian," in which she traces the disappearance of female intimates, Terry Castle turns to specifically literary questions in a movement she argues is characteristic of the representation of lesbian desire in English literature, from Defoe to Jeannette Winterson. Calling Defoe's 1706 *The Apparition of Mrs. Veal* "that first (and strangest) of lesbian love stories," Castle establishes eighteenth-century fiction as the inaugural moment and mode of lesbian representation. Castle's readings, while *tours de force*, leave us with little sense of the specificity of either period or genre in generating a culturally readable image of love between women. Carolyn Woodward's essay on "lesbian disruptions in eighteenth-century fiction" examines the conjunction of the rise of the novel and the representation of female same-sex desire and thus takes on the form and history of the novel more directly than does Castle.[18] Unlike Castle's, however, Woodward's is a salvific account of the radical status of "lesbians in the eighteenth century" and even of representations of love between women.[19] Whereas Woodward draws our attention to the ways in which "lesbian love unsettles prevailing expectations,"[20] both social and generic, my own readings identify not only the disruptive aspects of such representations but also the way in which they were recruited into a larger project of bourgeois hegemony, one that required such sexual stories as part of its own narrative of self-legitimation. Woodward concludes that "realist conventions cannot contain stories of lesbian love";[21] I aim to demonstrate that some stories of lesbian love are central to the consolidation of realist conventions and the arguments about personal and public desires such conventions implicitly and insistently make. Readers of the following pages will not find lesbian heroines transgressing norms and advancing progressive causes; instead, they will find a complex cultural relay in which the sapphic woman, as the site of competing discourses and material relations, plays several roles. As Vicinus concludes, "Many lesbian histories, contradictory, complicated, and perhaps uncomfortable, can be told."[22]

This new work is valuable because it offers a revisionist context for understanding the "romantic friendship" paradigm of the early 1980s that has hitherto dominated lesbian work on pre-twentieth-century culture. That paradigm remains an important one, however; the relationships that I examine are constructed in some reference—be it straightforward, parodic, or outright critical—to the term "romantic friendship," widely popularized by Lillian Faderman, one of the first feminist historians of intimacy between women. According to Faderman, this is the eighteenth-century term for the "love relationships between women" that were known as "Boston marriages" and "sentimental friendships" in the nineteenth century.[23] The following chapters not only broaden the terrain within which passionate, sometimes lifelong friendships between women must be conceived but also suggest that the representation of such friendships itself helps manage the diversity of female sexual acts and identities in limiting and potentially homophobic ways. My account of how romantic friendship was viewed in the eighteenth century, however, differs markedly from Faderman's. She claims that romantic friendships were widely approved of and idealized and therefore were never conceived of as sexual, even by romantic friends themselves. My argument, on the other hand, emphasizes the conflict between approbatory accounts of the chastity of these relationships and the virulent eighteenth-century discourse about the present dangers of female homosexuality in such relationships.

Faderman's book shares with the other well-known feminist study of the history of women's intimacy, Carroll Smith-Rosenberg's essay "The Female

World of Love and Ritual: Relations between Women in Nineteenth-Century America," the assumption that intimate female friendship of the past, far from being a problematic or contested category, was straightforwardly valued and encouraged by the middle-class society in which it was found. Faderman claims, for example, that romantic friendship in the eighteenth century "signified a relationship that was considered noble and virtuous in every way,"[24] and Smith-Rosenberg stresses the extent to which these friendships were "socially acceptable and fully compatible with heterosexual marriage."[25] Such accounts draw very partially on the evidence of how these relationships were viewed by contemporaries. Faderman's and Smith-Rosenberg's studies obscure the wariness and even prohibition that sometimes surrounded women's friendships, leaving us with a flattened notion of the contesting constructions of female sexuality in late-eighteenth-century and early-nineteenth-century English culture. Further, such studies do little to illuminate the way in which these approbatory accounts of intimacy between women came to have any wide cultural acceptance. What were the histories, the ideological functions, the effects—and the failures—of these assertions of the harmless and sexless female friendship?

Many of the limitations of Faderman's and Smith-Rosenberg's arguments spring from their reliance on the category of gender to the exclusion of a systematic consideration of sexuality in their efforts to understand women's intimate friendships.[26] For Faderman, sexuality is a "limited" vantage point from which to regard these relationships, for it is only "in our century that love has come to be perceived as a refinement of the sexual impulse."[27] By dismissing sexuality from her account of romantic friendship, Faderman can forge a link between the women she is studying and the particular lesbian-feminist community out of which she is writing—a link that refuses to see lesbian community as importantly constituted by sexuality. "In lesbian-feminism," she writes, "I found a contemporary analog to romantic friendship in which two women were everything to one another and had little connection with men who were so alienatingly and totally different. . . . I venture to guess that had the romantic friends of other eras lived today, many of them would have been lesbian-feminists; and had the lesbian-feminists of our day lived in other eras, most of them would have been romantic friends."[28] Their (gendered) difference from men, then, rather than their (sexual) desire for women draws romantic friends and lesbian feminists to one another. This polemical interpretation of contemporary lesbian feminist communities and relationships, Faderman makes clear, is an attempt to intervene in the misogynist medical and psychological view that "lesbians" relate to "women" in the same way men do—as failed and ridiculous pseudomen. But important as such interventions have been in feminist theory, Faderman's approach limits the parameters of feminist criticism unnecessarily. Faderman purports to offer an account of lesbianism as woman-centered, having nothing to do with men or masculinity (although, paradoxically, it is their difference from men that defines lesbians) and everything to do with feminism. In such an account, gender becomes the primary analytic category, and sexuality is seen at best as a subcategory of gender and certainly completely determined by it.

Smith-Rosenberg's argument, although more careful and less polemical, nonetheless shares this basic analytic grid. She argues that the "emotional segregation of men and women" in nineteenth-century United States society produced "a specifically female world . . . built around a generic and unself-conscious pattern of single-sex or homosocial networks."[29] For Smith-Rosenberg, the basic pattern of women's interactions was "an intimate mother-daughter relationship," and she frequently describes the relationships between the women she studies in familial terms, for example, as "sisterly bonds." Thus, although she takes pains to point out the "intensity and even physical nature" of women's intimate friendships, Smith-Rosenberg ultimately wants to locate that physicality within a set of nonsexual, family-like interactions between women.[30] Like Faderman, Smith-Rosenberg opposes an account of same-sex relationships that sees them "only in terms of the dichotomy between normal and abnormal." Instead, she suggests an approach that "would view [these relationships] within a cultural and sexual setting rather than from an exclusively individual psychosexual perspective."[31] This relocation from the individual to the social, for Smith-Rosenberg, is a move from analyses of sexuality to those of gender. This conceptual reframing, however, obliterates the possibility of an analysis of sexuality as a phenomenon both distinct from gender and social (rather than "merely" psychological or emotional) in its production and effects. My own exploration of the late-eighteenth- and early-nineteenth-century discourse of romantic friendship gives priority to the ideological work of sexuality as a social category related to but distinct from the operations of gender. The argument that sexual identity is private, psychic, and interior, I contend, constitutes one of the social and ideological effects of the history of representation traced here—the rise of identity as a modern category. As an effect of historical change rather than a transhistorical truth, the idea of sexuality as psychic rather than social must be interrogated.

One problem I seek to address, then, is that the genealogy of contemporary lesbian identities and practices is sharply attenuated: we know much more about the emergence in the early twentieth century of the term "lesbian" in sexology and popular culture—and the women, communities, and texts through which its current meaning has been constructed—than we do about the historical lineages that made such a meaning possible. Indeed, we have been cautioned by feminist historians not to look for "lesbians" in the eighteenth and nineteenth centuries; curiously, however, this caution against anachronism has most often taken the form of an ahistorical prohibition against reading sex between women in history. In insisting on such a reading—on reading lesbian sex—I do not attempt to find "lesbians" in the eighteenth- and early-nineteenth-century texts examined; rather, these texts demonstrate how powerful a part the category of "sapphism" played in the cultural imaginary of the period. Such images, while not representations of "lesbians" as we now understand the term, are nevertheless part of the history of those representations and as such warrant our careful scrutiny. The conflicts these texts express and contain have their legacies both in the construction of current lesbian identities, practices, and communities and in the history of the specific forms of misogyny and homophobia with which we struggle today.

Historically as well as politically, we need to understand the role of the relationships of concern in this book. As an identity category that developed over the last half of the eighteenth century, "sapphism" played a constitutive role in establishing the authority of a range of discourses, including religion, medicine, the law, and the heroine-centered novel. By reading the tension between "sapphism" and "romantic friendship" across both fiction and nonfiction, I seek to establish the status of that tension as a basic, if sometimes unstated, cultural assumption—fundamental to the establishment of both the bourgeois private and the bourgeois public spheres. As such, it formed an important part of the construction of specifically modern versions of sexuality, gender, the body, and the family, as well as of class and colonial relations, public order, and the rule of law. By implication, then, if bourgeois culture has a stake in effacing the symbolic role played by representations of sapphism in its own rise to power, contemporary feminist and lesbian criticism has a stake in exposing that role.

## Constituting and Contesting the Bourgeois Subject

The story of virtuous bourgeois femininity in the novel, a story in which the dangerous, potentially sapphist female friend provides the heroine with the opportunity to risk and then refuse sexual immorality, helped the bourgeoisie reckon with its central moral paradox: how its rise to power could be predicated on its greater virtue than that of the aristocracy or the peasantry, yet how that virtue could somehow countenance the bloody consequences of national rivalry and colonial trade and imperialism.[32] The racial and national hierarchies that worked to justify and incite colonial violence decisively shaped the story of domestic feminine virtue told by these novels. The sexual category of feminine virtue,[33] then, is crucially predicated on various colonial violences: slavery, the extermination of indigenous peoples, the exploitation of Europe's poor as indentured servants and transplanted laborers, revolution at home, and wars of imperial dominion abroad. The sexual Other of the virtuous bourgeois woman is often her slightly sapphic female friend; the unconscious logic of these texts links that freakish figure with a variety of characters drawn from nationalist and colonial discourses: decadent French and Italians, sensuous barbaric Turks, simple but savage Africans, sexually aberrant Indians, slaves, monsters, and voodoo witches. Such characters haunt the margins of these texts, often most urgently at precisely those moments when the insularity and virtue of the domestic space is being firmly asserted, when its Others have been banished, mutilated, or killed off. These readings, however, provide a series of cautions against seeing the mutilated or excluded sapphic woman as merely standing in for or paralleling colonial and national Others. Rather, the domestic novel develops a convention by which representations of sex between women are incorporated into stories of female virtue. The embodied and physically located images of women's intimacy that characterize the novels of the mid–eighteenth century disappear into subtextual and implicit plots and characters in early-nineteenth-century domestic fiction, providing an acceptably interior, psychic form of difference the novel can "solve" through the resolution of the heterosexual love plot, a resolution that allows for (sexual) threat without representing political violence. It is this process which accounts for the canonization of the kind of domestic realism we see in Jane Austen's *Emma* and which came to stand for the origin point of the novel as high art in critical history. In effecting an archaeology of lesbian identity in these novels, then, I always have had to contend with the intersections between the emerging categories of racial, national, and sexual identities as they collide at the representational site of the virtuous bourgeois woman, even as they help create it.[34]

In attempting to account for the status of a "sapphic" sexual identity as an emergent cultural category, then, I attend not only to the history of sexuality but also to the history and function of identity itself. Feminism and now gay and lesbian studies have both been preoccupied for some time with the question of what poststructuralists call subjectivity. How are we to understand the notion of identity? Once, it is argued, subjectivity was a coherent, unified, masculine, and European entity; now it is under assault both from the position of the various Others of this exclusive canon of selfhood and from the vantage point of postcolonial unravelings of the colonial world's tightly woven social structures. Here, I want to problematize the historical narrative that links a coherent, unified self with the European Enlightenment, and its dissolution with the present postmodern moment. I want to examine the contest and struggle surrounding the consolidation of a discourse of identity in the late eighteenth century in England, especially as it developed in that paradigmatic modern form of literary representation, the novel. The fiction of a coherent self was always already a fiction, even (and perhaps particularly) at its inaugural moment; its struggle for hegemony was marked by the persistent intrusion of its Others, as the story of "rational man" turned out to require other stories to justify its telling. Stories that castigated sexually aberrant women marked by their improper relations to racial, class, and national Others were especially powerful narratives of legitimation for the rise to power of bourgeois identity as a cultural norm.[35] I trace the marks left by these stories on the form and canonization of the novel, understanding the discursive struggle that produced it as one of the major technologies in the production of the modern self.

The relationships between nation, race, and sexuality differ widely among the four novels discussed in this study. Although slavery is insistently present in the frame narrative and figurative language of *Millenium Hall,* the subject of Chapter 1, the novel nonetheless produces a powerful silence about the trade in human beings. The concluding pages of *Memoirs of a Woman of Pleasure,* as I argue in Chapter 2, satirically celebrate the distinctiveness of English male homosexuality, soliciting an analysis alert to representations of national identity. In Chapter 3 I contend that it is only in *Belinda* that Africans and Creoles are explicitly represented; such figures demand attention to the novel's colonial plot. And the conclusion of the final chapter on *Emma* turns on the success with which Austen's canonical domestic realism eviscerates such explicit representations of racial and colonial Others in favor of representations of class and sexuality that relocate difference within the English domestic space and the bourgeois psychic interior. This argument, then, begins and ends with significant silences and absences in novelistic representations of a racialized, Anglicized notion of sexual identity. Thus in the interests of clarity I will sketch out the assumptions about race, nation, and colonialism that undergird the following readings.

The category of race in domestic fiction is itself a site of historical and ideological contestation. Margo Hendricks and Patricia Parker point out, " 'Race' as that term developed across several European languages was a highly unstable term in the early modern period."[36] This instability means that descriptions of and arguments about race could be deployed for a variety of purposes: English readers in the eighteenth century, for example, heard that "Africans" (itself a historically new generalization of the tribal, cultural, and ethnic diversity of the continent) were "noble savages" and that they were monkeylike beasts.[37] Both images, like the ethnographic conventions that they helped inaugurate, functioned not primarily as information about Others but as stories about the white Self whose observing eye and recording hand decisively represented the bodies under scrutiny, shaping them to particular ends.[38] Whether marshaled in the service of abolitionist or anticolonialist critiques or arguments in favor of the continued slavery and subjugation of the peoples rapidly being exposed to imperial depredations, these images used the fiction of observable, bodily "fact" to anchor and stabilize the upheavals imperialism brought in its wake.

Like sexuality and gender, race functions in these novels as a naturalized identity category, one assumed to be "of the body" and therefore unchangeable. Reading the sexual status of these narratives of bourgeois identity formation, then, has meant noticing their racial status as well. The two discourses often powerfully intersect and incite each other. While in no way pretending to treat race in systematic detail, then, I hope to clarify the ways in which racialized representations, whether explicitly present or symptomatically absent, form part of the logic of gender and sexual ideologies in the period.

As differences between Europe and its Others gained cultural force, the value of differences *among* European nations shifted. National rivalry, under the pressure of the imperialist land grab, mutated into a powerful new discourse of national identity. But English nationalism was also a response to internal pressures, appealing to a notion of "Englishness" that transcended local differences of class, region, and idiom. In the context of the increasing social mobility documented by the British domestic novel, an Anglicized British nationalism offered some discursive management of the threatening social differences now juxtaposed by urbanization and upward mobility. Like racial identity, English nationalism both depended on and supported increasingly naturalized notions of sexuality. Race and sexuality, however, emerge in this study as identities more insistently embodied than national identity. Indeed, we might speculate that it is through the construction of specifically race- and sex-marked bodies—the truth-telling bodies of Foucault's modern subject—that national claims in the sphere of international politics were made legitimate and convincing, made visceral, in the British domestic novel.

Near the end of his landmark study of nationalism, *Imagined Communities,* Benedict Anderson turns to a question for which other historians of the phenomenon seem unable to account: the question of love. He writes, "It is useful to remind ourselves that nations inspire love, and often profoundly self-sacrificing love."[39] Although Anderson has in mind the kind of *amor patriae* that results in a willingness to die for one's country, not the sexual love with which I am concerned, his observations about the ways in which "nation-ness" produces desire and solicits pleasurable connection suggest the usefulness of examining the specifically national character of the representations of sexuality considered here. As Anderson notes about the sense of fidelity to co-nationals one has never met: "It may appear paradoxical that the objects of all these attachments are 'imagined.' . . . But *amor patriae* does not differ in this respect from the other affections, in which there is always an element of fond imagining."[40] Fantasy and desire, "fond imagining," are crucial to the articulation of a national identity. And inasmuch as these categories are also always sexual categories, it becomes pertinent to ask what kind of sexual acts and practices came to be identified as proper to English national character during the period in which all three—acts, practices, and character itself—were beginning to consolidate into that quintessentially modern construct, identity.

The colonial project was the rubric under which discourses of race and those of nation collided. While both categories had intra-European histories,[41] sustained European contact with Africa, Asia, and America—a fundamental aspect of English culture by the eighteenth century—considerably expanded the field within which racial and national differences could be distinguished, as well as increasing the ideological urgency of making such distinctions. The discursive technologies for producing such differences exploded under these circumstances, generating ever more refined and specific racial and national hierarchies in the service of granting moral legitimacy to a process of colonial expansion that had always been contested within England.[42]

This contestation brought into high relief the fundamental contradiction on which the notion of the virtue of bourgeois ascension was based. As Mary Louise Pratt notes: "Euroimperialism faced a legitimation crisis. The histories of broken treaties, genocides, mass displacements and enslavements became less and less acceptable as rationalist and humanitarian ideologies took hold. Particularly after the French Revolution, contradictions between egalitarian, democratic ideologies at home and ruthless structures of domination and extermination abroad became more acute. Yet the demands of capital remained."[43] The instability created by these contradictions helps account for the rapid rise in popularity of the novel as a new literary form. Most often authored by bourgeois writers, most often featuring bourgeois characters, and always centered on "questions of virtue" (to borrow Michael McKeon's phrase)[44] and narratives of identity, the novel emerged as an ideological tool that could offer an imaginary space in which these contradictions could be addressed and resolved. Of course, this resolution itself was another fantasy; as we will see, the novel's heterogenous form reflected and produced ideological fissures even as it attempted to explain them away. The cultural work performed by the novel capitalized on its open and uncanonized form in the late eighteenth century, giving it a special status in relation to the middle class, colonialism, and nationalism; in Suvendrini Perera's words, "Empire is not simply expressed or reflected in the novel. . . . [I]t is rather processed and naturalized by it."[45]

Ian Watt's is only the most famous formulation of the link between the rise of the novel and the rise of the middle class in eighteenth-century England. In the almost four decades since publication of *The Rise of the Novel,* each of the central terms of his analysis ("rise," "novel," "middle class") has been challenged and reconceived. Even as ambitious a revision as Michael McKeon's 1987 *Origins of the English Novel,* however, which sets out explicitly to challenge Watt's thesis that the novel's formal realism is linked to the empirical tastes of the newly emerging bourgeoisie, is not able to disarticulate novelistic conventions and bourgeois social power. Rather, McKeon demonstrates persuasively that archaic generic forms such as romance and archaic social structures such as the aristocracy "persist" in the face of bourgeois culture's increasing investment in realistic representation.[46] The centrality of the novel to bourgeois culture's understanding of itself, however, remains intact in McKeon's account.

Other critics, however, have specified this thesis to identify the ways in which the novel is not only a bourgeois form but also one involved in the central project of eighteenth- and nineteenth-century European economic and political culture: the project of imperialism. Edward Said calls the novel "*the* aesthetic object" in "the formation of imperial attitudes, references, and experiences."[47] He continues: "The main battle in imperialism is over land, of course, but when it came to who owned the land, who had the right to settle and work on it, who kept it going, who won it back, and who now plans its future—these issues were reflected, contested, and for a time decided in narrative. . . . The power to narrate, or to block other narratives from forming and emerging, is very important to culture and imperialism and constitutes one of the main connections between them."[48] The importance of colonialism to understanding the novel is true not only of novels containing explicitly colonial characters and settings but also of novels set entirely in England, novels that seem to refuse to engage with any question whatsoever beyond whom the heroine will marry. One function of such domestic fictions, in Said's terms, is to "block" the emergence of hotly contested political questions that arose in the wake of imperial expansion, such as abolition, economic speculation, and revolution. But these novels, in obsessively mapping out the English domestic space, are also performing a directly imperial function. Maps of home, then, inevitably also map what is not home because they delimit home's boundaries. But they are also colonizing gestures that universalize the English domestic interior, even as English settlements imposed themselves on far-flung colonial landscapes.[49]

Perhaps paradoxically, this study of the sexual valence of romantic friendship begins with a novel of romantic friendship that completely denies sexuality. Chapter 1 offers a reading of *Millenium Hall,* Sarah Scott's 1762 novel about a group of women who withdraw from the public world of marriage and heterosexual courtship to live together in virtuous seclusion, demonstrating one side of the midcentury discourse about women's friendships. Here, sexuality is defined as characteristically male; as opposed to heterosexuality, romantic friendship between women is sexless and safe. Scott draws on images of slavery, which resonate not only with abolitionist discourse but also with the plot of her own earlier novel set in Jamaica, to dramatize the situation of Englishwomen by emphatically redefining "slavery" away from its material reference to the trade in human beings. In contrast to this chaste and immaterial world, John Cleland's 1748–49 *Memoirs of a Woman of Pleasure,* discussed in Chapter 2, represents women's relationships, including their relationships with other women, as by definition sexual. The novel both represents female (and male) homosexual acts and produces various sapphic (and sodomitical) points of view from which heterosexual acts are reimaged in the service of homosexual subjectivities. In the process, the novel insists on the existence of a specifically English homosexuality in implicit defiance of the nationalist convention that demarcates France and Italy as "cradles of sodomy"; instead, the novel offers an implicit homosexual geography of England. These two chapters, then, demonstrate the conflicting and contradictory ways in which romantic friendship was represented in the mid–eighteenth century: on the one hand, as paradigmatically chaste and, on the other, as excessively, inevitably sexual. This polar representational economy reduces colonial violences such as slavery to the status of metaphor and links such an erasure to the virtues of chastity, but it also allows for an anxious awareness of the bawdy and potentially subversive uses to which a discourse of English nationalism can be put when pornography satirically adopts the forms of domestic fiction.

In the last two chapters I explore the legacy of this double discourse in the domestic fiction of the early nineteenth century, tracing the effects of its contradictions in the textual anxieties of a form of fiction that had become central to bourgeois narratives of self-legitimation. In Maria Edgeworth's 1801 *Belinda,* the cautionary figure of Harriot Freke, derived from both Fanny Hill's brothel and the feminist agitation of the 1790s, repeatedly exceeds her function as foil to Belinda's virtue, connecting the heroine not only with the very sexual excesses she is supposed to be defined against but also with the sex-saturated colonial world she must repudiate in order to marry. The final chapter reads Jane Austen's 1816 *Emma* in terms of the three female friendships that structure its narrative of class consolidation and domestic female power. I emphasize the limitations of that power by showing how the heroine's choice of a friend, initially an emblem of her economic and social independence, is ceded to Mr. Knightley so as to make the novel's heterosexual closure possible. The colonial and extranational plots, characters, and references found in the earlier novels have here been recoded into minute distinctions among members of the English middle class. And in this novel, compared with the others under discussion, resistance to heterosexual heroineship is closed down most firmly, albeit with the irony characteristic of Austen's dark and truncated finales.

This relative impermeability to the disruptive images and conflicts that rendered the earlier eighteenth-century works formally uneven, at times incoherent, and certainly noncanonical suggests that as the nineteenth-century novel begins to define itself (and as its origin point is retrospectively defined by the critical tradition), a decisive struggle over the interpretation of female sexuality has been resolved. The eruption of embodied sexualities (whether the male sexual violence of *Millenium Hall* or what the *Memoirs* calls a sapphic "byass") and of literally colonial plots and characters (as in *Belinda*) no longer poses an unassimilable contradiction to the dominant narrative of female sexual virtue and bourgeois self-legitimation; rather, homosexual desire on the part of the heroine is recoded as class transgression and, as such, conflicts with the particularly metropolitan form of power available to the middle-class domestic woman. Female friendship in *Emma* comes full circle from *Millenium Hall,* in which the incursion of sexuality into the domestic space represents "slavery" and the limited form of power wielded by bourgeois women over peasants and what the novel calls "monsters" in a domestic sphere emphatically screened off from sexuality represents safety, if not freedom. In contrast, the representation of Emma's sexual attraction to her female friends is an unremarkable aspect of young ladyhood and a necessary lesson in heroine-ship. The heroine's renunciation of her intimacies with other women is the price she pays for the ascension to domestic female power. Sapphism, as a form of sexual (and thus psychic, interior) difference, can be successfully represented and then contained by the ironic realism of *Emma*. This form of difference comes to stand in, in the domestic novel, for the racial and national forms of difference that the domestic sphere excludes as the sign of its non-violent virtue and disciplinary power. Sapphic desire has been carefully disentangled from its colonial associations and is no longer an eruptive threat to the bourgeois ascension narrative; it has been domesticated into a necessary and controllable part of that narrative, essential to the formation of the identity of the heroine, as the emblem of bourgeois identity itself. The truth of the subject has become a sexual truth, and dangerous intimacies between women have been written into the narrative of hegemonic culture as its foundational violences have been written out.

My method here is both textual and cultural. While emphasizing close readings of particular novels, I make varied and differential attempts to read those novels in relation to texts from other, often nonliterary, genres. Thus, I hope to suggest that the ways these ideological struggles are played out in novelistic discourse has wider cultural resonance; novelistic representation both draws from the textual matrix surrounding it and decisively shapes that matrix. Given my interest in the disavowed aspects of Enlightenment self-hood, it is perhaps predictable that formally these readings should explore the textual and cultural unconscious of the novels discussed; their unintentional effects, excesses, and contradictions; their moments of ironic loss of control; and their resistances to their own conventions of realist representation and formal closure.

The final chapter deviates somewhat from the contextualizing method of the others. As a paradigmatic text of what would come to be nineteenth-century realism, *Emma,* it has seemed to me, has demanded a different treatment. The seamlessness of its plot, in which subplots and minor characters are woven inextricably into the fabric of the central narrative of Emma's discipline and punishment, required that the novel be treated as a whole, rather than read for its interesting subplots and fragments as were the earlier texts. The canonical status of Austen's work also created its stringencies:

*Emma*'s critical history, by now, is as much a part of reading the novel as reading the novel itself, a claim that cannot be made for the much more infrequently noticed texts that center the earlier chapters. And finally, as I argue, in Austen's novel it is precisely this kind of context—the existence of anything outside the novel—that the conventions of Austenian domestic realism have rendered invisible. To bring it back into the picture requires the context set up by the preceding chapters. Managing female sexuality through regulating female friendship is all the conflict the Austen novel can manage— and in the novel's terms, all it needs to manage to secure the virtue of the domestic woman, with all that figure's political purchase and all its inherent violences and exclusions.

# CHAPTER ONE

# Resisting Reform: *Millenium Hall*

*Millenium Hall* and the Lesbian Canon

Sarah Scott's 1762 novel begins this study because it seems to have summarized assumptions about female friendship that were circulating throughout early-eighteenth-century culture,[1] codifying them into a form that became influential for both novelists and readers throughout the latter half of the century.[2] The novel depicts a community of women who eschew marriage and live together, performing charitable works, educating and employing the surrounding villagers, and engaging in pursuits of "rational piety" themselves, including reading, drawing, and music. Such a scene would seem to nominate the novel for a prominent place in the canon of lesbian-feminist representation. In the first full-length article to appear on the novel since its 1986 republication, George Haggerty summarizes nearly a decade of published and unpublished opinion when he claims that *Millenium Hall* constructs "narrative authority for women-loving-women and offers women in general an escape from the prison-house of patriarchal narrative."[3] Haggerty finds the novel a powerful affirmation of "lesbian narrative" (117) that transgresses "the boundaries set for women in the eighteenth century" (118). The novel's popularity, however, seems to conflict with such an account of its destabilizing effect on its eighteenth-century reading audience. *Millenium Hall* went through four editions in the sixteen years following its publication in 1762, which indicates a fairly wide readership. What are the grounds of the novel's appeal for the middle-class readers (probably both men and women) whose interest in "romantic friendship" kept it in circulation? How can we reconcile claims about the novel's radical effects with its widespread popularity and undeniable conservatism? Why is its separatist vision neither a threatening nor a subversive one in terms of eighteenth-century culture?

To address these questions, we must examine the novel's careful construction of a particular form of power—bourgeois, domestic female virtue—as the legitimate property of the middle-class women characters of *Millenium Hall*. Defined in opposition to public, political, and particularly sexual power, this class-specific form of female agency sketches out the possibility of female homosocial institutions and practices that work with rather than against class and gender hierarchies. In constructing a space within which upper-class ladies might live together rather than with men, the novel works to further, rather than problematize or hinder, the spread of a bourgeois modernity crucially predicated on the centrality and naturalness of the heterosexual family. (This structure is itself a historically specific form of the much older social hierarchy of men over women.) The novel thus presents a paradox for feminist criticism: an all-female utopia that nevertheless strenuously resists the possibility of a critique of the emerging gender and sexual norms of the mid–eighteenth century.

What was seductive for women readers in particular about the women characters of *Millenium Hall,* women praised for their sexual unattractiveness and resistance to pleasure? The women of Millenium Hall, I would argue, represent a specific form of power that was available to bourgeois women within the patriarchal family structures that during the eighteenth century came to be central in the construction of bourgeois hegemony across society. To define this new category, we can turn to Nancy Armstrong's account of "the power of domestic surveillance," which provides the means for a necessary gender-marking of Foucault's notion of the "panoptic gaze." For Foucault, modern disciplinary society functions by means of this gaze: "Inspection functions ceaselessly. The gaze is alert everywhere."[4] Power operates through the constant play and possibility of the gaze, creating for itself "a perpetual victory that avoids any physical confrontation and which is always decided in advance." But Foucault's Panopticon, like Scott's Millenium Hall, did have physical effects. In its power to deform and reform bodies, "it could be used as a machine to carry out experiments, to alter behaviour, to train or correct individuals."[5] Although the women of Millenium Hall disclaim the title "reformer," their community sets the stage for various social experiments, sometimes carried out on their own bodies but more often on those of the poor around them. In enabling these bodily marks and changes, the Millenium Hall women consolidate their own power as agents of the panoptic gaze.[6]

Armstrong argues that the emergence of modern bourgeois subjectivity was crucially predicated on the development of a particular gendered identity, that of the virtuous domestic woman. Her characteristic activity was "domestic surveillance," the ceaseless observation of the intersections of power and subjectivity in the household.[7] The domestic woman, according to Armstrong, "was inscribed with values that addressed a whole range of competing interest groups and, through her, these groups gained authority over domestic relations and personal life. In this way, furthermore, they established the need for the kind of surveillance upon which modern institutions are based."[8] Given these high stakes, then, the appeal of the constrained role of the domestic woman for Scott and her woman characters and readers becomes clearer. The confinement of women to the domestic space actually placed them at the intersection of the competing sets of hierarchies struggling to achieve hegemony over the formation of modern subject relations; in Armstrong's words, "the notion of the household as a specifically feminine space established the preconditions for a modern institutional culture." To occupy the position of operating those intersections through surveillance was indeed, as Armstrong claims, "a form of power," one that beckoned beguilingly to middle-class women from the pages of many eighteenth-century domestic novels.[9] But how could women who refused to participate in heterosexual norms, who "failed" to marry, come to occupy such a central position? How is female sexuality constructed in Scott's novel such that the power of domestic surveillance becomes an attribute of romantic friendship?

In the following reading of *Millenium Hall*, I aim to exemplify the extent of domestic female power in mid-eighteenth-century culture but also to move away from Armstrong's emphasis on its success by identifying the limitations and constraints it posed for the very women who hoped to be enabled by it. Armstrong's account fails to distinguish between the agency of the middle-class women whom eighteenth-century novels placed at the heart of culture and that of the culture such a placement served. She claims that "the power of all the domestic clichés we have grown half ashamed to live by . . . was given to women and exercised through them," without appearing to notice that to have power "given" to them, women must not have been in complete control of the forms, effects, and distribution of that power.[10] The effectiveness of power was guaranteed, according to Armstrong, by its ability to pass for a "natural" psychological state, desire. Thus, "the domestic woman exercised a form of power that appeared to have no political force at all because it seemed forceful only when it was desired."[11] In such a formulation, desire, pleasure, and sexuality adhere seamlessly to the interests of bourgeois politics as its primary naturalizing agents. To point to the powerlessness of bourgeois women, according to Armstrong, is to participate in a "rhetoric of victimization" that garners them even more power.[12] In contrast, I want to offer an account of the contested construction of female sexuality in Scott's novel that renders desire a much more recalcitrant and complicated category than these statements allow. In my view, the argument that domestic female power was able successfully to mask and naturalize itself as mere "desire" takes the claims of novels such as *Millenium Hall* too much in their own terms; this promise of a seamlessly successful form of female power was exactly the lure that bourgeois ideology was beginning to hold out to women in the eighteenth century. In the second part of the chapter, then, I will document the novel's inadvertent portrait of the mutilating, abusive "experiments" performed by bourgeois women themselves in the service of domestic ideology, to discipline them into agents of a bourgeois hegemony in which the bodies and desires of women become objects, rather than agents, of this new form of patriarchal culture.

Thus the novel tells a conflicted story about domestic female power. On one hand, bourgeois women can operate such power in ways that produce hierarchies in which they are privileged; on the other hand, these very hierarchies are the locations in which the novel's female characters are abused and dominated. This contradiction helps account for the emptiness of the novel's most persistent metaphor—that is, slavery. Enslavement is the image the novel uses most frequently to express the conditions the Millenium Hall ladies are trying to escape or ameliorate, and the rhetoric of abolition informs the novel's language at crucial points. Sarah Scott was familiar with contemporary antislavery arguments; twelve years after the publication of *Millenium Hall,* in *The History of Sir George Ellison* she wrote a detailed critique of the cruelty of Caribbean slave masters, which culminated in an economic and moral argument for the humane treatment of slaves (though not for abolition itself). Strangely, however, the English trade in slaves is never mentioned in *Millenium Hall*. The metaphor of slavery keeps the historical fact of the trade in human beings always hovering at the edge of the novel, but within the language of the novel itself, slavery is an empty category, drained of historical and social reference in the service of British domestic ideology. In the final section of this chapter, then, I will investigate how the rhetoric of slavery illuminates both the privilege of the Millenium Hall ladies and the limits of that privilege. The precarious balance between protofeminist critique and bourgeois accommodation turns out to depend on the simultaneous invocation of physical force and its insistent attenuation to the status of empty metaphor. Scott's novel offers an early instance of the way in which the emergence of British feminist argument depended not only on abolition but also on slavery itself.[13]

By examining the rhetoric of slavery that structures certain key conflicts in the representation of female friendship in *Millenium Hall*, I point to the novel's involvement in an important Enlightenment discourse of liberation: abolition. As Moira Ferguson has demonstrated in her landmark study *Subject to Others: British Women Writers and Colonial Slavery, 1670–1834*, abolitionist discourse was an important precursor to English feminism, a relationship that created an uneasy, often one-sided, alliance between Englishwomen and the Africans they almost never knew. Women arguing for their own education or enfranchisement, Ferguson notes, "were prone to refer loosely to themselves as slaves" throughout this period.[14] Thus, over the course of the century, the term "slavery" in Englishwomen's writing acquired layers of meaning that drifted away from direct reference to the trade in human beings. Slavery became a popular metaphor for all kinds of oppression, in the process often losing its directly political charge and contestatory status and serving instead to refer to any of the purely personal limitations that Enlightenment theories were discovering as hindrances to human progress. This detachment of discussions of slavery from any acknowledgment of its most obvious and literal example in the experience of eighteenth-century English people, however, grounds the metaphoric use of "slavery" on a contradiction that constantly threatens to undo the discursive work whereby the moral charge of antislavery sentiment could be marshaled against the evils plaguing the bourgeois self and home. In *Millenium Hall*, the recurrent metaphor of slavery signals both the text's conscious invocation of a depoliticized discourse that seeks to contain social critique and its unconscious awareness of two other sets of relations on which the text depends. The first is social: the privilege that permits the Englishman who "discovers" Millenium Hall and makes its story public depends on the leisure afforded him by his Jamaican plantations— depends, that is, on slavery. The second is discursive: for the women of Millenium Hall to call themselves or the people around them "slaves" depends on the absence of actual slaves—Africans enslaved in English colonies in the Americas—from a narrative that nonetheless depends on their labor to produce the conditions of its own existence. The rhetoric of slavery in the text, then, demonstrates how and at whose expense the privilege of the Millenium Hall ladies is constructed. Thus, I trace an expanding and contracting dynamic in my account of the emergent form of power accorded to Englishwomen by bourgeois culture.

Power and the Panoptic Gaze

*Millenium Hall* begins as the epistolary account of an unnamed male traveler. In company with a young male friend, Lamont, this man is making his leisurely way from London to his family's country estate. One day they pass by the extremely well kept grounds of the house they dub Millenium Hall and decide to pay a call. There the narrator meets a "near relation," Mrs. Maynard, and prevails upon her to tell the story of the several happily employed women he sees around him in the house and garden. The novel is then divided into sections narrated by Mrs. Maynard and entitled "The History of Miss Mancel and Mrs. Morgan," "The History of Lady Mary Jones," "The History of Miss Selvyn," and "The History of Miss Trentham." The novel ends with the conversion of the narrator's companion, Lamont, fired by the ladies' pious example, from a worldly and secular point of view to that of devout Christianity.

Toward the middle of the novel, Lamont registers his anxiety about the high moral standards the ladies set for themselves and, implicitly, for him as their listener/reader. He admits that "if any people have a right to turn reformers, you ladies are best qualified";[15] Miss Mancel, horrified at the title that links her and her companions with the feminists and political radicals of their day, insists: "We do not set up for reformers . . . we wish to regulate ourselves by the laws laid down to us, and as far as our influence can extend, endeavour to enforce them; beyond that small circle all is foreign to us; we have sufficient employment in improving ourselves; to mend the world requires much abler hands" (118). The "foreignness" of the world beyond Millenium Hall—the masculine, public world of law and government to which "reformers" direct their critiques—emphasizes the clear boundaries set on the authority of these bourgeois women. Instead of changing "the world," they confine their feminine "influence" to the private sphere of the household.[16] Here, in the tentative language coded as appropriate to the domestic woman, they "endeavour to enforce" the hierarchized standards of morality and social life that buttress patriarchal law. Their positions as the conduits through which the law speaks and operates attest to the absolute functionality of domestic female virtue in the formation of modern narratives of power and pleasure. Because they take up the constrained position of the domestic woman, then, the characters in *Millenium Hall* achieve a very material authority over the privatized social space to which that ideology limits them.

The novel opens with an account of the visual pleasure furnished for the male narrator/spectators by the sight of women working in a field outside Millenium Hall. The narrator notes that "in them we beheld rural simplicity, without any of those marks of poverty and boorish rusticity which would have spoilt the pastoral air of the scene around us" (5). The marks of class ("boorish rusticity") and even of labor itself have been erased from this static tableau. This language of male fantasy in the novel, according to Melinda Alliker Rabb, represents "a mode of discourse never shared by the women in describing their own habitation"; for the women, she claims, "the garden is not idealized . . . it is not a timeless paradise."[17] Nonetheless, this passage attests to the effectiveness with which the Millenium Hall women have performed the ideological work of producing working-class women as a spectacle for male pleasure. Two crucial definitions for the rest of the novel are put into play in this early scene: the association of pleasure with masculinity, and the production of working-class women as the object of the bourgeois gaze.

Rabb is right, however, to insist on the distinction between masculine and feminine modes of representation in the novel. For while bourgeois women are important agents of the gaze later in the novel, theirs is the gaze of discipline, never that of pleasure. They observe the poor women of the surrounding village in order to enforce bourgeois standards of piety, cleanliness, morality, and rank on them: to discipline their bodies into the shapes required by bourgeois hegemony.[18]

The women are particularly concerned with marriage, as it is a central institution in perpetuating this hegemony. They give small dowries to the kitchen workers and laborers who serve them; but to "merit" such a "gift," the young women must place themselves under the surveillance of the Millenium Hall ladies. The following account attests to the material power of the domestic female gaze over poor households:

> [The ladies] watch with so careful an eye over the conduct of these young people as proves of much greater service to them than the money they bestow. They kindly, but strongly, reprehend the first error, and guard them by the most prudent admonitions against a repetition of their fault. By little presents they shew their approbation of those who behave well, always proportioning their gifts to the merits of the person; which are therefore looked upon as the most honourable testimony of their conduct, and are treasured up as valuable marks of distinction. This encouragement has great influence, and makes them vie with each other in endeavours to excel in sobriety, cleanliness, meekness and industry. (119–120)

The "careful eye" of the agents of domestic surveillance is substantially buttressed by "the money they bestow," as class position is transformed into a gendered idea of virtue. The careful scrutiny that distinguishes among behaviors ("the first error") and measures them ("always proportioning their gifts") forms a dense web of ideological and material incitements to conformity with hegemonic norms. The "marks of distinction" the ladies impose are "treasured up" rather than spent, becoming material artifacts that transform such qualities as "sobriety, cleanliness, meekness and industry" into the very furniture of the poor household. Significantly, these qualities, particularly "meekness and industry," are valuable not to the young women who bear them but to their social superiors—the Millenium Hall ladies. By scrutinizing, marking, and measuring the behavior of poor women, these middle-class women create "valuable marks of distinction" that attest to their own importance. Their transmission of bourgeois ideology produces poor women's bodies as such material marks: the downcast eyes, still tongues, and quiet footsteps of "meekness," and the exercised, roughened, and injured bodies of "industry."

The female gaze of domestic surveillance also produces the physical structure of the dwellings of the poor. The careful elaboration of the physical
spaces within which the poor may dwell transforms the "privacy" of the
home into what Foucault calls "a network of mechanisms" which are "elabo-
rated in specific, relatively enclosed places" and which provide "the basic
functioning of a society penetrated through and through" with the marks of
discipline.[19] One of the elderly women who has been put to work since the
arrival of the ladies gives the following detailed account of her new home to
the male narrator:

> There are twelve of us that live here. We have every one a house of two
> rooms, as you may see, beside other conveniences, and each a little garden,
> but though we are separate, we agree as well, perhaps better, than if we
> lived together, and all help one another. Now there is neighbour Susan, and
> neighbour Rachel; Susan is lame, so she spins clothes for Rachel; and
> Rachel cleans Susan's house, and does such things for her as she cannot do
> for herself. (13)

The divinely ordained hierarchy that empowers the ladies to arrange the
houses of the poor becomes explicit:

> The ladies settled all these matters at first, and told us, that as they, to please
> God, assisted us, we must in order to please him serve others. . . . There
> never passes a day that one or other of the ladies does not come and look all
> over our houses, which they tell us, and certainly with truth, for it is a great
> deal of trouble to them, is all for our good, for that we cannot be healthy if
> we are not clean and neat . . . nor do they ever come here without giving us
> some good advice. (13–15)

The buildings in which the poor live ("two rooms . . . and each a little
garden"), like the bodies of the laboring women themselves, become monu-
ments to the power of the Millenium Hall ladies. But these dwellings also
extend the possibilities of surveillance, providing more domestic spaces that
the ladies can "come and look all over."

Within the domestic realm, then, the bourgeois woman may lack power on
her own behalf, but as a conduit of the patriarchal gaze and a discipliner of the
female bodies under her scrutiny, she can certainly produce her own privilege.[20] This distinction between power and privilege identifies a difference

between structurally guaranteed power (that is, when a subject is located in a superior position within a hierarchical system that operates to maintain that superiority) and revocable privilege (a relatively ad hoc assignation of benefits to a subject located in one of several positions, any of which can aid the functioning of the hierarchy). Foucault insists on the impersonality, the arbitrariness, of these positions in disciplinary society: "Power has its principle not so much in a person as in a certain concerted distribution of bodies, surfaces, lights, gazes. . . . Consequently, it does not matter who exercises power. Any individual, taken almost at random, can operate the machine. . . . The more numerous those anonymous and temporary observers are, the greater the risk for the [person being observed] of being surprised and the greater his anxious awareness of being observed."[21] Clearly, for feminists the question of "who exercises power" certainly does matter; a concrete analysis such as this one must work to inflect the smooth surface of Foucauldian archaeologies with the marks of the forms of power generated in particular historical moments and texts. This passage, however, aptly describes the vertiginous awareness of those at the heart of a particular representation—those who "operate the machine"—that such a representation, precisely because it depends on the operation of that position, is not constructed to empower them but to render them functional for power.

The women of Millenium Hall, then, enjoy their privilege only to the extent that they are willing to serve a hierarchized ideology in which they are inferior to the men who visit them from the "foreign" realms beyond the domestic sphere. Thus their efforts to extend their privilege cannot take the form of challenging that hierarchy; rather, they must attempt to extend the domestic sphere itself. As a material practice, charity is their most effective strategy. As explained in the novel, "In every thing their view is to be as beneficial to society as possible, and they are such economists even in their charities as to order them in a manner that as large a part of mankind as possible should feel the happy influence of their bounty" (112). By making over poor households in the image of bourgeois domesticity, the women of Millenium Hall recruit "as large a part of mankind as possible" into the ideology that produces their own privilege and distinction. This privilege consists in their economic security—before coming to Millenium Hall, most of the women somehow inherited or acquired fortunes, and they pool their resources with those that didn't—and the leisure and education such security produces, as well as in their position at the center of the ideology of the Christian household, with an obligation to proselytize the true faith.

## The Danger of Pleasure and the Limits of Domestic Female Power

*Millenium Hall* is an explicit portrait of the powers of domestic female virtue. But it also represents, in a less conscious and systematized way, the violence necessary to confine bourgeois women to this limited sphere. This pattern of representation in the novel undermines the extent to which limitation to the domestic sphere can be seen as "natural" or "chosen." Instead, it dramatizes the ruthlessness and danger of bourgeois ideology, with its explicit hierarchies of men over women, heterosexuality over homosexuality, English over national and colonial Others. In this way, it exposes domestic female power as a coerced position rather than simply an inevitable one.

Perhaps the most important structure of coercion in the novel is its representation of pleasure and sexuality. The novel consistently represents pleasure, particularly sexual pleasure, as masculine and therefore inherently dangerous for women. Several of the characters come to live at Millenium Hall after having been victimized by male sexual power; female friendship is defined in opposition to the violence of male sexuality, as a refuge from it. The importance of such a distinction for a novel that represents a secure female utopia helps clarify the interest for women in constructing a discourse of female intimacy that cordons off sexuality to avoid male sexual violence. Sarah Scott, the survivor of an early, disastrous marriage to George Lewes Scott, followed just such a pattern, extricating herself from her marriage to live with her intimate friend, Lady Barbara Montagu.[22] When Scott's characters encounter sexuality, the result is violent catastrophe.

When ten-year-old Louisa Mancel is orphaned, Mr. Hintman, a traveler who happens to be staying at the same inn as the little girl, moved by her great beauty, agrees to educate and provide for her. At boarding school, Louisa befriends an older girl, Miss Melvyn, and shares Mr. Hintman's generous presents with her friend, cementing their intimacy.[23] Louisa grows up into a "dazzlingly handsome" (44) young woman, well educated and financially well provided for by Mr. Hintman. She regards these attributes "rather as snares than blessings," however. The description of Louisa's situation brings together a cluster of images of sexual attractiveness as the most extreme kind of danger. Louisa, "like a person on the brink of a precipice could not enjoy the beauty of the prospect, overawed by the dangers of the situation" (45). This generalized threat becomes specific when male protection turns to dangerous sexual interest: Mr. Hintman's "caresses, which suited her earlier years, had now become improper" (46), yet he continues to touch and fondle his teenage ward.

In such a situation, the contradictions in the code of domestic female virtue seriously constrain a woman from protecting herself. Louisa is "in great difficulty how to act, between gratitude and affection on one side, and necessary caution and reserve on the other" (47). Her filial duty prevents her from acting for her own protection, yet the responsibility for altering this dangerous situation also rests with her. Her tutor, Mr. d'Avora, insists that Mr. Hintman's behavior is subject to his dependent's control: the latter "would alter it, and if he was not immediately sensible of the difference a small addition of age makes, yet her behaviour would lead him to recollect it" (46). Paradoxically, the ideology of domestic female virtue insists that Louisa has the greatest degree of responsibility for her relationship with Mr. Hintman at precisely the moment at which her power and agency are most seriously hindered.

There is a narrative break at this point in the text; the woman telling the story, Mrs. Maynard, is interrupted by one of the male travelers whose visit to Millenium Hall occasions her narrative. The novel here clarifies and insists on the revision of male sexuality in terms of almost apocalyptic danger for women:

"You see gallantry in a very serious light, madam," said Lamont.

"I do indeed, sir," answered Mrs Maynard, "I look on it as the most dangerous of vices, it destroys truth, honour, humanity, it is directly contrary to the laws of God, is the destruction of society, and almost as inconsistent with morality as with religion."

"I beg pardon, madam," interrupted Lamont (who felt himself a little touched with what she said), "for breaking into your narrative, and must beg you will continue it." (52)

The woman narrator insists on the seriousness, the danger, and the viciousness and destructive power of what the male auditor wants to call merely "gallantry." Much of the rhetorical energy of the entire novel repeats this gesture, coding the danger of male sexuality as an interruption in the lives and stories of women.

There is no possibility in *Millenium Hall* that women might enjoy their own sexuality or beauty. Indeed, female beauty is consistently presented as a handicap and liability for a woman. For one thing, it renders women unable to work to support themselves. When Miss Melvyn searches for genteel employment, her elderly friend Mr. d'Avora tells her that "she must not expect, while her person continued such as it then was, that a married woman would receive her in any capacity that fixed her in the same house with her husband" (53). Indeed, the two agree that as long as Miss Melvyn remains beautiful, her plans of becoming a governess or companion to support herself must be postponed, since "her beauty was the great obstacle to its being put in execution" (86). The novel's universe accepts the terms of this argument—that no employer wants to hire a beautiful woman for the kinds of work available to indigent ladies—so completely that they form the basis of Mr. d'Avora's appeal to the widow Mrs. Thornby to take on Miss Melvyn. Both agree that Miss Melvyn's "person would justly deter a married woman from receiving her, and might make a cautious mother avoid it, since her good conduct would rather add to than diminish her attractions" (97); therefore, Mr. d'Avora argues, "it was only with a single lady" such as Mrs. Thornby that "she could hope to be placed" (97). The "justice" of such "cautious" scruples is never called into question—Mrs. Thornby hires Miss Melvyn out of a charitable recognition of the "cruelty" of her situation.

The novel presents a grotesque solution to the double bind in which women's beauty places them in the novel's final narrative, the story of Miss Harriot Trentham. Beautiful, wise, and good, Harriot attempts to cure her broken heart when her lover, Mr. Alworth, marries another woman by throwing herself into the dissipation of fashionable city life. In the course of a charitable excursion, she contracts smallpox and her face is seriously disfigured. Mrs. Maynard records Harriot's response to this event:

> When she came to her senses, she at first seemed mortified to think Mr Alworth had seen her in that disfigured condition; but on reflection told me she rejoiced in it, as she thought it must totally extinguish his passion; and her greatest solicitude was for his happiness. . . . When she recovered, she perceived that the smallpox had entirely destroyed her beauty. She

acknowledged she was not insensible to this mortification; and to avoid the observation of the envious or even of the idly curious she retired . . . to a country house. . . . In a very short time she became perfectly contented with the alteration this cruel distemper had made in her. (199)

The public, sexual pleasures of town flirtations are replaced with the activities characteristic of "rational piety":[24]

> Her love for reading returned, and she regained the quiet happiness of which flutter and dissipation had deprived her without substituting any thing so valuable in its place. She has often said she looks on this accident as a reward for the good she had done . . . and that few benevolent actions receive so immediate a recompense, or we should be less remiss in our duties. . . . In the country she had time to reflect on the necessity of conquering [her love for Alworth] if she wished to enjoy any tolerable happiness; and therefore took proper measures to combat it. (199–200)

The face of a beautiful woman must be disfigured, her beauty "entirely destroyed," before she can achieve "any tolerable happiness" in this novel. Harriot's "reward" for the loss of love, beauty, and sexuality is the return of "her love for reading" and the possibility of "the quiet happiness" of a retired country life devoted to "reason and piety" (200). The terror of public, sexual life—and in this novel those two categories are repeatedly linked—is so great that illness, disfigurement, and isolation are preferable for the women characters, as long as they can achieve some measure of safety from male sexuality and the violence it repeatedly brings in its wake.

Mr. d'Avora's conclusion that Miss Melvyn's dangerous beauty would be safely defused "only with a single lady" also implies that the sexual provocation of such beauty occurs only in the presence of men—husbands and sons. Two women together, then, are safe from the inroads not just of male sexuality but also of sexuality per se—because the novel defines sexuality per se as male. Women characters speak of the terrors of marriage in terms that emphatically distance their own interests from those of the heterosexual institution. Such representations preclude the possibility of any safe expression not just of female homosexuality (because to acknowledge the sexual possibilities inherent in intimacy between women would be to compromise the safety of that relationship) but also of heterosexuality.

The hyperbolic language used by Miss Melvyn to describe the prospect of her marriage to the man her parents have chosen for her exemplifies the extremity of the sexual danger that marriage represents for women in *Millenium Hall*:

> When I reflect . . . on the step I am going to take, my terrors are inexpressible; how dreadful is it at my age, when nature seems to promise me so many years of life, to doom myself to a state of wretchedness which death alone can terminate, and wherein I must bury all my sorrows in silence, without even the melancholy relief of pouring them forth in the bosom of my friend, and seeking, from her tender participation, the only consolation I could receive! For after this dreaded union is completed, duty will forbid me to make my distresses known, even to my Louisa; I must not then expose the faults of him whose slightest failings I ought to conceal. One only hope remains, that you, my first and dearest friend, will not abandon me; that whatever cloud of melancholy may hang over my mind, yet you will still bear with me, and remove your abode to a place where I may have the consolation of your company. (78–79)

Miss Melvyn's terror, dread, wretchedness, melancholy, distress, and wish for death at the prospect of marriage are rooted here in the anticipation of a significant deprivation: that of her friendship with Miss Mancel. Miss Melvyn's marriage, she assumes, will result in radical social isolation, even imposing "silence" between herself and her intimate friend. Later in the narrative, we learn that Miss Melvyn's husband refuses to permit Miss Mancel to live with them (as Lady Barbara Montagu lived with Sarah Scott and her husband, even accompanying them on their honeymoon).[25] He charges, "I will have no person in my house more beloved than myself" (80), indicating that even the novel's male characters accept the assumption that a woman finds happiness more readily in female friendship than in marriage: that the friend would inevitably be "more beloved" than the husband.

Despite this vivid pattern of association between marriage, terror, and isolation, the women of Millenium Hall are quick to defend themselves from the charge that they oppose marriage. Indeed, this careful defensiveness animates one of the novel's central conflicts. For although it celebrates the safety, rationality, and piety of a sexless community of middle- and upper-class women, it attempts to do so without condemning the oppressive conditions from which the women are liberated in their retirement: the dangers of male sexual violence, the impossibility of finding adequate work, the radical isolation of marriage. The following passage, in which two of the women explain the community's support of marriage, dramatizes the paradox of the novel's deep conservatism most acutely.[26] Mrs. Morgan asserts:

> We consider matrimony as absolutely necessary to the good of society; it is a general duty; but as, according to all ancient tenures, those obliged to perform knight's service, might, if they chose to enjoy their own firesides, be excused by sending deputies to supply their places; so we, using the same privilege substitute many others, and certainly much more promote wedlock than we could do by entering into it ourselves. . . . [Miss Trentham continues:] to face the enemy's cannon appear[s] to me a less effort of courage than to put our happiness into the hands of a person who perhaps will not once reflect on the importance of the trust committed to his or her care. (115–116)

The image of marriage as a war (complete with enemy cannon) paradoxically insists upon just the critique of marriage that this passage attempts to deny. Even in its most explicit statement of support for the heterosexual institution, then, the novel describes it in terms of unmistakable danger.

Sexual relationships are dangerous for women in *Millenium Hall;* but women also avert such relationships because sexual desire itself is consistently portrayed as disgusting. Elderly people, for example, ought not to experience sexual desire, for "the most whimsical of the poets never fancied a grey-bearded Cupid, or represented Hymen with a torch in one hand, and a crutch in the other" (55). When old Mr. Morgan marries Miss Melvyn, his desire disgusts her: we are told that her husband "was indeed fond of her person; he admired her beauty but despised her understanding. . . . [S]he suffered less uneasiness from his ill-humour, brutal as it was, than from his nauseous fondness" (85). Picking up on the eighteenth-century usage of "fondness" for sexual desire, Rabb notes the remarkable compression of this account of "marital rape and abuse"; Rabb claims that the indirection of such passages "minimizes their description (not necessarily their impact)."[27] The impact of such compression, I would argue, attests to the force of the paradox outlined above; like the women's defense of marriage, this passage manifests a taut and suppressed energy, the energy of denial necessary to the novel's paradoxical attempts to outline an all-female utopia without criticizing the society from which its inhabitants withdraw. Women's sexual affection for men can even excuse men's brutality; Mrs. Parnel, reflects the narrator, "had disgusted [her husband] with the continual professions of a love to which his heart would not make an equal return. This fondness teased a temper naturally good into peevishness and was near converting indifference into dislike" (192). The rational "disgust" of the Millenium Hall narrator is even more pronounced than Mr. Parnel's.

When less discredited characters than Mr. Morgan and Mrs. Parnel experience sexual desire in the novel, they simultaneously experience pain or sorrow. When Sir Edward Lambton declares his love to Miss Mancel, for example, "her heart return[s] his passion," but she also experiences "real sorrow" (90) that they should have fallen in love against the wishes of Sir Edward's mother. Later, when she attracts other lovers, she is "hurt with the serious attachment of those who more particularly addressed her" (108). In even stronger terms, Lady Emilia's sexual encounter with Lord Peyton is described as "a lasting affliction; a grief never to be washed away" (168); the child that results could never afford Lord Peyton "a pleasure that was not mingled with the deepest affliction" (171). Sorrow, hurt, affliction, and grief await the rational man or woman who succumbs to desire.

The dichotomy between rational friendship and animalistic sexual love recurs frequently in the novel. Miss Mancel and Mrs. Morgan, for instance, agree "to retire into the country, and though both of an age and fortune to enjoy all the pleasures which most people so eagerly pursue, they were desirous of fixing in a way of life where all their satisfactions might be rational and as conducive to eternal as to temporal happiness" (110). Friendship, then, is figured as a "retirement" from the "pleasures" of public life; we see the women "fixing" themselves into a static situation in which rational "satisfactions" replace pleasures, and the importance of life on earth gives way to that of the Christian vision of "eternal happiness." Repeatedly, in choosing their female friends over their male lovers, this novel's women characters direct their attention away from their current lives toward "the life to come." Miss Mancel reflects that

had she married Sir Edward Lambton, her sincere affection for him would have led her to conform implicitly to all his inclinations, her views would have been confined to this earth, and too strongly attached to human objects to have properly obeyed the giver of the blessings she so much valued. . . . Her age, her fortune and compliant temper might have seduced her into dissipation and have made her lose all the heart-felt joys she now daily experiences, both when she reflects on the past, contemplates the present, or anticipates the future. (112)

In this formulation, (hetero)sexual love must be eschewed because it is too good: it tempts one to think too much of this world. The love between Miss Mancel and her lifelong friend is in no danger of "seducing" her into a too great attachment to "human objects." Female friendship, then, provides an alternative to pleasure, sexuality, and the material world.

Despite the sustained argument against pleasure implicit in the movement of women away from the public world and marriage into the private sphere and friendship, the novel provides an explicit statement defending the women from the charge of opposing pleasure itself. As in the representation of marriage, the novel's association of pleasure with danger and disgust comes perilously close to social critique; the attempt to disarm this possibility and sustain the novel's conservative social vision results in a tension-filled paradox between the ladies' statements and their actions. In a characteristic narrative interruption, Lamont, the masculine, Frenchified listener who remains to be converted by the ladies' English rationalism, demands, "Do you think it incumbent on people of fashion to relinquish their pleasures, lest their example should lead others to neglect their business?" (117). Miss Trentham answers "in the affirmative," but when Lamont acknowledges their "right to turn reformers . . . since you begin by reforming yourselves," the ladies quickly cede their authority. To recall the quotation marked above, "we do not set up for reformers. . . . we wish to regulate ourselves by the laws laid down to us, and as far as our influence can extend, endeavour to enforce them; beyond that small circle all is foreign to us; we have sufficient employment in improving ourselves; to mend the world requires much abler hands" (118). The women of Millenium Hall, then, observe the pernicious effects of "the laws laid down to us" but never attempt to speak of them or their effects. Rather, patriarchal law (legislative, religious, and cultural) speaks through them, effectively silencing the possibilities of critique or reform inherent in the distance between the social world they have built for themselves and the one they have left behind.

Slaves to Friendship and Desire

Thus, the ideology of domestic femininity, which maintains power through the discursive penetration and surveillance of subjects, perpetually threatens to dissolve into simple force. Nowhere is the difficulty of maintaining this distinction clearer than in the repeated image of slavery as it is used and avoided by various speakers. This pattern of silence and assertion produces implicit support for the antislavery arguments that were beginning to reach popular middle-class consciousness in 1760s England. It also exposes the ways in which such arguments worked to extend and solidify bourgeois hegemony, advocating the "enlightened" labor methods of the emergent factory-based capitalist economy (and the Panoptical surveillance it entailed) over the labor-intensive systems of a feudal and slave-owning culture that depended on physical force for their operation.

Indeed, Scott herself makes such an argument in *The History of Sir George Ellison,* a novel praised by African British abolitionist Ignatius Sancho in a 1766 letter to Laurence Sterne.[28] On his arrival in Jamaica, Ellison, a "man of real sensibility," objects to "the cruelty exercised on one part of mankind; as if the difference of complexion excluded them from the human race."[29] He swears to "find a means of rendering our slaves obedient, without violating the laws of justice and humanity" (*Ellison,* 12). Instead of corporal punishment, he tells the slaves that he will deprive them of holidays after a first offense and of a day's food for a second; after a third offense, he will sell them to the first bidder (*Ellison,* 14–15). Ellison never considers freeing his slaves, and this shift from force to coercion (with its threat of exposing recalcitrant slaves to the physical brutality of another owner) is really only a shift in emphasis. But in the novel, this "humane" treatment results in Ellison's plantation becoming the most successful on the island; he is able to extract more labor from his slaves by attending to their health and safety than other owners can by torturing theirs.

The object of abolition in the novel—the slave who must be freed—is Ellison himself. His excessive attempts to avoid giving pain to others result in his being taken advantage of first by a disobedient slave, who gets him to reverse his "irreversible" sentence after a third offense (*Ellison,* 19). At this point the action shifts from the plantation fields to the domestic interior, where the weak and jealous Mrs. Ellison holds sway. She successfully keeps her husband from leaving her side by complaining that if he loved her, he would never displease her by absenting himself. The narrator evaluates her policy as follows: "Had Mrs. Ellison openly shewn an intention of enslaving her husband, she would have found him better acquainted with the relative duties of matrimony, than to have submitted to a disgraceful and unnatural yoke. But, on their first marriage, she restrained only with silken threads" (21). Mrs. Ellison's "silken threads," like her husband's humane labor practices, make possible an enslavement not open but covert, dependent not on force but on the solicitation of loyalty, affection, desire. Although Ellison's friends "seriously and sensibly, advised him to free himself from his bondage" (23), his fidelity to the canons of sensibility make it impossible for him to refuse his wife anything when she calls on his love. This narrative stasis is resolved by the sudden intervention of a fever that kills Mrs. Ellison, leaving Ellison free to return to the metropolis to repair "a constitution much hurt by the heat of the climate" (38) and to educate his son without his wife's damaging inter-ference. When Ellison leaves Jamaica, his enslavement ends; he arrives in England ready to extricate women from forced marriages and spring debtors from prison. Although he never liberated his slaves the way he does these enslaved English people, the novel imagines these actions as consistent with the sensibility demonstrated by his practices as a slave owner.

This problem is anticipated in *Millenium Hall,* which Ferguson calls a "com-panion volume" to *Sir George Ellison.*[30] The continuity between the two novels is made explicit in the character of Lamont, the young dandy of *Millenium Hall* who appears as the "eminent merchant" (*Ellison,* 6) to whom George Ellison is apprenticed in the later novel. Once again, the novel invokes slavery only to imagine English people, in this case especially women, as slaves, but in *Mille-nium Hall* the relationship between the Caribbean trade and the domestic balance of power is even more attenuated.

The occasion for the narrative in *Millenium Hall* is the return of the un-named male narrator from his plantations in Jamaica. Back home in England, he now hopes "to enjoy the plenty and leisure for which a few years labour had furnished [him] the necessary requisites" (2). This is as close as the novel comes to any reference to the slave trade, at its height in England's Caribbean colonies in the mid–eighteenth century. But as we saw in *Sir George Ellison,* this passage figures the evils of the Jamaican plantation in terms of the destruction of the body of the master rather than that of the slave: "I was advised by an eminent physician to make a very extensive tour through the western part of this kingdom, in order . . . to cure the ill effects of my long abode in the hot and unwholesome climate of Jamaica, where, while I increased my fortune, I gradually impaired my constitution" (2). Both abolitionist rhetoric and popular slave narratives echoed these intersecting images of illness, a hot climate, and physical (and, by extension, moral) impairment. Olaudah Equiano, for example, an Ibo man kidnapped and sold into slavery in about 1755, writes in his 1789 memoirs of an exceptional British seaman in the West Indies "whose heart had not been debauched by a West India climate." Cruelty among those who work the slave trade is more typical, he argues: "Such a tendency has the slave-trade to debauch men's minds and harden them to every feeling of humanity" when their business is to deprive Africans of "the freedom which diffuses health and prosperity throughout Britain."[31] The slave trade itself and the hot climates in which it is carried on are conflated in this account; if the slave trade debauches, the pure air of England "diffuses health." Such a nexus of images, then, has a discursive meaning produced by the interaction it opens up between texts such as Scott's and Equiano's. The scrupulous avoidance of any mention of slavery in Scott's description of the "unwholesome climate of Jamaica" fails to banish its specter from the rest of the text. "Slavery" is invoked in a variety of contexts by both the male narrator and his companion, Lamont, and the ladies of Millenium Hall themselves. This anxious reinscription of slavery, the marked absence of the novel's opening pages, endows it with unavoidable significance to the social world of the novel.

The first explicit discussion of "slavery" in the novel sounds very much like an argument against the Caribbean trade. Miss Mancel remonstrates that "to see a man, from a vain desire to have in his possession the native of another climate and another country, reduce a fine and noble creature to misery, and confine him within narrow inclosures whose happiness consisted in un- bounded liberty, shocks my nature" (18). Equiano uses a similar appeal to generosity, happiness, and equality when he argues that slavery "gives one man a dominion over his fellows which God could never intend! For it raises the owner to a state as far above man as it depresses the slave below it, and with all the presumption of human pride, sets a distinction between them, immeasurable in extent and endless in duration."[32] In fact, the passage from *Millenium Hall* is a discussion of the injustice of imprisoning wild animals in zoos, circuses, or parks. Miss Mancel continues: "I imagine man has a right to use the animal race for his own preservation, perhaps for his convenience, but certainly not to treat them with wanton cruelty, and as it is not in his power to give them any thing so valuable as their liberty, it is, in my opinion, criminal to *enslave* them, in order to procure ourselves vain amusement, if we have so little feeling as to find any while others suffer" (19; emphasis added). The auditors for this polemic are Lamont and the male narrator whose Jamaican planta-tions, presumably run by slaves, have given him the leisure to tarry and observe Millenium Hall society for as long as he likes. The irony here both undermines the text's explicit social conservatism and paradoxically supports it by clearly establishing the social boundaries of the world of Millenium Hall and its visitors. The enlightened sentiments against "enslavement" uttered by Miss Mancel and the consequent edification of her male auditors are made possible by the profits of British mercantile expansion in the Caribbean. Thus the occasion for this argument against "enslavement" is produced by the West Indian slave trade.

The next mention of slavery comes even closer to acknowledging this destabilizing irony, for it is a discussion of human beings used or treated as slaves. One of the charitable ventures of the Millenium Hall ladies is to provide housing for "those poor creatures who are rendered miserable from some natural deficiency or redundancy" (19). These "monsters"—giants, "dwarfs," "one grey-headed toothless old man of sixteen years of age"—live in an enclosed acreage surrounded by a fence and a thick hedge to protect them from the scorn of public scrutiny. The ladies have rescued the "poor creatures" from circuses and "monster-mongers" who exhibited them for profit. Mrs. Morgan explains: "This miserable treatment of persons, to whom compassion should secure more than common indulgence, determined us to purchase these worst sort of slaves, and in this place we have five" (20). By comparing the "monsters" with other sorts of slaves (especially by clarifying the ladies' acquisition of them by "purchase") this passage paradoxically both summons and erases the slaves whom the Millenium Hall visitor—and per-haps the *Millenium Hall* reader—would have used on his or her own planta-tions. The language of eighteenth-century English debates over abolition continues the metaphor, when the visitor remarks that he and Lamont "were very desirous of seeing this enfranchised company" (20). The extension of the franchise to slaves was an element of the most radical abolitionist arguments in the period; in a letter to an American acquaintance, for example, the well-known antislavery writer Granville Sharpe told American revolutionists that "they should realize that if Congress had acted 'nobly' in forbidding further importations of slaves, 'the business is but half done, 'till they have agreed upon some equitable and safe means of gradually enfranchising those which remain.' "[33] Lamont's reference to "this enfranchised company" obscures the "purchase" of the "monsters" in the first place—obscures, in fact, their continuing status as slaves. Because they are no longer publicly abused, he implies, they are free. This conflation of safety with freedom in other discussions of the basis for community at Millenium Hall marks one of the most crucial ideological slides in the novel's construction of female power. As we saw above, the notion of liberty as "freedom from" persecution, rather than "freedom to" act on one's own behalf, animates the depiction of the power of the Millenium Hall women. This paradoxical construction of power reveals the limits of female power in the bourgeois patriarchal culture that places the virtuous domestic woman at the center of its own narrative of self-legitimation.

The image of slavery empties further, from this deracialized metaphor to one actually disembodied in its next incarnation in the text. Here, it is emotions, not bodies, that are confined. In this shift, the responsibility for slavery is transferred from master to slave, just as Sir George Ellison actually ends up enslaved by the Africans he owns. Miss Melvyn's father, Sir Charles, lets himself be "totally guided by" his wife, Miss Melvyn's evil stepmother. Mrs. Maynard explains: "His mind was so entirely enslaved that he beheld nothing but in the light wherein she pleased to represent it, and was so easy a dupe, that she could scarcely feel the joys of self triumph in her superior art" (53). Sir Charles's culpability and weakness are clearly the causes of his "enslavement." This reversal of responsibility draws the metaphor of slavery even further away from the specific physical, economic, and political conditions of the eighteenth-century slave trade, suggesting that something about the "slave" himself or herself produces the condition. Slavery is not, then, a matter of inequality (a condition that inhabitants of the English domestic scene might observe all around them) but of constitutional weakness.

Slavery next becomes a question of mutual responsibility and religious duty when it is compared with friendship, moving the discussion even further away from the question of force acting on the body into the realm of abstract philosophical discussion. In response to Miss Mancel's description of how people achieve happiness—which she argues "consists in fulfilling the design of their Maker, in providing for their own greatest felicity, and contributing all that is in their power to the convenience of others"—Lamont worries that she wishes "to make us all slaves to each other" (62). "No sir," she replies. "I would only make you friends. Those who are really such are continually endeavouring to serve and oblige each other; this reciprocal communication of benefits should be universal, and then we might with reason be fond of this world" (62). In this reinscription of Lamont's anxious interruption, slavery becomes a "contribution" rather than an enforced servitude. Lamont's position as the friend and fellow traveler of the plantation owner/narrator suggests that the metaphor of slavery in the text circles back to the character with whose story it first entered the text, but with a difference. Instead of an evil that brings ill health, slave labor and the wealth it generates become voluntary "contributions," part of a system of "reciprocal communication" in which people confer benefits on one another from positions of contractual equality, just as Adam Smith's "invisible hand" regulated supply and demand in Enlightenment economic theory. Labor and hence the physically confined and tortured bodies that produce it have disappeared from this account, leaving "slavery" available as a philosophical and moral category empty of any specific political charge.

Such a redefinition in the novel's appropriation of "slavery" as a metaphor had significant social resonance in the mid– and late–eighteenth century. Historically, as David Brion Davis argues in *The Problem of Slavery in the Age of Revolution,* "the antislavery movement . . . reflected the needs and values of the emerging capitalist order" at least as much as it represented a humanitarian desire to liberate enslaved Africans. Davis notes that "the first decades of antislavery agitation [from 1770 on, in his account] also witnessed an outpouring of tracts on the problem of labor discipline [in England]. And the chief figures who helped to revise the traditional paternalism toward the 'laboring poor' were all outspoken opponents of Negro slavery." He contends that "an attack on the slave system could thus become a permissible means of responding to change without a weakening or discrediting of class hegemony."[34] On the contrary, antislavery activism focused on the West Indies and North America helped direct attention away from the human costs of the massive economic shift to industrialization in England. As Davis argues:

The abolitionist movement cannot be detached from its defining social context—from the accelerating pace of enclosures, which augmented a drifting population of rural paupers; from the problem of disposing of convicts, who could no longer be shipped to America; from the trade in pauper apprentices, who were being sent by the wagon- or barge-load from London to the mill towns; from the growing desire for utility, efficiency, productivity, and order; or from the industrial employment of small children. . . . If British abolitionists could express horror over the iron chains of the slave trade, their acts of selectivity and definition helped to strengthen the invisible chains being forged at home.[35]

Such a context helps explain the great interest in *Millenium Hall* in the household and labor arrangements of the poor and its connection to the ladies' philanthropy and enlightened charity. The network of images of slavery thus performs the ideological work of both erasing from the text the racial hierarchy of the Caribbean slave trade and naturalizing the expanding economic system on which the emergence of bourgeois English culture was based in the period. The charity of romantic friends, like their performance of domestic surveillance, works to legitimize imperial power relations. Their homosocial relations are asserted on the grounds of the specific class and racial hierarchies that the ideology of domestic virtue works to naturalize.

Women, Slaves, and "Monsters"

The ultimately static position of the women of Millenium Hall—safe and powerful only when cut off from the world—eerily echoes that of the "monsters" that the ladies protect in the heart of their estate, immuring them behind high hedges and sharp palings. Like these "unfortunates," the Millenium Hall women have been rescued (by themselves or by one another) from their abusive keepers—fathers or husbands—in the outside world. Rendered frail by the batterings they have received, neither the ladies nor the "monsters" need now work for their keep. Instead, they merely recover from the abusive outside world. The ladies are physically "monstrous" as well; whether marked and made ugly by disease or simply represented as sexless, these women have failed to conform to the expectations of heterosexual femininity. So like those they protect, the women must be shielded from public ridicule. They are safe only in an enclosed space that others, more powerful than they,

can enter and leave at will. But because the novel refuses the possibility that
the dangers of the public world could or should ever be "reformed," it imagines the fragile characters at its center safe only when confined—for life.
Lamont suggests that the ladies are "slaves"—slaves to friendship. As we saw
earlier, Miss Mancel revises this metaphor to suggest that the labor of slaves is
a voluntary contribution to a mutually beneficial economy—that slaves are
really free, as the ladies are "free" to choose friendship with one another over
heterosexual family life. The equation between slavery and friendship, despite
such a revision, ironically suggests the limited conditions under which they
make such a choice—the constraints of violence and coercion under which
relations between women take place in the form of patriarchal culture emerging in this period as bourgeois modernity. Crucially, however, the very terms
of this equation between friendship and slavery work to obscure and deny the
existence of the economic and political realities of the trade in human bodies
being conducted at the margins of English culture, as at the margins of Scott's
novel, in order to secure its center. The economic and political privilege such
an effacement produces makes possible the assertion of the particular form of
female homosociality that the ladies enjoy—a form that buttresses rather than
challenges the terms in which bourgeois heterosexual culture is being articulated in the mid–eighteenth century.

The analogy between the ladies and the "monsters" they protect underscores the central paradox at work in *Millenium Hall*'s portrait of domestic
female power. In its intransigent conservatism, the novel identifies and supports a social hierarchy that spreads out in detail below the bourgeois women
who operate it. This detail, however, obscures the machinations of power that
lie above them in this hierarchy. The novel tries to solve the problem of male
power—sexual violence, economic inequity, political disenfranchisement,
physical danger—by constructing a world without men, a world based on
class privilege in which bourgeois women become powerful. In its idealiza-
tion of such a world, however, the novel inevitably testifies to the powerlessness of women in the public world of men; it represents Millenium Hall as a
refuge for women stripped bare and humiliated by the material effects of the
hierarchy of men over women. Thus, the homosocial world that the ladies
inhabit can never be a sapphic one, never a space in which women exercise
agency in the service of their own desires. To construct this space aside from
patriarchal violence, the novel must represent the ideological work of Mille-

nium Hall as contributing to the emergence of a figure of bourgeois female power that finds her more typical place in later domestic fiction at the heart of a new, specifically bourgeois version of the heterosexual family, one based on a companionate marriage of mutual affection anchored in female virtue. The novel's brutally accurate description of the unequal distribution of power and sexual agency in patriarchal culture clarifies the enormous appeal of a utopian all-female space for mid-eighteenth-century, middle-class women. In representing this inequality as natural and desirable, however, the novel constructs and guarantees the limits of that safety and shuts down the radical potential of such a vision. The "safety" of Millenium Hall is made possible by the refusal to critique the social hierarchies that make such a refuge necessary. This gesture of refusal guarantees that there will always be a function for this all-female "utopia," for the conditions outside its walls, left intact and operative, will continue to populate it with "monsters," women, and other victims.

# Domesticating Homosexuality:

## *Memoirs of a Woman of Pleasure*

In this chapter I begin by examining a mid-eighteenth-century moment in which certain conventional excoriations of both homosexuals and foreigners come together in the articulation of a specifically English sexuality. This moment, exemplified here by the satirical pamphlet *Satan's Harvest Home,* is modified and its major premise—that homosexuality is distinctly foreign— subtly repudiated in John Cleland's *Memoirs of a Woman of Pleasure.* The latter text produces pornographic pleasure by soliciting a series of desiring gazes mediated through the voice of the heroine, Fanny. The multiple bodies and pleasures observed by Fanny, however, complicate the notion of a single, properly English, properly heterosexual reader. Cleland's text brings the fe- male homosexuality that *Satan's Harvest Home* locates in Turkey into the En- glish domestic interior, saturating it with the language and social structures of *Millenium Hall*–style romantic friendship. The text also marks certain male homosexual bodies as particularly English, distinguishing them from the homosexuality of "other climes" on the basis of how easy they are to read. In these ways, *Memoirs of a Woman of Pleasure* domesticates homosexuality, mark- ing it out as English, whether it is depicted as relatively harmless (in the case of women) or as a singularly horrible vice (in the case of men).

This Anglicization of homosexuality is also produced by the narrative structure and points of view in the novel. I consider these formal elements in the latter part of this chapter, arguing that the multiple desires and identifica- tions produced by their intersection with the conventions of pornographic representation end up cracking apart the naturalized heterosexuality on which those conventions depend.

## Xenohomophobia: *Satan's Harvest Home*

The proliferation of homosexual acts, identities, desires, and objects, both male and female, in Cleland's text constitutes its potentially radical incoherence. Such possibilities make the text available for a variety of readers and readings, including gay and lesbian ones, against the grain of the novel's normative, bourgeois heterosexuality. But in the context of the midcentury discourse about homosexuality, perhaps the most subversive claim the novel makes about homosexuality is a national rather than a sexual one.[1] I want to turn briefly to a contemporary diatribe entitled *Satan's Harvest Home* to underscore another set of ideological problems created by the intersection of the generic conventions of pornography with those of the narrative of bourgeois ascension. Published in 1749, the same year volume 2 of *Memoirs* appeared, *Satan's Harvest Home* is a satiric pamphlet condemning "the present state of whorecraft, adultery, fornication, procuring, pimping, sodomy, and the game at Flatts" in mid-eighteenth-century London.[2] ("The game at Flatts" is a bizarre euphemism for lesbianism.[3]) It concerns itself with many of the same issues and images as *Memoirs,* but from a distinctly horrified, rather than curious and titillated, point of view. It asserts the natural amorousness of women, describes country girls going to the city to become whores, and details varied sexual practices similar to those described in the novel. An important difference between the representations of lesbianism and male homosexuality in the two texts, however, is that in *Satan's Harvest Home,* such practices are definitely not English. The pamphlet participates in the widespread convention of locating all forms of homosexuality in places marked Other—Italy and France in the case of male homosexuality, and France and Turkey in the case of lesbianism.

In *Memoirs of a Woman of Pleasure,* Mrs. Cole comforts Fanny after she has witnessed two men having sex together by telling her that "whatever effect this infamous passion had in other ages, and other countries, it seem'd a peculiar blessing on our air and climate, that there was a plague-spot visibly imprinted on all that are tainted with it, in this nation at least."[4] Here the narrative invokes the convention of a foreign origin for sodomy only to discount it. English sodomy, according to this logic, is superior to that found elsewhere because of the "blessing" of the English "air and climate," which imprints a visible "plague-spot" on its practitioners. This bodily marking, of course, renders sodomites undeniably Other in relation to the norm that Fanny's outrage is supposed to guarantee, but this is an account of a difference within national character that contrasts sharply with the resolute deportation of homosexuality in *Satan's Harvest Home.*

The insistence in the pamphlet on the foreignness of homosexuality helps construct not only the homosexualized Other but the proper Englishman and -woman as well. For example, in its argument that the fashion of men kissing each other in greeting is the first step toward "unnatural Vices," the pamphlet constructs the following myth of national origins:

> This *Fashion* was brought over from *Italy* (the *Mother* and *Nurse* of *Sodomy*); where the *Master* is oftner *Intriguing* with his *Page,* than a *fair Lady.* And not only in that *Country,* but in *France,* which copies from them, the *Contagion* is diversify'd, and the Ladies (in the *Nunneries*) are criminally *amorous* of each other, in a *Method* too gross for Expression. I must be so partial to my own *Country-Women,* to affirm, or, at least, hope they claim no Share of this *Charge;* . . . Have we not *Sins* enough of our own, but we must eke 'em out with those of *Foreign Nations,* to fill up the Cup of our *Abominations,* and make us yet more ripe for *Divine* Vengeance? (51–52)

Interestingly, the declarative certainty with which the passage traces the geographical journey of male homosexuality is compromised in its description of the status of "crimes" between women. The diminution of certainty ("affirm, or, at least, hope") with which the passage indicates the possibility of English female homosexuality suggests both that women may be more firmly relied on to resist the foreign "contagion" and that the relative lack of information about women may mean that female homosexuality is a less easily knowable and hence more threatening possibility.

Indeed, the section that directly addresses "the game at Flatts" is the one that insists most explicitly on the foreignness of homosexuality; it is also the sole passage in the pamphlet that describes a setting outside England. This two-page "chapter" is the only sustained narrative in *Satan's Harvest Home,* a brief story with characters, dialogue, and plot. These singularities suggest that the attack on sex between women is rather uneasily incorporated into the otherwise gleeful catalogue of vices that characterizes this satire. The logical transition between the rest of the diatribe and this narrative, appended to the very end of the pamphlet, is strangely insufficient. To convince the reader that "a new and most abominable Vice has got footing among the W——n of Q——y," an assertion the author admits may appear "incredible," the pamphleteer turns not to London gossip or personal observation, the previous kinds of evidence offered, but to an unnamed "Author of very great Credit" who speaks not of the English, but of "the Turks" (60). As Felicity Nussbaum points out, Turkey's imperial history was often cited as an object lesson about the failures of despotism in the modern commercial world. In particular, what the English saw as the sexual license and luxury of the Turkish elite—and its requirement that women be endlessly available and endlessly imprisoned in the harem—was singled out as the preeminent cause of the decline of the Ottoman Empire over the course of the eighteenth century. Nussbaum claims that "by the end of the century the Turkish empire was near complete dissolution and its political leaders were characterized as slothful and sensual. . . . The East is represented as a failed power defeated by its sensuality and vulnerable to European penetration."[5] Such fantasies provided a rationale for English curiosity about English sexual practices, as a kind of prophylactic against imperial failure. Thus, our pamphleteer begins in an ethnographic mode:

> A *Turk* hates bodily Filthiness and Nastiness, worse than Soul-Defilement; and therefore, they wash very often, and they never ease themselves, by going to Stool, but they carry Water with them for their Posteriors. But ordinarily the Women bathe by themselves, bond and free together, so that you shall many times see young Maids, exceeding beautiful, gathered from all Parts of the World, exposed naked to the view of other Women, who thereupon fall in Love with them, as young Men do with us, at the Sight of Virgins. (60)

The effect of this passage is to establish the habits of the Turks as utterly foreign, their bodies marked by peculiar habits and their desires comprehensible only by analogy to love among "us." The language here, however, also has the effect of naturalizing the act of women falling in love with one another, at least in this exotic locale, making it something as quotidian as bathing and as inevitable as the love at first sight of myth or romance.

Indeed, the brief tale is filled with romance conventions. The historical location is vague ("It happened one Time"); the geographic location, exotic ("Constantinople"). The virginal love object is "the daughter of a poor man"; to win her, the lover "attempted to perform an Exploit almost incredible; she feigned herself to be a Man . . . and pretended he [*sic*] was one of the *Chiauxes* of the *Grand Seignor*" (61). After the marriage, when the lover is discovered as a woman, she faces with fearless words the governor who condemns her to death, refusing to deny her love: "Away Sir! . . . you do not know the Force of Love, and God grant you never may" (61). Her death also comes from the vocabulary of romance: instead of hanging like an eighteenth-century English criminal, the woman is "pack'd away and drown'd in the Deep" (61).

The language of romance distinguishes this account of love between women from the rest of *Satan's Harvest Home*. Such language does not match the conventions of political satire that structure the rest of the pamphlet. True, the passage insists on the horror of women's desire for one another, calling it a "mad Affection," "so notorious a Bestiality, and so filthy a Fact" (61); it ridicules the lover's pretensions to heroism at the end, when the "Governor could scarce forbear Laughter" at her defiant words. The tone of such moments provides some continuity between the "game at Flatts" chapter and the rest of the pamphlet. But the fablelike structure of the tale, the naturalized account of how Turkish women are struck by one another's beauty, the language of romance—all these elements mark the uneasiness with which the pamphlet addresses love between women, even to excoriate it. Describing the behavior of English "women of quality" by telling the story of a poor Turkish girl renders this form of desire even less English than male homosexuality. For while the misogynist and presumably male pamphleteer can support his condemnation of sodomy and effeminacy by describing what he sees on the streets of London, he can render the possibility of sex between women and female cross-dressing only through the highly distanced medium of this fabulous tale.

*Memoirs of a Woman of Pleasure,* then, while it breaks with the surrounding satirical discourse on sexuality in representing female and male homosexuality in explicit detail, differs much more from that discourse in representing (even satirically) such practices as natural to England, an unsurprising part of the English character. Given the greater difficulty, for this discourse, of imagining sex between women actually happening in England, Cleland's reading of romantic friendship and domestic ideology—the female homosocial spaces that are supposed to guarantee English moral purity—as saturated with sexual meaning may perhaps have been the most troubling aspect of the novel for contemporary readers. Thus the novel's attempt to recuperate itself through insisting on a moral, heterosexual ending has implications not only for how members of the English reading public imagined themselves sexually but also for how they imagined themselves as English.

*Satan's Harvest Home* makes explicit the emerging sexual hierarchy that distinguished between adultery and fornication, on the one hand (which, although condemned by the pamphlet, are easily imaginable and clearly English), and the sexual "crimes" of sodomy and sapphism, on the other. The pamphlet also anxiously connects the latter to questions of national identity. To render masculinity heterogenous (rather than heterosexual) threatens not only the hierarchy of men over women and procreative over pleasure-oriented sex but also that of England over the rest of the world. There is a distinctly English sexuality—procreative, heterosexual, active for men and passive for women—emerging in this discourse, struggling to define itself in opposition to the national and racial Others being exposed to English readers through the literature of nationalist superiority in Europe and the colonies. In contrast, *Memoirs* insists on domesticating homosexuality. It makes sex between men in England better than sex between men on the Continent because English sodomites are clearly marked and therefore recognizable and manageable; it makes the proper location of sex between women the same pretty parlor in which romantic friends read or sew. English sodomy is superior because of its visibility; English sapphism is the natural property of romantic friendship and the domestic ideology that such a relationship complements and legitimates. Thus representations of sex between women, though less threatening in the novel's world than those of sex between men, are actually a more significant revision of the discourse of women's sexlessness because they puncture the national assumptions of that discourse more thoroughly. This "domestication"—the insistence on the Englishness of homosexuality—provides an example of the text's excessive, even unconscious parodic force, a narrative force that requires the operation of a powerful nationalism to reframe perversity as patriotism and accomplish the novel's bourgeois closure. The generic requirements of pornography complicate this closure and provide a structure within which this ambivalence can play itself out. The multiple and heterogenous identifications solicited by the text's commitment to readerly pleasure are also the sources of its unstable point of view, an instability that militates against the putative moral.

### Sodomitical and Sapphic Subjectivities in *Memoirs of a Woman of Pleasure*

*Memoirs of a Woman of Pleasure* justifies itself in the first sentence as the response of one woman to another woman's desires. Fanny Hill begins her memoirs thus:

> MADAM,
>
> I sit down to give you an undeniable proof of my considering your desires as indispensible orders: ungracious then as the task may be, I shall recall to view those scandalous stages of my life, out of which I emerg'd at length. . . . [I will] paint situations such as they actually rose to me in nature, careless of vitiating those laws of decency, that were never made for such unreserved intimacies as ours. (1)

Many feminist critics of the novel, however, have cautioned feminist readers against taking pleasure in such representations of female desire, arguing that the *Memoirs* constructs an oppressive male fantasy of female sexuality.[6] The representation of sexuality in the *Memoirs,* according to these critics, is an artificial construction aimed only at producing pornographic pleasure in male readers, unproductive for feminism because it provides neither an authentic representation of female sexuality nor an empowering articulation of a female voice.[7]

Although this view is well supported by the text itself, one of my tasks in this chapter is to complicate it by reading Cleland's eccentric authorial position less schematically. Beyond the question of whether the *Memoirs* is a misogynist text (which, of course, it is) lies the potentially more fruitful question of the relation between the text's representation of female sexuality and the discourses of romantic friendship and domestic ideology we saw interwoven in Scott's *Millenium Hall.* As the story of a prostitute who becomes a bourgeois wife, *Memoirs* offers an account of female power and pleasure beyond the domestic realm that illuminates the construction of that realm from outside to inside. Because *Memoirs,* like Richardson's 1740 *Pamela,* charts the ascension of the heroine from sexual danger to secure domestic virtue, domestic ideology and the representation of woman it requires provide one of the novel's major frames of reference. But as a pornographic narrative, its relation to narratives of domestic virtue is something other than straightforwardly celebratory. In particular, the novel's representations of intimacy between women, of female virtue, and of female community often parodically expose the sexual and social alternatives from which the bourgeois norms of the *Millenium Hall* or *Pamela* worlds must be wrenched. At times, however, the power of these representations in relation to one another exceeds even parody, spilling over the text's conscious satirical, pedagogical, and heteropornographic intentions to produce pleasure and sexual agency outside those norms. Working against the conservative and conventional closure of Cleland's text, then, is an alternative account of the phantasmal status of domestic female virtue that undercuts the novel's investment in bourgeois ascension and by implication exposes the illusory naturalness of such plots in domestic fiction. Surely there is feminist pleasure to be taken in such a representation.[8]

The novel enacts this denaturalizing gesture most powerfully through its inability to maintain a heterosexual point of view. Feminist critics are right to characterize Cleland as a man writing pornography for the pleasure of other men; in this chapter, I want to explore the sexual charge of such a relation and its effects on the structure of sexuality and the desiring gaze in the novel. Nancy Miller's important article inaugurated the critical convention of referring to Cleland's construction of a female narrator for pornography aimed at men as a character in "drag," enacting a "female impersonation."[9] Miller argues that "the assumption of the Other's sexual identity through an 'I' in drag constitutes an exemplary—if extreme—model of the erotics of authorship in the eighteenth-century novel: a mode of production calibrated not so much to seduce women readers as to attain recognition from other men."[10] She concludes that for the "memorial fiction" of which the *Memoirs* is an example, "the founding contract of the novel as it functions in the phallocentric (heterosexual) economies of representation is homoerotic."[11] Miller's parentheses, however, collapse the very categories I would like to distinguish and analyze: is the "phallocentric" always "heterosexual"? Philip E. Simmons assumes so when he takes up Miller's image in order to argue for the inauthenticity of female characters in Cleland's novel and of its female readers, claiming that the novel's conservative investment in "chastity, heterosexuality, and patriarchal authority . . . ultimately contains any radical energy that might be produced by transgressions of the sexual code."[12] Fanny's letters to a female friend, he claims, create an "ideal female reader" of male pornography, one who has "so internalized the pornographic conventions of female surrender to male pleasure that she becomes little more than a male reader in drag."[13] The "trope" of one woman recounting her sexual adventures to another, Simmons argues, "is a female version of the locker room. Only in saying this we must be aware of an even more fundamental level of disguise: the female narrator is, after all, ventriloquized by a male author. What we have, in fact, is a men's locker room; these jocks are in drag."[14] Curiously, all this talk of "drag" in Cleland's novel never seems to raise the question of homosexuality, the twentieth-century language and culture of which provided the term in the first place. Indeed, Miller's reference to the "homoerotic" relation between male author and male reader is rhetorically positioned to insist on the phallocentrism and therefore (in her terms) the heterosexuality of this relationship. While I would not want to collapse Eve Kosofsky Sedgwick's useful distinction between the homoerotic, which enables a culture of male heterosexual supremacy, and the homosexual, which profoundly threatens it,[15] I do wish to broaden the critical terrain of "phallocentrism" slightly to take seriously the difference it makes when this textual relationship is set up around a pornographic work, one conventionally intended to arouse and even satisfy sexual desire. The dismissive language Simmons uses when he invokes the image of drag (*"little more* than a male reader in drag" [emphasis added], "jocks") exposes the critical attitude that I am attempting to displace: the implicit assumption that homosexuality is a kind of joke, its presence only ever an unimportant, subservient structure undergirding the triumph of heterosexuality in the *Memoirs*. To be sure, the novel itself insists on this reading, especially in the last two anxious pages, in which Fanny's "tail-piece of morality" attempts to paint "the delicate charms of VIRTUE" (187) in convincing enough colors to make a moral tale out of a pornographic narrative. Instead of taking this attempt at heterosexual closure entirely on its own terms, however, I want to examine the ways in which the text produces and represents male and female homosexual desires and subjectivities, in characters and implied readers.[16] Feminist criticism cannot afford to buy patriarchal culture's seamless representation of male sexuality as monolithically heterosexual; in the interest of better understanding how such a monolith is made "natural" in bourgeois culture, I wish to consider the construction in *Memoirs of a Woman of Pleasure* of a "phallocentric" male homosexuality and to trace its relation to female homosexuality and female sexual agency in the novel.

More recent gay critics have done much to revise the joking tone with which homosexuality in the novel is often discussed. For Donald H. Mengay, the question of "drag" works not as a dismissive metaphor but as an account of the structure of address in the novel, one that exposes "a homoeroticized male 'I' under Fanny's rhetorical make-up." To argue for the presence of a "hypothetical he-Fanny" with whom male homosexual readers would identify, Mengay carefully reads the novel's diction and patterns of imagery, establishing the pervasiveness of this narrative possibility, its integration into all elements of its language and structure.[17] Kevin Kopelson's account of the anomalous status of the sodomitical scene underscores the instability of Fanny's point of view, its tendency to wobble away from the novel's norm even at the moment when that norm is most vehemently asserted. Kopelson notes that this is "the only voyeuristic episode in the novel in which the voyeur unwittingly discovers herself, as well as the only such episode in which the voyeur is stationed in a position of instability or insecurity."[18] Read together, these critics offer a way of understanding how Fanny's point of view slips away from that of normative heterosexuality and offers a space for male homosexual desire in both that point of view's representations and the kinds of spaces it makes for readerly intervention. For these critics, however, "homosexuality" in the novel is male. Either Fanny herself represents male homosexual desire or the sodomy scene is the privileged location of homosexuality in the novel. Taking female homosexuality seriously as a narrative and representational category in the novel, as I do here, offers a fuller account of the struggles over subjectivity and sexuality that the novel enacts.

Peter Sabor's 1985 edition of the *Memoirs* restores, for the first time since the novel's initial printing in 1748–49, the male homosexual episode that Fanny witnesses near the end of the novel.[19] Initially deleted after the first printing to avoid scandal, the incident, according to Sabor, was "groundlessly" attributed to authors other than Cleland throughout the nineteenth and the twentieth centuries.[20] In his own time, however, Cleland's contemporaries found it understandable "that he should pass under the Censure of being a Sodomite," in Josiah Beckwith's words. Sabor speculates that such a reputation may have arisen from Cleland's writing of the homosexual episode in the *Memoirs,* buttressed by the fact that he "seems never to have married."[21] Whether the spur is textual, biographical, or both, it seems clear that part of the scandal surrounding *Memoirs of a Woman of Pleasure* is the scandal of homosexuality.

In such a context, we can take seriously Fanny's opening stance of address—perhaps the encoded textual version of the male homosexual politics of address enacted by Cleland's writing of a pornographic novel for the pleasure of other men[22]—as a representation not only of heterosexual male desire "in drag" but of female homosexual desire as well. Janet Todd notes the way in which Fanny's "narrative of her sexual life, sent to her friend, forms an erotic encounter through which the friend comes to 'know' Fanny as Fanny herself came to know her numerous sexual partners."[23] She addresses her interlocutor as "MADAM," a term whose meaning ironically reverberates between a class-coded title of honor and the name of a bawd, the madam of a whorehouse. Domestic female virtue, then, is called into question in the very first word of the novel. The language of the opening paragraph emphasizes the play of desire within the relationship between Fanny and "Madam"—and by implication between whore and madam—displacing the conventional demarcation of the brothel as the site of unmediated heterosexuality. Fanny considers (the) Madam's "desires as indispensible orders"; her production of pornographic narrative, she tells her reader, occurs in response to "*your* desires" rather than those of the heterosexual male reader or client. The brothel, then, is established in the novel's first paragraph as the site of "unreserved intimacies" between women, and women are clearly identified as desiring agents. Finally, Fanny's servicing of the desires of her female internal reader also raises the possibility that her adventures might prove arousing to female readers outside the text. Todd discusses the "confusing" way in which vice in the novel proves "exemplary";[24] the text implies exactly the kind of female reader later antinovelists such as Maria Edgeworth were to deplore, a female reader who might come to identify too strongly with the heroine and become dissatisfied with life outside the text.[25]

Representations of female homosexual desire and agency such as this opening scenario continue to challenge the novel's explicit plot of heterosexual social ascension. Fanny's first sexual encounter takes place when she meets "Mrs. *Phoebe Ayres,* the name of my tutress elect, to whose care and instructions I was affectionately recommended" (9) by Mrs. Brown, the bawd who recruits Fanny for her brothel from a domestic servants agency.

Phoebe's job is to accustom Fanny to "lewdness" so that Mrs. Brown can secure "a good market" for Fanny's maidenhead (10). The language in which the incident is described, however, sometimes slips outside this explicitly heterosexual narrative frame. For example, Fanny refers to Phoebe as "this precious substitute of my mistress's" (10); the ambivalent article ("this") here opens up the possibility that Phoebe acts as a sexual surrogate not only for male clients but for Mrs. Brown herself, rendering Phoebe's seduction of Fanny not just a homosexual act but a complex construction of a homosexual voyeurism unmediated by heterosexual economics.[26]

Such an unmooring of the normative codes of heterosexuality seems to cast conventionally gendered bodies adrift as well. Fanny excuses her complicity in the scene by explaining her ignorance of the "strange, and till then unfelt pleasure" (11) of sexual activity: "Knowing no ill, I feared none; especially from one who had prevented all doubt of her womanhood, by conducting my hands to a pair of breasts that hung loosely down, in a size and volume that full sufficiently distinguished her sex, to me at least, who had never made any other comparison" (10–11). Despite the emphatic assertions of gender identification in the first part of this sentence, the curious qualifying phrases at the end introduce some doubt as to whether Fanny can accurately judge the gender of someone with whom she is having sex, even when she feels the most "womanly" parts of her partner's body. Phoebe's large breasts make Fanny think she is a woman, but having "never made any other comparison," perhaps Fanny does not know what a woman's body really feels and looks like—or perhaps one cannot judge gender from the body. Significantly, Fanny fails to consider her own body as a basis for comparison here, as if she has never examined it as a gendered object. Phoebe's behavior is equally ambiguous:

> In the mean time the extension of my limbs, languid stretchings, sighs, short heavings, all conspired to assure that experienced wanton, that I was more pleased then [*sic*] offended at her proceedings, which she seasoned with repeated kisses and exclamations, such as "Oh! what a charming creature thou art!—what a happy man will he be that first makes a woman of you!—Oh! that I were a man for your sake!"—with the like broken expressions, interrupted by kisses as fierce and salacious as ever I received from the other sex. (11)

By representing Phoebe's wish to be "a man," the passage indicates that she is not one; but her "kisses as fierce and salacious" as a man's suggest that at this moment Phoebe's sexual body might just as easily be a man's. Interestingly, throughout this passage Phoebe never claims to be a woman. And even Fanny, having not yet passed through the process that "makes a woman," is left with her gender undefined. In this homosexual encounter, gender becomes a diffuse and relatively insignificant category; a distinct gender identity is unnecessary for the operation of desire. Amid this vertiginous dislocation of the gender and sexual norms of domestic fiction, Fanny can only assert her heroineship as the suspension of identity: "I was transported, confused, and out of myself" (11).

The novel's somewhat confused account of Phoebe's character offers the possibility of a distinct female homosexual identity as a meaningful category in mid-eighteenth-century culture. Fanny reflects:

> *Phoebe* herself, the hackney'd, thorough-bred *Phoebe,* to whom all modes and devices of pleasure were known and familiar, found, it seems, in this exercise of her art to break young girls, the gratification of one of those arbitrary tastes, for which there is no accounting: not that she hated men, or did not even prefer them to her own sex; but when she met with such occasions as this was, a satiety of enjoyments in the common road, perhaps too a secret byass, inclined her to make the most of pleasure, where-ever she could find it, without distinction of sexes. (12)

This passage vacillates between anxious reassurance that Phoebe must prefer men "to her own sex" and the contradictory assertion of an "arbitrary" taste, "a secret byass" toward women. And contradicting both possibilities is the final statement that she made sexual choices "without distinction of sexes." In our terms, then, this passage slides through the possibilities that Phoebe is heterosexual, lesbian, or bisexual; all three categories are invoked. The competing claims of these eighteenth-century gender and sexual practices can, however inconsistently, make space for not just sapphic acts but also identities.

Sexual relations between women, then, are tightly woven into the fabric of identity formation in the *Memoirs*. This interdependence gives rise to a representation of female community that arranges many of the same elements as were at play in *Millenium Hall* into a different pattern, one that makes female sexuality central rather than dangerously unthinkable. For example, Fanny's second residence in a brothel marks her ascension from the lower-class environs of Mrs. Brown's to a community of "ladies" whose standards seem to rival those of their virtuous counterparts at Millenium Hall. Like Miss Mancel and her friends, Fanny is drawn to this all-female household by the appeal of romantic friendship. Of the madam of the house, she says:

> For Mrs. *Cole* had, I do not know how, unless by one of those unaccountable invincible simpathies, that nevertheless form the strongest links, especially of female friendship, won and got intire possession of me. On her side, she pretended that a strict resemblance, she fancied she saw in me to an only daughter, whom she had lost at my age, was the first motive of her taking to me so affectionately as she did. . . . [S]he had by degrees insinuated herself so far into my confidence, that I threw myself blindly into her hands, and came at length to regard, love, and obey her implicitly: and to do her justice, I never experienc'd at her hands other than a sincerity of tenderness, and care for my interest, hardly heard of in those of her profession. We parted that night, after having settled a perfect unreserv'd agreement; and the next morning Mrs. *Cole* came, and took me with her to her house, for the first time. (92–93)

Here, the likeness drawn between familial relations and female friendship, which such accounts as *Millenium Hall* offer so as to guarantee the sexual innocence of intimacy between women, instead expedites a relationship created by women's sexual activity. This passage performs a parody of the romantic language of female friendship, in which "unaccountable invincible simpathies" and "fancied" likenesses created "the strongest links" of "regard, love, and obe[dience]" between women. In *Millenium Hall,* this language attempts to rule out sexuality; its parodic appropriation in *Memoirs of a Woman of Pleasure* attempts to make sexuality not just possible but inevitable as well. This shift, however, necessitates a resituation of female agency—from the virtuous domestic heroine to the willing prostitute—that moves beyond the limits of parody to produce textual effects that divert Fanny's ascension to happy heterosexuality.

The paragraph that follows the description of Fanny's friendship with Mrs. Cole continues to emphasize the gentility of Mrs. Cole's house and the purity of the relationships among women within it. The young prostitutes offer up the perfect simulacrum of the female friends of *Millenium Hall*.

> Here, at the first sight of things, I found every thing breath an air of decency, modesty, and order.
>
> In the outer-parlour, or rather shop, sat three young women, very demurely employ'd on millinary work, which was the cover of a traffic in more precious commodities: but three beautifuller creatures could hardly be seen: two of them were extremely fair, the eldest not above nineteen, and the third, much about that age, was a piquant brunette. . . . Their dress too, had the more design in it, the less it appeared to have, being in a taste of uniform correct neatness, and elegant simplicity. These were the girls that composed the small, and domestic flock, which my governess train'd up with surprising order and management. . . . Thus, had she insensibly formed a little family of love, in which the members found so sensibly their account in a rare alliance of pleasure with interest, and of a necessary outward decency, with unbounded secret liberty, that Mrs. *Cole*, who had pick'd them as much for their temper as their beauty, govern'd them with ease to herself, and them too. (93)

Like the Millenium Hall ladies, the women of Mrs. Cole's brothel live in a "little family of love," a well-"train'd" "domestic flock" engaged in the virtuous feminine activity of millinery. The vacillation in this representation of female community between surface and depth, outwardly unimpeachable "modesty" and inwardly "unbounded" sexual "liberty," gains parodic force from its allusion to the Richardsonian standards of purity for novelistic heroines, the standards that buttress the sexless account of female friendship supported by *Millenium Hall*. If successful prostitutes can appear to be, even at times think of themselves as, modest and virtuous female friends, then the representation of female virtue that stands at the heart of domestic fiction is fragile indeed.

The sexual "liberty" of this female community is employed most frequently and explicitly in the service of heterosexuality in the novel. Adhering to the canons of pornographic narrative, the novel depicts women's sexual interest in men (especially in their penises, the sizes of which increase dramatically as the story proceeds) as inevitable, insatiable, "natural." Of course, in following this convention, *Memoirs* directly unseats the assumption of women's sexlessness that is central to domestic fiction; in its representation of female sexuality, Cleland's novel becomes not a parody of but something entirely different from and in opposition to the construction of domestic female virtue offered in *Millenium Hall, Belinda,* or *Emma.*[27] This representation of female sexual agency is clearest in certain "point-of-view shots," moments of concrete visual description in which Fanny surveys the sexual possibilities of the body before her. Receiving Mr. H's well-endowed servant, for example, Fanny notices that "his hair trimly dress'd, clean linnen and above all, a hale, ruddy, wholesome country look, made him out as pretty a piece of woman's meat as you should see, and I should have thought any one much out of taste, that could not have made a hearty meal of such a morsel as nature seem'd to have design'd for the highest diet of pleasure" (80). The frank voraciousness of this description, Fanny's cool appraisal of the "young minion's" body in terms of its capacity to satisfy appetite, constructs a female speaker for whom sexual agency is a defining characteristic. In such a moment, as Miller and other feminist critics have argued, the novel constructs a particular ideal subject/heroine of male pornographic fiction, one whose service to male heterosexual desire is flawless because of its continuity with that desire: Fanny wants men absolutely, needs to have sex with men as she needs "meat," to survive. The absoluteness of this insistence on female heterosexual agency actually means that the male heterosexual reader need never trouble himself over the question of female desire. He can assume that, although Fanny may distinguish between more and less "pretty" pieces of "meat," her need for sex with men is as incontrovertible as her need for food.

The very excessiveness of the novel's investment in female desire, however, produces "queer" disruptions in this account of the naturalness of heterosexuality. At times, the bodies we see through Fanny's eyes imply that they are viewed by a different subjectivity, a less absolute heterosexual agency. Early in Fanny's sojourn at Mrs. Cole's, for example, the other women in the house prepare an evening of debauchery in which they and their male customers demonstrate the various sexual techniques she will need at this new stage in her career. Fanny's position as the female spectator at this event creates strange fissures in the representation of the heterosexuality of the other women. Their attentions occasionally slip from the men's pleasure to Fanny's. Of Louisa's encounter, for example, Fanny says, "We could easily see the signs [of satiation], in the quiet, dying, languid posture of her late so furious driver, who was stopp'd of a sudden, breathing short, panting; and for that time, giving up the spirit of pleasure. As soon as he was dismounted, *Louisa* sprung up, shook her petticoats, and running up to me, gave me a kiss, and drew me to the side-board" (114). In the space left by the "dying" man who "give[s] up the spirit of pleasure," Louisa turns to Fanny to conclude the event and bestow meaning on it by her approval. The next incident begins with another such appeal: "*Harriet* then was led to the vacant couch by her gallant, blushing as she look'd at me, and with eyes made to justify any thing, tenderly bespeaking of me the most favourable construction of the step she was thus irresistibly drawn into" (114). Fanny becomes not just the arbiter of pleasure but also of female virtue itself. As the incident progresses, then, she comes to occupy more and more the space of sexual agent, deciding on the proper limits as well as the proper objects of female desire. Fanny's admiration of the "eyes made to justify any thing" signifies the possibility that Harriet herself, within these redefined limits, could become such an object.

The implication is drawn even more clearly in the slippery point of view with which Fanny describes Emily's body:

> Her gallant began first, as she stood, to disengage her breasts, and restore them to the liberty of nature, from the easy confinement of no more than a pair of jumps; but on their coming out to view, we thought a new light was added to the room, so superiorly shining was their whiteness; then they rose in so happy a swell as to compose her a well-form'd fullness of bosom, that had such an effect on the eye as to seem flesh hardening into marble, of which it emulated the polish'd glass, and far surpass'd even the whitest, in the life and lustre of its colours, white vein'd with blue. Refrain who could from such provoking enticements to it in reach? (117–18)

"Her gallant" completely drops out from this account, as its point of view shifts from that of one man to encompass both the men and women in the room ("we thought") and finally circles back to the single "eye" of the speaker, Fanny herself. As a frankly sexualized subject, Fanny now asks the passage's final question: "Refrain who could from such provoking enticements?" Inverting its rhetorical structure produces the clear implication that Fanny, at least, cannot refrain. This image of Fanny reaching for the gleaming breasts of pornographic fiction's ideal creates a vertiginous disruption of the heterosexual conventions by which such narratives justify themselves. Fanny's sexual agency, which is supposed to guarantee her insatiable desire for men, intersects with the conventions of memoir form and heroine description to produce a female homosexual gaze.

In this act of production, Fanny's point of view bursts the bounds of parody as jubilantly as Emily's breasts leap from their restraining clothing. At times, Fanny's "innocent" language, mixing as it does both conventional heroine description ("a piquant brunette") and double entendre ("flesh hardening into marble"), seems intended as a joke between the male author and the male reader—a joke, at Fanny's expense, that exposes both her ignorance and her licentiousness. Her difference from the virtuous heroine of domestic fiction cements the relationship between male author and reader. But at these moments, when Fanny vacates the position of heroine, the representation of female agency and female sexuality comes loose from the bourgeois heterosexual ascension narrative that has held it in place. No longer a retrospective narrator who, like Mrs. Morgan in *Millenium Hall*, has learned from her mistakes and offers her story for the moral edification of others, Fanny's narrative becomes indistinguishable from her "mistakes." The truth of her narrative, like that of Pamela's, is the truth of the moment; but in Fanny's pornographic narrative, this truth becomes an assertion of the female desiring gaze autonomous from the bonds of masculinity, a masculinity that can cope with the possibility of such a gaze only by making a joke of it. This desire to ridicule and dismiss Fanny's use of language, the language on which the "truth" of the narrative depends, makes visible the ideological conflict between two pornographic conventions: masculinist heterosexism and a voracious female. Their juxtaposition is the source of considerable textual instability here.

The absolute separateness of sexual bonds between men outside the text and women within it helps account for the differing treatment of male and female homosexuality in the novel. The liminal possibility of female homosexual desire raised in my readings contrasts strongly with the marked and explicit discussion of male homosexuality at the end of the novel. Female homosexuality is never condemned in the strong terms reserved for male homosexuality; it is seen as more easily recuperable, mere "preparation" for heterosexual sex. Of course, Cleland was following the assumptions of English law and custom in presenting sex between women as trivial. This status was both reflected and produced by the fact that "lesbians in England (unlike their sisters in Europe) were not criminal under the law."[28] This distinction, however, can be held in place only intermittently in Cleland's text. The power of Fanny's point of view—and the compelling representation of female sexual agency it produces—also accounts for much of the male homosexual pleasure in the text. The nexus between these two categories—female sexual agency and male homosexuality—creates a powerful web of representation that undermines the ideologically produced "naturalness" and "obviousness" of the external conditions of the text's production and the assertion of exclusive male knowledge and pleasure it assumes.

Although ostensibly in the service of heterosexuality and the hierarchy of men over women, Fanny's appraisal of the sexual attractiveness of male bodies puts them in the same category as female ones: as objects of the gaze, to be dissected with the same detail used in conventional heroine description, in both pornographic and domestic fictions. This objectification of male bodies could be said to "feminize" them; instead, I want to argue that it produces them as objects not only of Fanny's desire but also of the specifically masculine desire that *Memoirs of a Woman of Pleasure* is intended to serve. In other words, I am less concerned with the effect of such objectification on the representation of male bodies themselves than with the kinds of readerly subjectivities such a representation implies and produces. The unusual prominence and availability of male bodies in the novel both assumes and creates a male homosexual gaze and desire.

Fanny's description of Charles, her first love and future husband, extends for almost two pages and repeats many of the conventions of heroine description. It begins with Fanny's emphatic self-positioning as the agent of desire and consumer of beauty:

> I hung over him enamour'd indeed! and devour'd all his naked charms with only two eyes, when I could have wish'd them at least a hundred, for the fuller enjoyment of the gaze.
>
> Oh! could I paint his figure as I see it now still present to my transported imagination! a whole length of an all-perfect manly beauty in full view. Think of a face without a fault, glowing with all the opening bloom, and vernal freshness of an age, in which beauty is of either sex, and which the first down over his upper-lip scarce began to distinguish.

The passage then continues with a description of the parts of the body that readers of domestic fiction are schooled to admire in a heroine:

> The parting of the double ruby-pout of his lips, seem'd to exhale an air sweeter and purer than what it drew in: Ah! what violence did it not cost me to refrain the so tempted kiss?
>
> Then a neck exquisitely turn'd, grac'd behind and on the sides with his hair playing freely in natural ringlets, connected his head to a body of the most perfect form, and of the most vigorous contexture, in which all the strength of manhood was conceal'd and soften'd to appearance, by the delicacy of his complexion, the smoothness of his skin, and the plumpness of his flesh.
>
> The plat-form of his snow-white bosom, that was laid out in a manly proportion, presented on the vermillion summet [sic] of each pap, the idea of a rose about to blow. (44)

Again, Fanny takes up the position of the sexual agent in this passage, "devouring" the body before her, concerned only with her own "enjoyment," tempted even to "violence" to satisfy it. Her appraisal of Charles, however, weaves back and forth between noting the specifically masculine signs of "all-perfect manly beauty" and disavowing gender differences altogether. Charles's "beauty is of either sex"; his "manhood" is "conceal'd and soften'd" by a feminized body marked by "delicacy," "smoothness," and "plumpness." The appropriation of the metaphors of conventional heroine description—"opening bloom," "vernal freshness," "the double ruby-pout," "a neck exquisitely turn'd," "delicacy of . . . complexion"—create a sexually desirable body that would appeal not just to Fanny's pornographic voraciousness but also to male readers schooled to admire such bodies by the conventions—present in both pornographic and domestic fiction—themselves. This "heroinization" of male bodies in the text seduces male readers into responding to Charles's body "as if" it were a woman's—that is, to respond to it with sexual admiration and arousal. Not only Fanny's heterosexual desire, then, but also the male homosexual desire outside the text in writer and readers would be caught by "the idea of a rose about to blow."

Much has been made of Cleland's attention to the penis. Sabor notes that "there are over fifty metaphorical variations for the penis" and far "fewer, but similarly original terms for the vagina" in the novel.[29] Critics have paid less attention, however, to Cleland's glorification of the male buttocks. Juxtaposing the two patterns of representation makes clear that a glorification of the penis need not necessarily produce untrammeled male heterosexuality. For example, Fanny's friend Harriet describes a youth she encounters swimming naked: "He had now chang'd his posture, and swam prone on his belly, striking out with his legs and arms, finer modell'd than which could not have been cast, whilst his floating locks play'd o'er a neck and shoulders, whose whiteness they delightfully set off. Then the luxuriant swell of flesh that rose from the small of his back, and terminates its double cope, at where the thighs are sent off, perfectly dazzl'd one with its watery glistening gloss" (102). The euphemistic tone of this description suggests that in the *Memoirs,* the buttocks are as sexual a body part as the penis or the vagina, one that both deserves and requires figurative language. In another description, the sadomasochist Mr. Barvile's buttocks are endowed with an agency and desire of their own: "And now he lay, in all the fairest, broadest display of that part of the back-view, in which a pair of chubby, smooth-cheek'd, and passing white posteriours rose cushioning upwards from two stout, fleshful thighs, and ending their cleft, or separation, by an union at the small of the back, presented a bold mark, that swell'd, as it were, to meet the scourge" (146). Mr. Barvile's buttocks rise to meet Fanny's lash in an image of natural bodily desire that matches the frequent personification of the penis in the novel. In this way, at least, penises and male buttocks belong together in Cleland's novel.

Of course, the most explicit representation of male homosexual desire in the novel is also the text's most homophobic moment. The moral strictures that hedge this account of Fanny witnessing sex between men were not enough to keep the incident in the novel after the first printing; the publishers felt that representing such desires was too great a risk to take, even when the novel uses the representation to argue against toleration for homosexuality. And indeed, because this is the conceit of the entire novel—that vice "painted all in its gayest colours" (187–188) would repel rather than attract readers— arguments against any kind of sex are bound to clash with the assumptions the text has produced in its readers heretofore. Such a conflict undermines the force of Fanny's moral outrage because here she must speak out against vice in a novel in which vice is supposed to speak for itself. To make this possible, the text must construct a different reader from the one it has been imagining up to this point. This is the reader who will accept the narrative of bourgeois heterosexual ascent that quickly closes the novel after the homosexual incident. In the last few pages of the novel, Fanny meets her first ravisher, Charles, marries him, and settles down to distance herself from her sexual past by writing her memoirs. A certain kind of sexual agency—the female desire that has fueled Fanny's picaresque progress through the narrative—becomes impossible after the moral moment of homophobia in the novel.

To produce this closure, Cleland must distance the text from the homosexual desire it represents in the penultimate incident. Significantly, the novel at this point insists much more clearly on the importance of gender distinctions than at other moments when homosexual desire is implied rather than stated. This juxtaposition helps clarify the utility of rigid gender boundaries in holding in place normative heterosexuality in the novel.

The narrative justifies Fanny's voyeuristic interest in the two men having sex in the room next to her in an inn by stating that her ignorance of homosexuality is based on factual error. Peering at the men through a hole she makes in the wallpaper thus takes on the air of Enlightenment rational experimentation rather than the satisfaction of sexual curiosity or even the production of sexual desire through pornographic representation. After hearing Emily's account of how, dressed as a boy, she had resisted an attempt at anal penetration on the part of an older man, Fanny remarks:

> I could not conceive how it was possible for mankind to run into a taste, not only universally odious, but absurd, and impossible to gratify, since, according to the notions and experience I had of things, it was not in nature to force such immense disproportions; Mrs. *Cole* only smil'd at my ignorance, and said nothing towards my undeception, which was not effected but by occular demonstration, some months after, which a most singular accident furnish'd me, and I will here set down, that I may not return again to so disagreeable a subject. (156)

One of the running jokes in this novel is Fanny's disbelief, as she encounters ever larger penises, that she will ever be able to contain such "enormous" engines within "that tender, small part of me which was framed to receive" them (27). In attributing this recurring appraisal of her own body to that of the "passive" homosexual, Fanny produces a curious identification with his position that works against her professed inability to believe in homosexuality. Also, Fanny's insistence that "occular demonstration" alone convinces her of the possibility of anal intercourse contradicts an earlier incident, in which she feels a young sailor "knocking desperately" on the "wrong" door. When she tells him of his "mistake," he makes light of it: "Pooh, says he my dear, any port in a storm" (141). Although Fanny eventually talks him into "altering his course," there is no suggestion either that she doesn't know what he is talking about or that she is particularly offended by his interest in the "wrong door." These narrative slips render particularly anxious the repeated assertions of the later incident that Fanny watches homosexual sex only to dispel her "disbelief of the possibility of things being push'd to odious extremities" (158), that she watches the whole scene "purely that [she] might gather more facts" (159). These homophobic interpellations serve much the same purpose as the speeches in favor of marriage and pleasure in *Millenium Hall:* by bowing to convention, they make possible unconventional depictions that produce conflict and contradiction in their reverberation with the rest of the text.

The sodomy incident domesticates the "immense disproportions" of sex between men by naming one of the participants a woman. Indeed, this incident produces some of the novel's most emphatic language about the differences between men and women and how they are determined. Initially, Fanny simply takes the younger man for a woman: "For now the elder began to embrace, to press, to kiss the younger, to put his hands in his bosom, and give such manifest signs of an amorous intention, as made me conclude the other to be a girl in disguise, a mistake that nature kept me in countenance in, for she had certainly made one, when she gave him the male stamp" (157). The ambiguous relation between the last three clauses suggests a double reading. We read both the explicit sense in which Fanny and nature err—Fanny in thinking the boy a girl, Nature in making the "girl" a boy—and the sense the phrases make on first reading, in which Fanny's assertion that nature "had certainly made one" seems to allude not to a mistake but to a girl—nature has "certainly" made a girl, as we can tell by the way "she" is behaving. Next, Fanny observes the physical contact between male genitals, noting, no doubt as a "fact," the presence of penises on both men. Of the younger, she says, "His red-topt ivory toy, that stood perfectly stiff . . . shewed, that if he was like his mother behind, he was like his father before" (158). Bodily cavities are for "mothers" or women, whereas the "stiff" "toys" that penetrate them are for "fathers" or men. This distinction must be kept clear in this passage even at the risk of producing a slightly ridiculous picture of hermaphroditism. Male and female body parts are distinguishable even when they appear on the same body.

## Domesticating Homosexuality

Finally, when Fanny recounts her adventure to Mrs. Cole, the older woman observes, "with a declaration extorted from her by pure regard to truth," that English homosexuals are always readily distinguishable from actual men. In this penultimate section of the novel, the instabilities of gender contrast rather markedly with a carelessly confident assertion of national character. To quote more fully from the passage cited at the beginning of this chapter:

> Whatever effect this infamous passion had in other ages, and other coun-
> tries, it seem'd a peculiar blessing on our air and climate, that there was a
> plague-spot visibly imprinted on all that are tainted with it, in this nation at
> least . . . [homosexuals are] stript of the manly virtues of their own sex, and
> fill'd up with only the very worst vices and follies of ours . . . in fine, they
> were scarce less execrable than ridiculous in their monstrous inconsistency,
> of loathing and contemning women, and all at the same time, apeing their
> manners, airs, lisp, skuttle, and, in general, all their little modes of affecta-
> tion, which become them at least better, than they do these unsex'd male-
> misses. (159–60)

The worst thing about homosexuality, then, is nothing sexual at all; rather, it is the "inconsistency" of stable gender markers that poses the threat, that con-stitutes the "plague-spot." This passage offers a curiously anxious image of gendered subjectivity, the possibility of an identity "stript" of "manly virtues" but insufficiently "fill'd up with only the very worst vices and follies" of women—a monster "unsex'd" by its failure to line up with gender's rigid binarism. The binarism that stays firmly in place here, however, is that of nation (and, significantly, of time—suggesting the priority of modernity itself in this ideological task): "other ages, and other countries" can be cordoned off from "this nation." Thus, the passage appropriates much of the rhetoric of *Satan's Harvest Home,* positioning the "problem" in a timeless elsewhere that allows for the reification of a valued English present. But, here, the "prob-lem" is redefined: the danger is less homosexuality itself than its invisibility, its incorporation into everyday life (represented, for example, by the bathing habits of the Turks in *Satan's Harvest Home*). What is peculiarly and positively English, then, is the carving out of a distinctly "tainted" social space and body for the homosexual, "visibly imprinted" with just those confused gender markers that the author of *Satan's Harvest Home* condemns. The social margin of the brothel and the literary margin of pornography are thus required to operate as containers for a readable and therefore manageable sodomitical proto-identity. The novel is able to make space for such a radical innovation by calling it a "peculiar blessing" that confirms English national superiority. The perceived "obscenity" of this passage, then, may well lie in its ability to endow nationalist discourse (whether cynically or strategically, of course, would depend on the reader) with the power to make space for a distinctly English sodomy.

This useful relay between gender and nation dramatizes the status of pleasure as the novel's bedrock, unquestioned category. The novel considers, with Mrs. Cole, "pleasure of one sort or other, as the universal port of destination, and every wind that [blows] thither a good one, provided it blew nobody any harm" (144). The politics of pleasure in the novel, then, subsume other ideological agendas that the text may also intermittently serve. In this way, the novel sets up pleasure as "utopian"—as the final port of destination within which the contradictions that have produced so many different readers for the text will magically dissolve. Thus, although *Memoirs* provocatively offers feminist readers the spectacle of female sexual agency and the possibility of non-heterosexual desiring gazes, I would not want to argue that it simply and "progressively" valorizes the category—pleasure—that *Millenium Hall* ruled off-limits to women. Rather, the radical potential of this spectacle is contained for the novel's bourgeois readership by a violent swerve toward the pleasures of national superiority.

In fact, the slippage in point of view that I have identified as typical of the text's production of homosexual subjectivities is actually much more generally true of the way the novel works than this partial reading can demonstrate. Every sexual incident narrated in the novel exemplifies the shifting points of view that problematize any reader's identification with or pleasure in Fanny's sexuality and sexual agency. The novel's final appeal to a stable national identity is reiterated on the last page, when sexual knowledge becomes part of an enlightened English education for Fanny's emphatically gentlemanly son.

The last paragraph of the novel describes Fanny's husband's superintendence of their son's education, returning to the direct apostrophe of "Madam" that characterized its opening page:

> You know Mr. C—— O——, you know his estate, his worth, and good sense: can you? will you pronounce it ill meant, at least of him? when anxious for his son's morals, with a view to form him to Virtue, and inspire him with a fixt, a rational contempt for vice, he condescended to be his master of the ceremonies, and led him by the hand thro' the most noted bawdy-houses in town, where he took care that he should be familiariz'd with all those scenes of debauchery, so fit to nauseate a good taste. The experiment, you will cry, is dangerous. True, on a fool: but are fools worth the least attention to? (188)

This improbable swerve toward not only a "good estate" but "Virtue" productively manipulates a slippage that readers have been well schooled by the novel itself to experience as pleasurable because it is painful. Thus, national pride and bourgeois self-consequence are configured as kinds of pleasure, acceptable vehicles for containing the novel's other, more perverse offerings, together justifying all kinds of inadmissible and disavowed desires. In Benedict Anderson's words, "Nations inspire love"; in the idiom of this reading, we might say that nationalism produces specific desires and pleasures. Indeed, these pleasures might be exactly those for which the national subject is willing to die.

# Colonizing Virtue: *Belinda*

In Chapter 1 we saw that a certain disconnection from the body in *Millenium Hall*'s account of romantic friendship resulted in both a refusal of female sexuality and an avoidance of the material (as opposed to metaphoric) status of human slavery. This novel displaces sexuality away from relations between women into the male-gendered public sphere and finally, in the frame narrative, into an enervating colonial world that vitiates the body. By contrast, in Chapter 2 I argue that the discourse of romantic friendship is gleefully satirized and sexualized by *Memoirs of a Woman of Pleasure*, which recruits female sexual agency into the service of misogyny and of nationalism, producing an account of the culturally valued body as not only emphatically (homo)sexual but also definitively English, as evaluated by a frankly desiring and potentially sapphic female gaze. The claim to national superiority is premised here as a sexual claim, one that paradoxically guarantees the success of the bourgeois family imaged at the end of the novel by making a visible, easily readable space inside English culture for its Others. A heterogenous, often contradictory range of representations was thus available for making female friendship do the work of defining the superiority of bourgeois personal identity and its stories by the late–eighteenth century. Intense, lifelong attachments between women were often described by novelists, poets, and philosophers as definitionally chaste and virtuous, yet in low-culture sources such as pornography and newspapers, nonliterary ones such as legal transcripts and satiric pamphlets, and private records such as diaries, the lively specter of a freakishly sexualized connection between women haunted representations of female friendship.[1] In this chapter I examine the consequences of this tension in the representation of female friendship for a paradigmatic text in the tradition of domestic fiction—Maria Edgeworth's 1801 *Belinda*. The utility of both cele-bratory and satiric images of female friendship in making colonial and na-tional arguments by the turn of the century helps explain *Belinda*'s hetero-genous plotting: why should a heroine-centered novel also contain the story of a West Indian planter and an account of a meeting between that planter's slave and a sapphic woman? In a late-eighteenth-century novel about a middle-class girl's rise to power, what does colonialism have to do with En-glish female sexuality?

I attempt to explain how the cultural task of determining appropriate female sexuality and that of determining appropriate English identity, tasks unemphatically yoked together in Edgeworth's novel, have come to seem disparate and even at odds with each other to present-day readers. For a "theorist of global hegemony" such as Edgeworth,[2] the morality of the En-glish bourgeois household is a powerful warrant and a necessary precondition for the spread of an Anglicized ethnicity. For the Anglo-Irish Edgeworth, that such an ethnicity could not be defined solely in terms of national borders (or her own hegemonic position would be defined out of existence) should direct our attention to the way in which colonialism dynamically appropriates na-tionalist sentiment and racial hierarchy, fusing them into an Other who marks the psychic as well as geographical boundaries of the colonial Self. To draw attention to the ways in which colonialism works as a narrative—the ways in which it draws together the strands of nationalism, racial hierarchy, gender, and sexuality explored above—I emphasize the interactions between repre-sentations of female friends—Belinda, Lady Delacour, and Harriot Freke in Edgeworth's novel; Miss Pirie and Miss Woods in the Scottish trial record; diarist Anne Lister and her actual and potential women lovers—and the concomitant representations of national, class, and racial hierarchy that bour-geois institutions as disparate as marriage, the law, and personal identity seem to require to scrutinize these relations between women appropriately. Thus, Edgeworth's Juba, a Caribbean slave, functions both as an especially acute observer of female indecency (and is thus aligned with the novel's didactic voice) and as a marker of the social ridicule and physical danger that await the indecent women who could enter, even inadvertently, the scope of Juba's censure. Jane Cumming, the half-Indian schoolgirl whose observing eyes and ears set in motion the events chronicled in the Woods-Pirie case, occupies a similarly ambivalent position, her testimony sometimes used by the judges to limit and punish the sexuality of her teachers but at other moments used as evidence "against" Jane herself, evidence that supports British legal authority's location of sapphic sexuality outside not only the geographic borders of Britain but also beyond the physical and emotional powers or desires of British women themselves. Anne Lister, frankly capitalizing on the rank, wealth, and independence made possible by her central position in the culture of the colonizer, nonetheless also functions as an ambivalent reporter on her own life, one who alternately regrets and rejoices, scrutinizes and celebrates her own sexual agency and that of other women. Lister's diary and the Woods-Pirie case make explicit the variety and importance of cultural narratives pulled together by Edgeworth in *Belinda* as she seeks to represent the ideal hegemonic subject as romantic friend.

The most obvious candidate for the heroine's "romantic friend," as defined by *Millenium Hall,* is Lady Delacour, the rakish woman of the world who launches Belinda into society and finally, precariously, into marriage with Clarence Hervey. But the implicit pleasures and explicit dangers of intimacy between women cluster most clearly around a figure who might seem more appropriate to the satiric, pornographic world of *Memoirs of a Woman of Pleasure:* Harriot Freke, the cross-dressing *"man-woman"* whom Belinda supplants as Lady Delacour's intimate friend in the novel's second chapter.[3] This displacement from Lady Delacour's affections, however, fails to banish Harriot Freke from the narrative itself. Her several reappearances work to expose the political and moral ruin threatening young ladies who trust too much to intimacy with other women, as well as the grave consequences for society of such relationships. Thus, Belinda's judgment of Mrs. Freke also defines one of the chief didactic aims of the novel itself: she provides a "lesson to young ladies in the choice of female friends" (252). By placing Edgeworth's novel in the context of two other contemporary accounts of the consequences of "the choice of female friends"—a legal case in which two women teachers were accused of "indecent relations" by one of their pupils, and the diary of Anne Lister, a Regency Yorkshirewoman who records details of her sexual liaisons with other women—I hope to demonstrate some of the cultural and formal constraints within which Belinda's friendships were written and read in late-eighteenth-century England. As well, I will attempt to show the ways in which colonial narrative—meaning both stories about the colonies and colonialism *as* narrative—brings together previously distinct literary forms (the "high" form of *Millenium Hall*'s utopianism and the "low" form of Cleland's pornography, with their concomitant, generically appropriate representations of women's intimacy) in the hybrid form of the domestic novel, the novel form that was to dominate the early-nineteenth-century canonization of the new genre.

### Legal Contests, Legal Contexts

The utility of the category romantic friendship in securing colonial hierarchies is made explicit in a Scottish legal case that was tried in 1810, just nine years after the publication of *Belinda*.[4] The facts of the case are briefly these: Jane Pirie and Marianne Woods met in 1802 in Edinburgh and became intimate friends immediately.[5] In 1809, they opened a boarding school for young gentlewomen. In November 1810, the grandmother of one of their pupils and one of Edinburgh's most influential noblewomen, Dame Cumming Gordon, withdrew her half-Indian granddaughter, Jane Cumming, from the school for what she called only "very serious reasons" ("State of the Process," 135) and recommended that several other families do likewise. Jane Cumming had only recently been recognized and adopted as the "natural" daughter of Lady Cumming Gordon's son and an Indian woman whom he had met while stationed in India, and Jane's placement in a boarding school was clearly an attempt to render her acceptable within the domestic world of the British (in this case Scottish) aristocracy. The story that the child brought home from school—or what the grandmother made of it—pitted the appropriate femininity of Lady Cumming Gordon's granddaughter against that of the two genteel but not aristocratic teachers. Although, as far as we know, Lady Cumming Gordon made no explicit or public charge against the teachers, within a few days from her communication with the families of the other pupils, the school was emptied. In May 1811, Pirie and Woods brought a charge of libel against Lady Cumming Gordon. When the hearings began, Lady Cumming Gordon's lawyer, George Cranstoun, submitted a statement that accused Pirie and Woods of "indecent and criminal practices" ("Petition for Lady Cumming Gordon," 2). The central piece of evidence was the following testimony from Jane Cumming, in which she describes what happened one night while she was in the bed she shared with her teacher, Miss Pirie:

> She wakened one night with a whispering, and heard, Miss Pirie say, 'O do it darling, and Miss Woods said, 'Not to night;'. . . then Miss Pirie pressed her again to come in, and she came in, and she lay above Miss Pirie. . . . Miss Woods began to move, and she shook the bed, and she [Cumming] heard [a noise like] . . . putting one's finger in the neck of a wet bottle. . . . [Finally] she heard Miss Woods say to Miss Pirie, 'Good night, darling, I think I have put you in the way to get a good sleep to-night.' ("State of the Process," 70–73)

The libel case was ultimately decided, by a margin of one vote, in favor of Miss Pirie and Miss Woods—that is, the judges decided that they were innocent of the "indecent and criminal practices" of which they had been accused. However, Dame Cumming Gordon successfully petitioned Parliament to excuse the teachers' claims for damages. Unable to support themselves over the nine-year course of the trial, Woods and Pirie had separated, reduced from flourishing businesswomen to the ranks of the genteel poor.

The case turned on the problem of defining romantic friendship and on the relative claims to virtue of colonial versus British femininity. Witnesses were repeatedly asked if they had ever seen the teachers "kissing, caressing, and fondling each other, more than . . . could have resulted from ordinary female friendship" ("State of the Process," 49). The lawyer for the two women played heavily on the outrage to virtuous friendship that the charges represented: "They little thought, that that warm and interesting mutual regard, which springs from the finest and purest feelings of the human heart, and can only exist in pure and virtuous breasts, should be to them the source of the foulest condemnation, or be converted into the means of fixing upon them an imputation of the blackest and most disgusting atrocity" ("Petition of Miss Marianne Woods and Miss Jane Pirie," 3). The heavy stress on notions of fineness, purity, and virtue in these statements indicates the importance of a naturalized norm of emphatically nonsexual friendship between women to which the relationship between Woods and Pirie is implicitly compared. The language used to invoke this norm reveals that one of its major functions is to make "virtue" a quality "natural" to women—that is, to render women's sexuality and sexual agency *un*ordinary, complicated, devious, unnatural, impure, and vicious. But the necessity of reiterating these terms, often within the same sentence, points to the lawyer's anxiety over the instability of the norm that he must nonetheless invoke as stable and unproblematic.

The very possibility that sexual acts could occur between women in the absence of a man dislodged a whole system of interpreting women's "ordinary" acts and desires. The presiding justice, Lord Meadowbank, emphasizes what poor strategy it was for the teachers to sleep with pupils, rather than each other, during the school term if they really wanted to have sex together. This argument rests on the assumption that for the teachers to sleep in the same bed would have been a perfectly ordinary occurrence that would raise no suspicions—yet it also reveals the capacity of acts of "ordinary" female friendship to mask the indecent acts that were supposed to be their antithesis. Lord Meadowbank points out that "under the unsuspected state of female intercourse and habits in this country, they could have been under no difficulty, had it so pleased them, so to have arranged the household, as to have afforded them ample opportunity of every possible indulgence, without suspicion of any impropriety" ("Speeches of the Judges," 9). Inadvertently, this statement demonstrates the impossibility of successfully scrutinizing female friendship, since its "unsuspected state" makes its sexual status unknowable, at least to the male judicial observer. If you can't tell from the outside whether "female intercourse and habits" might be masking "every possible indulgence," how can you rely on the "unsuspected state" of such habits as the basis for a legal decision?

This challenge to cultural assumptions about sexless female friendship posed an interpretive problem for the judges—the problem of how to read women's representations of female homosexual desires. In their speeches, the judges repeatedly figure the very existence of this problem and the ambiguities it raises about female heterosexual virtue as threats not just to the students in the boarding school but to society itself as well. Lord Meadowbank asserts that besides the students, the teachers, and Lady Cumming Gordon,

> there is a fourth party whose interest is deeply at stake, I mean the public: for the virtues, the comforts, and the freedom of domestic intercourse, mainly depend on the purity of female manners, and that, again, on their habits of intercourse remaining, as they have hitherto been,—free from suspicion. [Thus your Lordships] have taken every precaution within your

power, though necessarily with small hopes of success, to confine this
cause by the walls of the Court, and keep its subject and its investigation
unknown in general society. ("Speeches of the Judges," 2)

The difficulty for the judges was to try to determine which was the more
unlikely: that a schoolgirl had imagined her teachers acting together in such a
way as to "supply the absence or neglect of males" ("Speeches of the Judges,"
16) or that the teachers themselves had not only imagined but carried out
such acts. Thus the question of the "truth" of the case comes to rest on a
choice between not women's sexual passivity and their agency but two equally
problematic forms of that agency.

Because the ideology of female sexual passivity requires that the "unsuspected state" of romantic friendship be considered unworthy of suspicion
and because, by the court's own admission, that "unsuspected state" is im-
penetrable to or unreadable by the judicial male gaze unless it is virtuous and
passive, the authority of the court rests on strictly preserving gendered power
relations. This impasse, in which establishing the sexual passivity of the two
teachers logically requires the recognition of the sexual awareness of a young
girl, threatens to disrupt a system of cultural authority in which women's
sexually passive virtue held in place and legitimated the very forms of gender,
class, and national power that authorized the court's investigation as the mere
safeguard of such virtue. In the attempt to shore up the "natural" status of
female sexual virtue and hence guarantee its own authority as overseer, the
court looked to factors other than gender to shift the origin of the no-win
choice between Jane Cumming's "truth" and that of her teachers. Thus,
evidence that women could imagine or carry out sexual acts without the
presence of a man placed an added burden on the explanatory powers of race,
in the context of colonialism, to locate the origins of the problem of stable
female virtue. Jane Cumming's identity as a half-"Hindoo" young woman
thus provides the judges with a way to explain the otherwise unthinkable
possibility of sapphic love. Sexual relations between women becomes not
only the cultural but also the bodily property of the colonial Other.

As noted above, Jane Cumming, the pupil who first described the teachers'
relationship to her grandmother, had been born in India of an Indian mother
and a Scottish father, Lady Cumming Gordon's son. Dark-skinned and illegitimate, she spent the first several years of her life in India with her mother's

family. Several of the judges felt that her "Hindoo" background was the source of her story. Lord Meadowbank refers to "two Hindoo laws" that, in his mind, establish the strictly foreign character of sex between women by marking out the activity of the deviant foreign body:

> There is no sort of doubt, that women of a peculiar conformation, from an elongation of the *clitoris*, are capable both of giving and receiving venereal pleasure, in intercourse with women, by imitating the functions of a male in copulation; and that in some countries this conformation is so common, that circumcision of the *clitoris* is practised as a religious rite. . . . [A]nd I dare say, it is also true enough, that as a provocative to the use of the male, women have been employed to kindle each other's lewd appetites. Nor is it to be disputed, that by means of tools, women may artificially accomplish the venereal gratification. . . . But if tools and tribadism [clitoral penetration] are out of the question, then I state as the ground of my incredulity . . . the important fact, that the imputed vice has been hitherto unknown in Britain. ("Speeches of the Judges," 7–8)

Ultimately, most of the judges were to use this argument—that race determines sexuality more importantly than does gender, at least in the case of deviance—to acquit the two Scottish teachers. Of course, Pirie and Woods were never examined to determine whether or not they bore the "peculiar conformation" that would make it possible for them to have sex together, according to this theory: rather, their "normality" was assumed on the basis of their race. The possibility that British female bodies or British female erotic imaginations were capable of sexual congress with each other was thus diverted in the trial through recourse to a racist myth of a deviant, sexualized Eastern woman's body that, like her sexual conversation, was unnaturally similar to a man's.[6]

In the judges' narrative, then, Jane Cumming plays a crucial role. In the colonizer's story, the "Hindoo" woman is the source of sapphic sexuality, the freak who holds in place the normality of the intact British virgin and hence requires that judgment be passed on her and not just the plaintiffs. Jane Cumming's South Asian ancestry allowed the judges to dismiss the possibility of sapphic love and sapphic sex as properly British. How then can a self-identified sapphist such as Anne Lister, whose sexual self-assertion depends on her class and colonial privilege and the independence it affords her, find a way to represent herself? Lister's challenge is to reject a powerful discursive "othering" of sapphism, such as that practiced by the Woods-Pirie judges, without rejecting their right to judge; it is, after all, precisely the rights and privileges of the British aristocracy that she must assert to justify and pursue her own desires for other women. This complex representational dilemma must also be examined if we are to understand all that is at stake in Edgeworth's representation of romantic friendship.

## "More Tender Still Than Friendship": Sapphic Identities and Practices

The Woods-Pirie case demonstrates the enormous pressure placed on intimacy between women as a way of distinguishing between the domestic and the colonial. In the context of such pressure on the virtuous status of romantic friendship to hold in place English bourgeois assumptions about gender, race, and class, it is not surprising that historical romantic friendships themselves should be the site of contradictory social meanings in the period. As I mentioned in the Introduction, the so-called Ladies of Llangollen, Lady Eleanor Butler and Sarah Ponsonby, eloped from their matchmaking families in 1778 and lived together in Wales until Butler's death in 1829. The two were often held up as exemplars of chastity, both by their contemporaries and by such historians as Faderman. Edmund Burke, for example, who corresponded with and visited them, wrote to Eleanor Butler of "the virtues that entitled you to the esteem of all who know how to esteem honour, friendship, principle, and dignity of thinking."[7] Faderman refers to their friendships with the Duke of Wellington, William Wordsworth, Robert Southey, Josiah Wedgewood, Edmund Burke, Hester Thrale, Sir Walter Scott, and Lady Caroline Lamb to bolster her assertion that "their society was happy to see them as the embodiment of the highest ideals of spiritual love and the purest dreams of romantic friendship."[8] Other sources reveal, however, that their relationship was regarded as often with suspicion as with encomium. In 1790 an account of the friendship, entitled "Extraordinary Female Affection," appeared in a local Welsh paper. The article described Butler's "tall and masculine" appearance, her "air of a sportsman," and how she appeared "in all respects as a young man if we except the petticoats which she still retains," contrasting these attributes with Ponsonby's "polite and effeminate, fair and beautiful" demeanor.[9] The account mortified the two women. They wrote to

Burke, asking whether they should sue the paper for libel. He wrote back tactfully advising them not to subject themselves to the suspicions produced by "the baseness of the age" by publicly raising the possibility of any impropriety in their relationship.[10] The possibility continued to occur to their contemporaries, however. When they reached old age, the actor Charles Mathews wrote to his wife that "as they are seated, there is not one point to distinguish them from men."[11] In such accounts, the Ladies of Llangollen begin to seem less like paragons of female virtue and more like Edgeworth's cross-dressing feminist, Harriot Freke.

Not only were Butler and Ponsonby attacked for transgressing gender boundaries in their dress, there were also contemporary doubts about the chastity of their relationship. Anne Lister, born in 1791 in West Yorkshire, kept voluminous diaries that recorded details—often in code—of her numerous sexual affairs with other women. In response to a letter from a lover, Marianne Lawton, speculating on whether the relationship between the Ladies of Llangollen "has always been platonic," Lister wrote: "I cannot help thinking that surely it was not platonic. Heaven forgive me, but I look within myself & doubt. I feel the infirmity of our nature & hesitate to pronounce such attachments uncemented by something more tender still than friendship."[12] Public (and private) opinion about the Ladies of Llangollen, then, was by no means unanimous. Here we see how fears about women "taking the place" of men—dressing like them, eloping with women like them—exist side by side with questions about women's sexual chastity. This conflation will recur in the representation of female friendship in *Belinda*.

But Lister's diaries raise another question at play in *Belinda*: that of the education of women and the effects of reading and representation on them. Lister took great pride in her own self-education, working daily to improve her Greek, Latin, and mathematics and hoping to write a philosophical treatise eventually. Yet in her accounts of her own reading, Lister clearly participates in turn-of-the-century assumptions that inappropriate reading will allow women access to information that might threaten their virtue. Interestingly, Lister is at different times both empowered and subjugated by this assumption. That is, she delineates a compelling relation between her reading and her self-conscious sexual identity, a relation that she experiences as both enabling, in the sense that it helps her identify her own desires and other women who might share them, and dangerous, in that certain kinds of reading, particularly that of novels, might generate desires which she cannot control and which would encourage her to engage in sexual acts that violate her own code of virtue. Thus, she implicitly accepts the notion that some representations harm women by rendering them sexually suspect. This is precisely the problem raised by the representation of Harriot Freke in *Belinda:* that of the simultaneous necessity of representing indecent female behavior as a warning to women readers (and thus, by implication, the necessity that women be educated and well read) and the danger that such representations might exceed their intended effect, allowing women access to the indecent behaviors and desires they read about and to those (perhaps different) that are produced by the act of reading independently for pleasure itself.

Lister depends on reading to identify other women whose sexuality is like hers and to identify herself to them. For example, a neighbor's guest, Miss Pickford, attracts Lister's attention because she is considered "blue [that is, a bluestocking] and masculine" by county society and is referred to satirically as "Frank Pickford."[13] Lister delicately attempts to probe her views on sexuality with a literary allusion: "Miss Pickford spoke of the moon being made masculine by some nations, for instance, by the Germans. I smiled & said the moon had tried both sexes, like old Tiresius, but that one could not make such an observation to every one. Of course she remembered the story? She said yes. I am not quite certain, though, whether she did or not. 'Tis not everyone who would (*vid.* Ovid *Metamorphoses*)."[14] Lister records using classical allusions frequently to identify women who, like her, "only love the fairer sex."[15] Allusions to the classics, especially to narratives of irregular sexuality, allow her to construct an atmosphere of exclusivity, even of intimacy, with her companion. Most obviously, only another "bluestocking" would be conversationally familiar with Ovid, and their "gentlemanly" interests, as Lister calls them elsewhere, mark them as members of a select community of learned women.[16] Her comment that "one could not make such an observation to every one" indicates a second level of exclusivity, one at which sexual subjects may be broached. Thus Lister's allusion to the classics marks her interest in reading as an interest in sexuality as well, especially in its less conventional forms.

Lister's views on the education of women outside this circle of exclusivity are completely conventional, however. Her identification with Miss Pickford is as a lover of women like herself rather than as a potential object of admiration. She places herself and Miss Pickford in a category separate from the women they court, asking, "Are there more Miss Pickfords in the world than I have ever before thought of?"[17] When Lister wrote these words in 1823, she had been sexually involved with at least three women; clearly, she does not consider them to be "Miss Pickfords." Although (or perhaps because) Miss Pickford's distaste for feminine dress mirrors Lister's own, Lister finds it as unappealing as her learning: "As to not noticing dress, etc., she supposes me like herself. How she is mistaken! She loves her habit and hat. She is better informed than some ladies & and godsend of a companion in my present scarcity, but I am not an admirer of learned ladies. They are not the sweet, interesting creatures I should love." Later, Lister complains, "She . . . is too masculine & if she runs after me too much, I shall tire."[18] It is as a "companion," then, not a potential lover, that Lister considers a woman who reads. Here, Lister concurs with the notion that education harms women's femininity, linking learning to masculine clothing and both to the spectacle of a sexually unappealing woman.

Perhaps because of her self-contradictory distaste for "learned ladies," Lister both relies on the relation between sexuality and representation to identify and define her sexual community and deeply distrusts it. This paradox produces telling contradictions in her representation of her own desires. In her account of her attachments to women, Lister tries to create and uphold a distinction between a "natural" propensity for her own sex and "learned" desire that comes from books. The moral value she assigns to each of these categories—and her own position with regard to each—shifts strategically according to how Lister represents her sexuality, whether to herself or others. When she records her private thoughts in her diary, Lister uses a discourse of "naturalness" as a rationale for her sexual identity and activity; when she wants to gain information, for example from Miss Pickford, without revealing herself, she uses this discourse as a way of distancing herself from that identity and activity.

For example, in an incident that seems to have the emotional and political force of a manifesto of sorts, Lister relies on notions of naturalness (appropriateness, requited love, the heart, physical revulsion) in defining her sexuality: "Burnt . . . Mr Montagu's farewell verses that no trace of any man's admiration may remain. It is not meet for me. I love, & only love, the fairer sex & thus beloved by them in turn, my heart revolts from any other love than theirs." And in the following passage, she seems to accept the judgment of her sometime-lover Isabella Norcliffe ("Tib"): "Talking of my sleeping with Eliza Belcombe [Marianne Lawton's sister], said I should not like it, & that I was much altered of late in all these matters. Tib laughed, looked incredulous, bade me not say so, & added, 'It would be unnatural in you not to like sleeping with a pretty girl.' I thought of M—— [Marianne], as I do perpetually & that for her I could & would do anything."[19] And in a quarrel with Lawton, occasioned because of Lawton's reference to "the objection, the horror she had to anything unnatural," Lister insists on her own "conduct and feelings being surely natural to me inasmuch as they were not taught, not fictitious, but instinctive."[20] In these moments, then, Lister accounts for her own desires as "natural" in order to authorize them to herself and her lovers.

This strategy shifts when she attempts to identify others like her. For example, while Lister wants to know whether Miss Pickford is involved sexually with the latter's friend, she needs to conceal her own liaison with Marianne Lawton, who is married and has sworn Lister to secrecy. To establish her own "innocence," then, Lister tries to convince Miss Pickford that her knowledge of such matters is theoretical only.

> Our subject, both driving and walking, was Miss Threlfall. I said I knew she could not have made the confession if she had not supposed I understood the thing thoroughly. She answered, "No, certainly." I dilated on my knowing it from reading & speculation but nothing further. She was mistaken. "No, no," said she, "it is not all theory." . . . Whether she credits my denial of all practical knowledge, I cannot yet tell.[21]

Her attempts to convince Miss Pickford of the truth of this "denial" persist for several weeks. During the course of these discussions, Lister refers to specific literary texts to bolster her "theoretical" arguments in favor of sexual relationships between women:

> There was no parallel between a case like this [Miss Pickford's relationship with Miss Threlfall] and the Sixth Satyr of Juvenal.[22] The one was artificial and inconsistent, the other was the effect of nature & always consistent with itself. "At all events," said I, "you remember an early chapter of Genesis & it is infinitely better than the thing alluded to there, meaning onanism. This is surely comparatively unpardonable. There is no mutual

affection to excuse it." ... "Now," said I, "the difference between you and me is, mine is theory, yours practice. I am taught by books, you by nature. I am very warm in friendship, perhaps few or none more so. My manners might mislead you but I don't, in reality, go beyond the utmost verge of friendship. Here my feelings stop."[23]

As we saw in the Woods-Pirie case, the "utmost verge of friendship" becomes a crucial boundary for holding in place epistemological and social categories, such as "nature" and "representation" here. Placing herself on the side of "books" rather than "nature" works to preserve Lister's virtuous safety—the safety of what we would now call "the closet."[24] Speaking from inside the closet, however, Lister also wants to establish the possibility of a "natural" desire between women that might provide another kind of safety, that of community. The "effect of nature" is thus importantly marked out as "comparatively pardonable" in the hierarchy of sexual irregularity. And earlier, Lister assures Miss Pickford that "many would censure unqualifiedly but I did not. If it had been done from books & not from nature, the thing would have been different."[25] Moving cautiously between self-disclosure and self-protection, Lister attempts both to occupy and to disavow the category of "naturalness" in order to create public and private spaces for her desire.

As we have seen, Lister uses reading strategically so as to construct her sexuality. But at other moments, she seems to fear that its effects will exceed her intentions and lead her beyond the fluctuating safety of the "natural." She occasionally reads novels, sometimes aloud to her friends, sometimes alone. Following an afternoon of reading aloud, Lister notes that the company agreed "that Lady Caroline Lambe's novel, *Glenarvon,* is very talented but a very dangerous sort of book." The danger seems to increase when Lister is alone:

From 1 to 3, read the first 100pp. vol. 3 *Leontine de Blondheim.* . . . It is altogether a very interesting thing & I have read it with a sort of melancholy feeling, the very germ of which I thought had died forever. I cried a good deal. . . . Arlhofe reminds me of C—— [Marianne Lawton's husband], Leontine of M—— [Marianne], & Wallerstein of myself. I find my former feelings are too soon awakened & I have, still, more romance than can let me bear the stimulus, the fearful rousing, of novel reading. I must not indulge it. I must keep to graver things and strongly occupy myself with other thoughts and perpetual exertions. I am not happy. I get into what I have been led with . . . Anne [a woman with whom she had had an affair that she kept secret from Marianne]. Oh, that I were more virtuous and quiet. Reflection distracts me & now I could cry like a child but will not, must not give way.[26]

One of the dangers of reading novels, then, is that it might lead one to compare the fictional situation too closely with "real life," thus creating a heightened emotional and sexual state that might work against virtuous determinations such as Lister's vow to see no more of Anne. To remain "virtuous and quiet," then, one must avoid "the stimulus, the fearful rousing, of novel reading."

That Lister could have recourse to the idea of "virtue" in describing herself—even if only in describing what she lacks—suggests the importance of this term as a marker, not just of heterosexual femininity (which Lister eschews) but also of subjectivity itself with all its reliance on class and colonial privilege. Her elite education, wrested—despite some protest, we must imagine—from a culture that at least sometimes equated women's reading and writing with being "unsexed," is nonetheless a powerful class marker.[27] Lister's references to Ovid and Juvenal cannot be considered casual, because both emerge from this hard-fought struggle for education for women and serve the fraught purpose of establishing secret sexual ties with other women. But their frequency and detail does denote how much she takes such references for granted, the extent to which they serve as a material resource derived directly from the benefits of a good library and an expensive tutor; such perks of wealth indicate the necessity of Lister's privilege, her installation at the heart of British hegemony, for her own sapphic self-construction. Her interest in her own emotional states and the links of those states to reading argue for the emergence of a psychologized, bourgeois self as the norm even for aristocrats such as Lister. That is, to call such a construction of subjectivity "bourgeois" is not to attempt to describe an economic position but to document a psychic one, one whose equation with British virtue (as in the Woods-Pirie case) justifies the physical, economic, and psychic violences of colonialism. And colonialism is the work of a bourgeois modern democracy, not an absolutist aristocratic state. For Lister to think of herself as crying "like a child" at the thought of her woman lover requires a notion of subjectivity that irons out the contradiction posed by Lord Meadowbank's idea that sapphism is wholly foreign. Sapphist Anne Lister joins sapphist-accuser Jane Cumming in her "freak" status in that she plays the role, in her own self-representation, of reconciling what would otherwise be unbearable contradictions for British authority in the emerging discourse of identity.

### Domestic Spaces and Sexual Stakes

These discursive contexts, then—the social and "public" functions of romantic friendship, the difficulty of distinguishing it from "indecent" relations between women, and the threat to sexual virtue posed by novels—allow for a fuller understanding of the representation of female sexuality and relations between women in *Belinda*. I want to begin by examining the Edgeworth character who most appears to resemble Jane Cumming, as seen by the judges, and Anne Lister's self-representation: Harriot Freke.

Lest her functions in the novel be misunderstood, Harriot Freke's name itself signals her unnatural status in the novel's terms. Her dress provides another unequivocal marker of her freakishness: from her first appearance at a masquerade, during which Lady Delacour looks for her dressed as "the widow Brady, in man's clothes" (21), until her final defeat when she is mistaken by Lady Delacour's gardener for "the fellow . . . who has been at my morello cherry-tree every night" (309) and is caught and wounded in the gardener's "man-trap," Harriot Freke exults in dressing like a man. Wearing men's clothes also allows Mrs. Freke to adopt gestures implicitly coded in the novel as "masculine": polishing a pistol on the sleeve of her coat (57), throwing her hat on the table (225), and striking the sole of her boot with her whip (226). The verbs used to describe her movement through the domestic spaces of the novel attest to the "unnatural" freedom that cross-dressing allows her. In the following scene, Mrs. Freke attempts to "carry [Belinda] off in triumph" from the home of the virtuous Percivals. All the activity of the attempted elopement is seen to be what Belinda calls the "knight-errantry" of Mrs. Freke; Belinda, whom her would-be rescuer calls a "distressed damsel," can only "draw back" from the spectacle of an active woman: "Belinda was alone, and reading, when Mrs Freke dashed into the room. 'How do, dear creature?' cried she, stepping up to her, and shaking hands with her boisterously—'How do?—Glad to see you, faith!—Been long here?—Tremendously hot to-day!' She flung herself upon the sofa beside Belinda, threw her hat upon the table, and then continued speaking" (225). Then follows a long speech by Mrs. Freke condemning the Percivals, the "good people" with whom Belinda is staying. The novel continues: "Belinda, who had not been suffered to utter a word whilst Mrs. Freke ran on in this strange manner, looked in unfeigned astonishment; but when she found herself seized and dragged toward the door, she drew back with a degree of gentle firmness that astonished Mrs. Freke" (225–226). The terms used to describe Mrs. Freke in this scene are varied and active: "dashed," "stepping up," "shaking," "boisterously," "flung," "threw," "speaking," "ran on," and "seized and dragged." Her masculine activity, of course, is the kind conventionally ridiculed in the domestic novel: Mrs. Freke's movement through the room is the inattentive bluster of the vain buck, like that of Austen's John Thorpe in *Northanger Abbey*. Belinda, by contrast, is described in much less detail as sedentary, silent, and passive: she "was alone, and reading," she "had not been suffered to utter a word," she "looked," she "found herself seized," and she "drew back."

The chapter in which this scene appears is entitled "The Rights of Woman," and in it Mrs. Freke produces several inconsistent "plump assertions" (229) purporting to represent arguments for the equality of women with men. These arguments, culminating in her cry, "I hate slavery! *Vive la liberté!* . . . I'm a champion for the Rights of Woman" (229), are firmly and reasonably opposed by Mr. Percival, who claims to be "an advocate for [women's] happiness" instead of their rights. Defending such female virtues as decency, delicacy, and shame, Mr. Percival thoroughly discredits Harriot Freke's position. Importantly, this scene also discredits her activity as such: by establishing the necessity of opposing Mrs. Freke's opinions, it also argues for opposing her actions. Belinda's calmness and passivity are set in opposition to Mrs. Freke's rapid speech and movements as clearly as Mr. Percival's rational, sustained argument contrasts with her scattered, shocking statements. Harriot Freke's clothing, then, is linked in this chapter to her freedom of movement and her opposition to the "slavery" of women.[28] All are coded as the ineffective dandyism of the failed suitor, and all are made to seem ridiculous and unnatural in a woman.

Although the violence of Harriot Freke's gender and sexual transgressions are startlingly unusual portrayals for women novelists of the period, the vivid parody of a whole cluster of "Jacobin" ideas—feminism, domestic and political revolution, opposition to slavery, sexual freedom—are utterly conventional in the work of Edgeworth's contemporaries such as Austen and Amelia Opie.[29] Harriot Freke's male-parodic behavior, however, links these ideas to the possibility of a female erotic agency directed not at men but at other women. Harriot Freke is the "wrong" suitor for Belinda, true; but that she could be represented as a suitor at all raises fundamental problems in this attempt to construct the sexuality of the domestic woman. Thus, although Harriot Freke is figured as a joke, she also poses a danger to Belinda—the danger of inappropriate female friendship. Clearly, to associate with such a woman would compromise Belinda in the eyes of her host and of her suitor, Mr. Vincent, who is also present during the scene. Thus, when Mr. Vincent asks if she is not afraid of making an enemy of Mrs. Freke, Belinda replies, "I think her friendship more to be dreaded than her enmity" (232). Belinda has successfully learned and reproduced the novel's most important stricture about female friendship: that women who attempt to usurp the position of men are not just inappropriate but also *dangerous* friends for young ladies hoping to marry well.

The novel opposes Harriot's freakish courtship of Belinda with Lady Delacour's ladylike attentions, establishing romantic friendship between "normal" feminine women as an appropriate relationship within which the women can express intense romantic feeling. Such a location is necessary because to establish Belinda's "aversion to the idea of marrying from interest, or convenience, or from any motives but esteem and love" (241), the novel must represent her as capable of desire. But, paradoxically, desire can take place only within the bounds of the heterosexual marriage, and such a marriage, in this genre of domestic fiction, does not occur until *after* the novel ends. This conventional constraint poses a distinct problem, for because we do not see the marriage itself within the novel, how can the heroine's desire be represented? The central strategy for managing such a difficulty in *Belinda* is this: to ensure that Belinda does not feel desire for her male suitors too soon, the novel displaces her desire onto a fascinating older woman. Thus, Belinda's relationship with Lady Delacour becomes the most consistently and intensely eroticized one in the novel.

In the first description of this relationship, the narrator corrects herself to emphasize its intensity: Belinda "was charmed with the idea of her visit to lady Delacour, whom she thought the most agreeable—no, that is too feeble an expression—the most fascinating person she had ever beheld" (10). The ungendered "person" here attests to Lady Delacour's primacy in Belinda's psychic life over both men and other women. Lady Delacour's response to Belinda is equally intense. She wonders: "What was Harriot Freke in comparison with Belinda Portman? Harriot Freke, even whilst she diverted me most, I half despised. But Belinda! Oh, Belinda! how entirely have I loved-trusted-admired-adored-respected-revered you!" (183). The rivalry and the comparison set up here between Harriot and Belinda suggest a troubling equation between two characters who are supposed to represent moral opposites.

The status of this equation becomes even clearer when Lady Delacour exonerates Belinda from the charge of concealing a (male) lover in her ladyship's boudoir: "*She,* the confidante of my intrigues!—*she* leagued with me in vice!—No, I am bound to her by ties stronger than vice ever felt; than vice, even in the utmost ingenuity of its depravity, can devise" (335–336). The possibility raised here that the tie between Belinda and Lady Delacour might be comparable to, or even seen as, one of "vice" betrays another locus of anxiety about the virtue of Belinda's attachment to Lady Delacour. To acquit her of inappropriate warmth toward or excessive interest in men and marriage, the novel overinvests in Belinda's relationships with women to the extent that their intensity finally becomes equally threatening. The most striking example of this consequence is the threat that Belinda's friendship with Lady Delacour may make it impossible for her to marry. When early in the novel someone facetiously congratulates Clarence Hervey on the rumor of his engagement to Belinda, he replies: "You don't imagine I go to lady Delacour's to look for a *wife?* . . . Do you think I'm an idiot?" (25–26). The self-evident idiocy of finding a virtuous wife in the improper home of Lady Delacour leads another character to observe that "miss Portman is in a dangerous situation" (108) as her ladyship's most intimate friend. The dangers of romantic friendship significantly undermine the stability of heterosexual marriage and thus of the domestic realm itself.

The public stakes of "the choice of female friends" become clear in an early scene. Lady Delacour recounts the many adventures in which she has been involved with Harriot Freke, adventures that culminate in Lady Delacour's being challenged by another woman, Mrs. Luttridge, to a duel. The occasion is an election, in which Lady Delacour and Mrs. Freke are canvassing for one candidate, and Mrs. Luttridge, for his opponent. Incensed by a caricature Lady Delacour has drawn of her, Mrs. Luttridge is heard to say that "she wished . . . to be a man, that she might be qualified to take proper notice of [Lady Delacour's] conduct" (58). Harriot Freke has read an essay by the novel's hero, Clarence Hervey, titled "The Propriety and Necessity of Female Duelling," the argument of which she uses to convince Lady Delacour to duel. Lady Delacour tells Belinda that she is persuaded by "the masculine superiority, as I thought it, of Harriot's understanding," as well as by Harriot's assurance that she "should charm all beholders in male attire." Both Mrs. Luttridge and her second appear in men's clothes as well. As the cross-dressed women fire into the air, a mob of the local electorate pours onto the scene. Lady Delacour suddenly realizes that "an English mob is really a formidable thing" (58), especially when she herself is the object of its wrath. She says she is "convinced that they would not have been half so much scandalized if we had boxed in petticoats" (58) rather than dueling in boots and jackets. Their danger increases until Clarence Hervey arrives driving a herd of pigs, convinces the mob to follow him in order to race a Frenchman driving a flock of turkeys, and diverts the crowd's attention to this nationalistic contest. Lady Delacour's improperly loaded pistol backfires, and she sustains a wound to her breast. Everyone else escapes without physical harm, but the political consequences are more serious. "The fate of the election turned upon this duel," Lady Delacour says. "With true English pigheadedness, they went every man of them and polled for an independent candidate of their own choosing, whose wife, forsooth, was a proper behaved woman" (60).

This scene turns on the novel's—and the period's—central anxieties about how improper female friendship can lead women to usurp the positions of men, resulting not only in confused gender boundaries but in personal and political violence as well. These anxieties underscore the simultaneous necessity and impossibility of policing the boundaries of romantic friendship. For while on the one hand such a friendship could be argued to guarantee female virtue because it fixed women's desires and attentions on one another and therefore *not* on possibly sexual relations with men, on the other hand female friendship could also result in a dangerous female autonomy from men, even an attempt to take the place of men, in this case by dressing or dueling like them.[30] The usurpation of male-gendered clothing and behavior by women, then, produces a dislocation in the social organization of sexuality. Female homoeroticism disrupts heterosexual norms, calling into question the gendered terms within which the domestic space is organized. And in the context of the domestic novel, wrenching sexuality from gender in this way sets in motion a whole set of political upheavals that threaten to collapse the tightly knit interrelations of gender, class, nation, and sexuality on which the novel's authority depends.

*Belinda* is one of those eighteenth-century texts that uneasily condemns the reading of novels on the grounds that they give their young women readers dangerous ideas about how to act in the world.[31] This self-undermining anxiety spills over into ambivalence about all acts of writing and reading—about who writes, who reads, and what effects these activities have on the susceptible minds of women. In this scene, women reading—Harriot Freke's and Lady Delacour's responses to Hervey's essay—has indeed produced women rioting, or women *and* rioting. And this nexus—of autonomous, indecent women and an enraged popular mob—is a potent threat in this scene, in this novel, and, I would argue, in the definition of romantic friendship as well. If inappropriate friendship between women can throw an election and rouse the common people of an English county to protest en masse, then the stakes of separating "virtuous" romantic friendship, in which women's reading is controlled by propriety, from "indecent" female intimacy, which fails to distinguish appropriate texts for women, are high indeed. The explicit anxiety in this scene might be political unrest, but such public consequences were also shadowed by the possibility of privatized, sexual indecency between women. Both spectacles of rebellion are linked to the fear that to mark the boundary between "virtuous" and "indecent" female friendships, one might actually have to represent an indecent character such as Harriot Freke so as to condemn her—but that such a representation might have the power, as it does *within* the text, to entice women to imitate her rather than to turn from her in horror. Such representations, in short, might give female readers access to the very acts and attitudes that the category "romantic friendship" exists to suppress.

As one of the most important consequences of the duel for the plot of the novel, Lady Delacour receives the terrible wound to her breast that haunts the rest of the narrative. Convinced she has cancer, Lady Delacour determines to keep her wound a secret and for this purpose dresses it in the privacy of her boudoir with only her maid, Marriott, and later Belinda in attendance. She refuses to consult a physician, fearful of exchanging the world's "admiration" for its "pity" (65). She vows to "act my part in public" (65) rather than have the world discover her illness. Lady Delacour's refusal to retreat to the privacy of the domestic sphere, even when wounded, powerfully marks her "unwomanly" desires in the novel's terms. The monstrosity of her desire to remain in public is figured by the unnatural act she contemplates in order to keep that act secret: she resolves, against Belinda's advice, to undergo "the amazonian operation" (194)—the removal, we infer, of the "cancerous" breast.

Lady Delacour's wound is, in terms of the novel's sexual economy, a wound to her femininity, the moral consequence of her transgression of gender boundaries in the duel. The wound—Lady Delacour's secrecy about it—compromises her reputation and hence her virtue—for as Belinda notes, "a woman ought not even to be suspected" (132) of sexual impropriety. Harriot Freke, Mrs. Luttridge, and especially Lord Delacour all assume that Lady Delacour has hidden a lover in the "mysterious boudoir" (294). Early in the novel, Lady Delacour cements her attachment to Belinda by revealing to her the "hideous spectacle" (32) of her wound, and from that point on Belinda's virtue too is involved in Lady Delacour's "amazonian" secret. This implication becomes clear in a scene during which Lady Delacour returns ill from a party and Lord Delacour returns drunk from a dinner. Belinda attempts to stop her host from entering the boudoir when Lady Delacour gives "a scream of agony" at the prospect: "Lord Delacour stopped short. 'Tell me, then,' cried Lord Delacour, 'is not a lover of lady Delacour's concealed there?' 'No!—No!—No!' answered Belinda. 'Then a lover of miss Portman's?' said lord Delacour. 'Gad! we have hit it now, I believe'" (128). The immediate transference of Lord Delacour's suspicions of his wife's virtue to Belinda indicates that Belinda's proximity to Lady Delacour's boudoir and to her wounded body place her close to the boundary of virtuous behavior herself. Indeed, the boudoir conceals the "truth" of Lady Delacour's body and sexuality and hence may be said to conceal the essential Lady Delacour herself: "a lover of miss Portman." Not only Belinda's proximity to Lady Delacour, then, but also Belinda's actual relationship to her, represented by access to the boudoir, is here figured as improper. Clarence Hervey has witnessed this scene, and his recurring suspicions about Belinda's honor retard the declaration of his love for her until the last few pages of the novel.

Lady Delacour's wound also demonstrates the relation between marital and class power; the secret of the wound gives her servant Marriott a power over her lady that rivals a husband's. In one of the novel's first scenes, Lady Delacour tries to decide whether she or Belinda should wear the costume of the tragic muse to a masquerade. She herself wants to go as the comic muse, but Marriott insists otherwise. Lady Delacour gives in, murmuring, "*Marriott knows her power*" (20). The narrative then presents commentary on the inversion of authority this "power" both bears witness to and produces: "Upon many occasions miss Portman had observed, that Marriott exercised despotic authority over her mistress; and she had seen, with surprise, that a lady, who would not yield an iota of power to her husband, submitted herself to every caprice of the most insolent of waiting-women" (20). Lady Delacour's submission to her maid inverts class relations by substituting the authority of a woman for that of a man. The implication that working-class people are, as Nancy Armstrong puts it, "insufficiently gendered," emerged at the end of the eighteenth century and became a convention of nineteenth-century social analysis. The portrayal of working-class "women as masculine" in nineteenth-century writing, according to Armstrong, had its roots in eighteenth-century domestic fiction.[32] The attribution of domestic power to Marriott marks her as "masculine" because a servant could never achieve the appropriate power of the domestic lady of the house. In succumbing to Marriott, then, Lady Delacour resists the authority of her husband and thus of the institution of marriage itself. Her actions here are governed by a hierarchy of domestic knowledge (organized in terms of access to the secret of her boudoir) rather than by one of class or gender. Because this knowledge is the product and property of the domestic space over which virtuous women are granted some authority, knowledge and the power within which it is imbricated fail to line up with patriarchal hierarchies of class and gender. Lady Delacour's wound, then, threatens the stability of both middle-class authority and heterosexual marriage.

The wound is Lady Delacour's; Harriot Freke's deviant body remains intact in the duel scene because the novel is not interested in disciplining her body into the shape of a virtuous woman. Although she is later brutally mangled, as we will see, such violence aims not to recuperate her into the domestic space inhabited by virtuous women but rather finally to do away with the threat of her deviance by severing her completely from that space. Most often, Mrs.

Freke is represented as a catalyst rather than an agent. She is the remote cause of the duel and the wound as opposed to a wounded duelist herself. Thus, in this scene she is never the victim of her own freakishness; that she is spared indicates another of the novel's ambiguities about the pleasures and powers of Harriot Freke's unnaturalness. It is her intimate friend, Lady Delacour, who receives the mark of Harriot Freke's gender and sexual transgressions on her own body.

Harriot Freke's distanced agency places her outside the world of conventional femininity in which the heterosexual plot of the novel takes place. Appropriately, then, the character who most clearly recognizes her as a transgressor of gender boundaries, bestowing on her the epithet "*man-woman*" (219), is the African slave Juba, whom Mr. Vincent, one of Belinda's suitors, has brought with him from Jamaica. Indeed, it is in her interactions with Juba, placed late in the novel, that the cultural work performed by the representation of Mrs. Freke's aberrant status is clearest. Just as this novel has two plots (the colonial story of Vincent's search for a wife and the domestic one of Belinda's search for a husband), so it has two "freaks," figures who here do the ideological work of Jane Cumming and Anne Lister in their respective narratives. Harriot Freke's relationship with Juba pivotally establishes the importance of female sexual "normality" in holding in place not just domestic and familial relations but class and colonial ones as well. The novel's anxiety over the possibility of sapphic sexuality is rerouted into a consideration of the quaint and perverted superstitions of the racial Other.

The major incident in which Juba takes part begins with a reference to Harriot Freke's characteristically distanced agency in the sexuality of the women around her: "It is somewhat singular that lady Delacour's faithful friend, Harriot Freke, should be the cause of Mr Vincent's first fixing his favourable attention on miss Portman" (219). In this incident, Juba takes Mrs. Freke's place in the carriage house in which both her vehicle and Mr. Vincent's are housed. She screams curses at him out the window and swears revenge. Juba's response is the only utterance in which the novel makes Harriot Freke's masculinity explicit; the narrator and other characters allude to qualities that are read, in the context of the novel's conventional construction of femininity, as masculine, but it takes a character as "freakish" (in the novel's world) as Mrs. Freke herself to name what is so shocking about her. Juba then ventriloquizes her, identifying those same aspects of Mrs. Freke's demeanor for Mr. Vincent:

> Mrs Freke, who heard and saw the whole transaction from her window, said, or swore, that she would make Juba repent of, what she called, his insolence. The threat was loud enough to reach his ears, and he looked up in astonishment to hear such a voice from a woman. . . . Mr Vincent, to whom Juba, with much simplicity, expressed his aversion of the *man-woman* who lived in the house with them, laughed at the odd manner in which the black imitated her voice and gesture. (219)

Of course, this scene establishes not only Mrs. Freke's inappropriate masculinity but Juba's appropriate or "normal" masculinity as well. In retelling the incident to Mr. Vincent, Juba is clearly a man among men, for this moment at least.

At the same time, however, Juba's ability to represent Harriot Freke's masculinity to Mr. Vincent rests on overlapping and contradictory assumptions about his racial difference from his master. This passage draws attention first to his "simplicity," the uncivilized propensity for seeing right to the heart of things manifested in his "astonishment" at hearing a woman swearing. Because he has not been perverted by the metropolitan fashion that makes Harriot Freke's oddities tolerable in the polite world, he can identify them as repulsive and oxymoronic by demonstrating an instinctual "aversion" to the "*man-woman.*" But equally important is Juba's affinity with her: his ability to imitate "her voice and gesture" not only indicates the racist notion that Africans are imitative, monkeylike, but also suggests that Juba can, because of his own "odd manner," successfully parody Mrs. Freke's. Juba, then, is as freakish in his colonial "simplicity" as Harriot Freke is in her metropolitan decadence. Both primitiveness and decadence help define the boundaries of the middle-class female virtue that is the novel's ideological ground.

To reinforce this similarity, the novel enacts Mrs. Freke's power over Juba in terms of an English notion of the voodoo culture of the Caribbean, masking but also alluding to the actual relations of power between eighteenth-century Englishwomen and Jamaican slaves. After offending Mrs. Freke, Juba receives nightly visits from a mysterious phantom whom he takes to be "one of the obeah-women of his own country" (221). The phantom is actually a figure drawn by Mrs. Freke in phosphorous outside Juba's window. The terms in which the obeah-woman's power is described indicate an implicit connection between Juba's identification of Harriot Freke's gender transgression and his sense of being punished for telling secrets. After telling Mr. Vincent and Belinda about being pursued by an obeah-woman,

> [Juba] calmly said, that he knew he must now die, for that the obeah-women never forgave those that talked of them or their secrets. . . . [T]he same figure of an old woman, all in flames, appeared at the foot of his bed every night whilst he stayed at Harrowgate; and that he was then persuaded she would never let him escape from her power, till she had killed him. . . . [H]e was sure of her vengeance for having spoken of the past.
>
> Mr Vincent knew the astonishing power, which the belief in this species of sorcery has over the minds of the Jamaica negroes; they pine and actually die away, from the moment they fancy themselves under the malignant power of these witches. (221–222)

This passage works to establish Mrs. Freke's power over Juba as resulting solely from his superstitious beliefs—but in doing so, it reveals the material reality of that power, which is actually the power of life and death. Thus, it ends up affirming Juba's "superstitious" fear of Mrs. Freke, pointing to the material power that an Englishwoman really did have over a slave in a colonial setting.[33] Juba has indeed "talked of " Mrs. Freke and brought the "secrets" of her gender and sexual transgression, hitherto represented only indirectly, into the discourse of the novel. Hence, he has earned her "vengeance," a mark of the "power" she holds over him, which, as the power of the white Englishwoman over the black slave—but also like that of the obeah-woman over her victim—means that she will "never let him escape from her power until she [has] killed him" (for his slavery will continue to his death). The image of Mrs. Freke's power, however, is also that of an indecently sexual woman: whether her sexuality is inappropriate because of her age ("an old woman, all in flames") or her mysterious powers ("a malignant witch").[34] These lurid images of female sexuality are produced by the novel's equation of Harriot Freke's obscene transgressions and the spectacle of a primitive woman powerful enough to control life and death—the equation between metropolitan and colonial perversity. Mrs. Freke's power over Juba, then, is as inappropriate as Marriot's over Lady Delacour. But instead of enacting a reversal of the relations of the bourgeois family, this incident dramatizes an eerie parody of it. As a "man-woman," Mrs. Freke cannot have the appropriate power of the white domestic woman over the black slave: her power, that of a grotesquely threatening, sexualized being, can be understood only in terms of a world defined in opposition to the bourgeois domestic scene, the voodoo-ridden slave culture that, like Harriot Freke, is the object of both fear and ridicule in the novel.

At the moment when Juba and Mrs. Freke clash, then, all the alternative possibilities for representing female sexuality that are being generated and unsuccessfully contained in Belinda's world of female domestic power break out into the larger national and international space. The incident underscores the importance of publicly identifying and repudiating Harriot Freke's aberrant power. Thus, she is punished for a trick similar to the phosphorus incident by being brutally mangled in a "man-trap" set to catch garden thieves, and the novel insists that as a result of her wound "the beauty of her legs would be spoiled, and . . . she would never more be able to appear to advantage in man's apparel" (312). Like Lady Delacour's wound, Harriot Freke's is a disciplinary mark on a transgressive body. But Lady Delacour's body is wounded to make it conform to the norms of gender and sexuality without which the powerful ideology of female domestic virtue is impossible, whereas Harriot Freke's is torn from the narrative when its compelling power as a spectacle threatens to overwhelm its exemplary function. We see no more of Harriot when she can no longer wear men's clothes—and very little more of Juba when he no longer functions to define Harriot.[35]

Because the novel's heterosexual plot has been so problematized, the act of ending the narrative becomes a problem as well. The last two pages of *Belinda* exhibit a remarkable anxiety about and resistance to conventional novelistic closure. Such resistance and anxiety allow us to speculate about the extent to which Edgeworth, as a conservative woman novelist in a period when the novel itself was identified primarily with progressive politics, might have found herself in a contradictory position in trying to "reform" Lady Delacour.[36] Marilyn Butler argues that the "virtuous domesticated matron . . . [is] the most typical heroine of Maria's early novels," but this assessment holds true for *Belinda* only if we consider the minor character of Lady Anne Percival as the novel's "heroine."[37] While awarding the heroineship to Lady Anne might help explain the novel's insistence that Belinda herself is no heroine, the novel is named for Belinda, and it is Lady Delacour who holds center stage. The representations of these two women, whose virtue is to varying degrees questioned in the novel, compete for the status of heroine. Indeed, this conservative novelist's investment in one of her most scandalous characters suggests that the representation of Lady Delacour serves as a space within which Edgeworth's own inevitable conflicts about female authority could find expression. For if Lady Delacour's "radicalism and . . . sexual promiscuity" link her with the indecent, Jacobin values associated with the novel form—the values from which Edgeworth was consciously trying to distance herself—these same qualities also foster her power in the domestic scene because they raise the possibility that she could disrupt it.[38] Because Edgeworth was a woman writer attempting to find a voice in a form, the novel, which was conventionally vilified because of its association with women writers and readers, her attempts to speak up about politics and sexuality were implicated in, because they were analogous to, Lady Delacour's scandalous wit. Although Butler claims that Edgeworth "joined the group of rational women writers of this period whose first novels were so to speak anti-novels," even such conservative women writers could not escape the consequences of writing in a genre that granted them an unprecedented cultural authority that was still often regarded as indecent.[39] Women novelists and the domestic form of knowledge they created became a major form of bourgeois cultural legitimation. According to Armstrong, "Middle-class authority rested in large part upon the authority that novels attributed to women and in this way designated as specifically female."[40] Thus, while Edgeworth might explicitly praise the retiring "lady Anne Percival in the midst of her children" (98), her own practice is much more like that of Lady Delacour, who congratulates herself on possessing "the true skill of a good story-teller" (52). Edgeworth's identification with Lady Delacour's powers of language becomes unavoidably explicit at the end of the novel. Here, Edgeworth confronts the difficulty of converting a good storyteller into the "domestic woman" (105) that Lady Delacour must become to satisfy the moral trajectory of the narrative. The uneasy position of the conservative woman writer is represented here as Edgeworth tries, through Lady Delacour, to end the story.

One of *Belinda*'s subplots concerns Hervey's Rousseauian attempts to train an innocent young girl into the perfect wife and his efforts to extricate himself from this relationship after he falls in love with Belinda. Eventually, his pupil

Virginia frees him by declaring her love for Captain Sunderland, to whose picture she has become attached in her retirement. Lady Delacour marks the narrative's uneasy awareness of the conventionality of such revelations by asking, "And now, my good friends . . . shall I finish the novel for you?" (477). The gesture of displacing the task of the text itself onto one of its characters indicates a desire to distance the problem of closure from the author/narrator. This strange masking of Edgeworth's own agency in relation to novelistic convention summarizes the many disavowals throughout of *Belinda*'s status as a novel: from Lady Delacour's warning that "you will be woefully disappointed if in my story you expect any thing like a novel" (35–36) to Belinda's refusal to use "any of the terms in the heroine's dictionary" (452) to respond to Hervey's proposal of marriage. Yet the heterosexual plot requires conventional novelistic closure; it is only by retelling this particular story about marital, family, and class relations that the woman novelist gains authority within the domestic sphere.

To defer the necessity of producing conventional closure, the novel turns from self-criticism to criticism of the endings of other novels. Indeed, these pages provide a minicatalogue of critiques of the convention in which *Belinda* itself is nonetheless enmeshed. On the second-last page, Belinda notes that "there is nothing in which novelists are so apt to err as in hurrying things toward the conclusion: in not allowing *time* enough for that change of feeling, which change of situation cannot instantly produce" (477). This argument resonates oddly with the narrative necessity it attempts to critique. Lady Delacour offers to "draw out the story to five volumes more" (477) but then withdraws the offer to propose a move to another genre entirely. She asks if she "might conclude the business in two lines," with a couplet resonant of the Restoration stage: "Ye gods, annihilate both space and time / And make four lovers happy" (477). Lady Delacour's aunt withstands this violation—even to the point of abandonment—of novelistic convention, invoking Richardson's *Sir Charles Grandison* as a model both to imitate and to resist:

O, that would be cutting matters too short. . . . I am of the old school; and though I could dispense with the description of miss Harriot Byron's worked chairs and fine china, yet I own, I like to hear something of the preparation for a marriage, as well as of the mere wedding. I like to hear *how* people become happy in a rational manner, better than to be told in the huddled style of an old fairy tale—*and so they were all married, and they lived very happily all the rest of their days.* (477)

Both Belinda and Mrs. Delacour, then, agree on the necessity of more narrative. Significantly, they also argue for representing the now permissible heterosexual desire that the flurry of recent revelations has made possible: Belinda wants to see a "change of feeling," and Mrs. Delacour assumes she will get at least the "mere wedding" (477). Lady Delacour's rejoinder to these suggestions, however, recasts them as a controversy: "But how shall I please you all? Some people cry, 'Tell me every thing', others say, that, 'Le secret d'ennuyer est celui de tout dire' " (477). In fact, Lady Delacour herself is the only one to voice the latter sentiment (that is, "the secret of being boring is to tell all"). Setting up the problem as one generated by the conflicting desires of her audience rather than by her own lingering desire to keep secrets allows her to return to her own solution, that of recasting the story in another genre. She proposes first "a characteristic letter of congratulation from Mrs. Stanhope to her *dearest* niece, Belinda." Mrs. Delacour approves: "Well, I have no objection to ending with a letter . . . for last speeches are always tiresome" (478). The approval of a member of "the old school" who reads Richardson reminds the reader that ending a novel with a letter is a highly conventional solution and perhaps not a shift in genre at all. Lady Delacour once again recasts the response, seeming to agree with it but actually using it to ground an even more radical suggestion:

> Yes . . . it is so difficult, as the critic says, to get lovers off upon their knees.[41] Now I think of it, let me place you all in proper attitudes for stage effect. What signifies being happy, unless we appear so?—Captain Sunderland— kneeling with Virginia, if you please, sir, at her father's feet. You in the act of giving them your blessing, Mr Hartley. Mrs Ormond clasps her hands with joy—nothing can be better than that, madam—I give you infinite credit for the attitude. Clarence, you have a right to Belinda's hand, and may kiss it too. Nay, miss Portman, it is the rule of the stage. . . . There! quite pretty and natural! Now, lady Delacour, to show that she is reformed, comes forward to address the audience with a moral—a moral! Yes,
>
> > Our *tale* contains a *moral;* and, no doubt,
> > You all have wit enough to find it out. (478)

The bizarre superimposition of a "stage effect" onto the end of the novel finally allows for the representation of Belinda's heterosexuality—as Clarence kisses her hand—but it also removes all agency from the scene, leaving the characters not the realist personalities of prose fiction but the flat types of the Restoration stage or eighteenth-century private theatrical. Even Lady Delacour must finally refer to herself in the third person, as if she were under the direction of someone else—perhaps a figure for Edgeworth's own inability to escape genre fully by throwing off the radical consequences of writing a novel. The reduction of novelistic relationships to flattened visual stereotypes and of the idiom of novelistic realism to an ambiguous couplet indicates Edgeworth's attempt to resolve the contradictions of the conditions of novelistic closure by deferring the final scene to another genre entirely, hence masking the contradictory discourse in which both she and her characters are caught up and by which they are compelled.

It is significant that the final couplet should refuse to identify the novel's "moral." This gesture indicates both Edgeworth's overt concern with moral questions and her inability to resolve successfully the central ones it raises. The absence of a moral from the conclusion signals the possibility that these questions have not been fully recuperated by the awkward and incoherent version of heterosexual closure. For the linchpin of *Belinda*'s moral universe is the purity of its namesake, a purity guaranteed by the reformation of her intimate friend. Central to this reformation is Lady Delacour's rejection of Harriot Freke, whose sexual irregularity renders the English domestic world penetrable by the gaze of the colonial and racial Other, whose "natural" sexual standards give him the threatening power to comment on the domestic arrangements of the novel's English characters. The novel tries to mend the aperture caused by Harriot Freke's sapphic status by having Lady Delacour cast off her friend in the second chapter. But because the issue of female friendship rests at the center of so many other systems of authority, Harriot Freke must be constantly summoned back into the story to demonstrate the threat posed by inappropriate female friendship to gender relations, sexual norms, nationalism, class hierarchies, and race and colonial relations—to establish these relations by constructing their opposites in the world of Harriot Freke's authority. In the context of the Scottish judges' fears about the power of the sapphic colonial body not only to sully the purity of the domestic woman but also to threaten public safety and Anne Lister's potent construction of her class power into a form of sapphic sexual agency, the novel cannot convincingly dismiss that world through satire and ridicule. The figure of Harriot Freke invokes both the spectacle raised by the Woods-Pirie case, that of the erotic recolonization of British women's intimate relationships by subaltern "indecency," and the potential, made manifest in Anne Lister's diaries, that elite women's reading and writing could create a sexual agency for women that would destabilize gender. The dangerous appeal of Harriot Freke's presence in *Belinda,* both for the women within the narrative and the women writer and women readers outside it, is marked by the masking of her freedom and power that takes place when her agency is mediated in the chaotic actions she is nonetheless blamed for causing. Harriot Freke, as the figure for indecent female friendship, plays the necessary Other to bourgeois women in the privatized domestic space where they hold and exert this power; however, she also threatens the sanctity of that space by revealing the conflict of the several systems of authority based on gender, class, and race that make it possible. Significantly, it is the production of specifically sexual figures within this female-gendered space that disrupts these systems. Only by reading these sexual figures—reading them precisely as sexual—can the bourgeoisie's story about the legitimacy of its own rise to power become visible. Sapphic sexuality, at once produced and banished in the invocation of romantic friendship, provides a unique category with which we can analyze a specific moment in the emergence of identity as a modern category, a category that continues to shape homosexuality and homophobia today.

In this chapter I have tried to demonstrate how representations of romantic friendship are used to construct domestic space, a sphere of activity created in the interests of the middle class, in which and through which it exercises its power. That space is both the space of affect and sexuality, the domestic interior; and simultaneously it is the domestic as opposed to the colonial, an insulated political space. Thus the term "domestic" designates a private and a public sphere; both are spaces constructed together through representations bent on the sexual regulation of women, so that only an analysis of the textual construction of bourgeois female sexuality will show us exhaustively how colonialism and racism sustain bourgeois hegemony.

*Belinda* is a formal aesthetic attempt to contain the active and powerful sapphic Other who threatens to emerge uncontained and contaminating from nonfiction accounts of female friendship such as the Woods-Pirie case and Lister's diaries, an attempt that deploys some of the same strategies for containment as legal discourse itself, such as the racializing and projecting of sapphic sexual activity onto the colonial Other. But this proves an insufficient strategy insofar as representation itself is implicated in stimulating sapphic agency, as can be seen in the diaries of the self-consciously powerful and active Lister, who mobilizes the categories of "natural" and "freakish/book-ish" sexualities to legitimate, to represent as a kind of virtue, her own activity.

I would like to return to a larger context briefly both to conclude and to proceed. In Chapter 1 on *Millenium Hall,* I considered the representation of romantic friendship in a supposed "high" cultural form (the utopian novel), whereas in Chapter 2 on *Memoirs of a Woman of Pleasure,* I looked at this representation in a form, the pornographic novel, that could be understood as "low." In this chapter I argue that *Belinda* exemplifies the way in which the domestic novel attempts and yet fails to incorporate and thereby contain the threat of "freakish" female sexuality and female agency represented in aesthetically "low" cultural forms, both literary ones such as pornography and nonliterary ones such as trial transcripts, newspapers, and diaries, while also profiting from the representations of female power available in such "low" sources. As we've learned from Peter Stallybrass and Allon White, the sphere of bourgeois hegemony is established in culture through prying apart the high and the low;[42] the domestic novel, as a heterogenous form that brings together high and low elements, metropolitan and colonial plots, and disparate generic conventions so as to create narratives of coherent identity that distinguish among these elements, thus emerges as the quintessential literary vehicle of bourgeois hegemony. *Belinda* fails to contain the threat it represents because the novel's generic strategy for achieving closure through representing a heterosexual union that depends on female passivity does not allow for the depiction of the active female novelist authorized by the writing of it. The implications of the novel's conditions of production—that women can have both sexual agency and literary authority—outrun the novel's didactic attempts to represent female passivity admiringly. This chapter, then, has shown the haunting of "virtuous," desexualized female friendship that *Belinda* depicts by a "freakish," sexualized version of that friendship: because the novel is written by a female author whose activity contradicts the passivity she wants to represent, there is a return of the low in the high. The consequences of this "return"—which I have also called a "haunting"—for the resolutely rational and successfully canonized world of Jane Austen's fiction is the subject of the next chapter.

# Desire and Diminution: *Emma*

Closing this book with a reading of Jane Austen's *Emma* poses certain rhetorical and political problems. For while readers might intuitively agree (or at least accept) that the novel offers rich resources to the history of female friendship and lesbian identity, its relevance to this argument's secondary strand, about the ways in which female friendship was recruited into the service of narratives legitimating the bourgeoisie's rise to power, is less obvious. Edward Said's essay on *Mansfield Park* joins with much of the feminist work on Austen in challenging, this time from the point of view of postcolonialism, older assumptions about the apolitical status of Austen's domestic interiors.[1] But as Said himself notes, *Mansfield Park* is "the most explicit in its ideological and moral affirmations of Austen's novels."[2] Sketchy as it is, the Antigua subplot of *Mansfield Park* brings the colonial world into the domestic home in a way that solicits analysis. No character in *Emma* has such wide-ranging holdings and interests as the master of Mansfield Park, who must leave England to attend to his colonial business; Emma's father's hypochondriacal focus is on his own body and his own fireside, and Knightley's interest in his own farm is only a more culturally valued version of the same narcissistic projection. The single representation of the cultural Other in the novel, an incident in which two young ladies encounter a band of importuning "gipsies,"[3] results in their rescue by one of the story's eligible bachelors, and as such the incident is instantly hustled inside the boundaries of the novel's sexual plot: "Such an adventure as this—a fine young man and a lovely young woman thrown together in such a way, could hardly fail of suggesting certain ideas to the coldest heart and the steadiest brain" (227). This coercive process, I would argue, is characteristic not only of this novel's treatment of representations of "outside" that interrupt or compete with its insistent focus on domestic and psychic interiors; more generally, such homogeneity comes to be associated with the successful novelistic "realism" for which Jane Austen was celebrated early on and consistently thereafter.[4] The multiply plotted narrative structure of *Belinda,* which can make room for Creoles, slaves, and feminists, thus comes to appear old-fashioned (or postmodern) in relation to a smooth and successful incorporation of violently imposed hierarchies of difference into the sexual plot of courtship and marriage. As plot dwindles, character becomes more and more the focus of the realist novel, and the fully psychologized subject of both modern culture and what will come to be seen as novelistic convention takes its place at the center of both culture and genre.

In this chapter I attempt to demonstrate how the representation of female friendship in *Emma* incorporates and subordinates other social differences— here, microscopic increments of class and status—into sexual questions about the heroine's relations with other women. This chapter, then, lacks the explicit references that colonialism, race, and nationalism presented in previous readings. This absence, I contend, is symptomatic of the very process the novel enacts—that is, naturalizing out of sight the national and international consequences of the bourgeois rise to power in favor of representations of domestic and psychic interiors, the "truths" of which are founded on sexuality.[5] My hope is that such a reading, by dramatizing what Said calls "isolated, venerated, or formalized experience that excludes and forbids the hybridizing intrusions of human history," can contribute to the much larger feminist project of understanding lesbian history as not only an object of power but one of its agents as well.[6]

As we have seen, by the time Austen wrote *Emma* (1816) the discourse of romantic friendship already had a complex and contradictory history both within and beyond novelistic representation. For readers of the novel, Emma's friendships with Mrs. Weston, Harriet Smith, and Jane Fairfax allude not only to the chaste ladies of *Millenium Hall* but also to the "unaccountable invincible simpathies" of "female friendship" that bind Fanny Hill to Mrs.

Cole as well as to the "ties stronger than vice ever felt" between Lady Delacour and Belinda. And all these fictional friendships are being read in a
context that also produced the self-conscious sapphic practice and identity of
Anne Lister and the horrified but deadly serious debate among the Scottish
judges about the ability of schoolteachers Miss Woods and Miss Pirie to
penetrate one another in the heat of "an unnatural passion for each other."
This history had built up an ideological investment in such representations
that by the early nineteenth century had become central to definitions not just
of the virtue of an individual woman but also of the family, class, and national
authority that her virtue centers and guarantees. Such a powerful ideological
category thus operates on a text such as *Emma* in ways that the text itself
cannot control. For a heroine-centered novel to represent female friendship
at all is to invoke the possibility of sapphism; even texts as didactic as *Emma,*
in which that possibility is raised only as a specter of the heroine's possible fall
from femininity and subsequent loss of power, inevitably contribute to the
importance of that specter by endowing it with the ability to threaten the
heroine's position within the firm boundaries of heterosexual femininity and
domestic female virtue.

The ideology of romantic friendship—the sum effect of all the ways it was
represented in the fictional and nonfictional discourses of late-eighteenth-
and early-nineteenth-century culture—exceeds the intentions of a single representation; indeed, it imposes the marks of its own contradictory history on
the text, making of it something besides a single story. In its interaction with
the other texts that speak of romantic friendship in the period, then, *Emma*
raises possibilities which are explored only marginally or intermittently in the
text itself but which are visible and effective in the relation between one
anxious textual representation of female friendship and another, as well as in
the relation between this text's anxiety and that of the others I have examined
in this book. Thus I will explore the explicit and implicit ways in which the
novel poses unregulated female friendship as a "danger" to Emma as a novelistic heroine because it makes possible for her "the power of having rather too
much her own way, and a disposition to think a little too well of herself" (1).
Such autonomy and self-approbation work against the necessary compliance
of the heroine with the social hierarchies to which her story, as a story of
marriage, contributes.

*Emma*, then, inherits the novelistic topos of female friendship as both a formal necessity and a narrative problem. The difficulties generated by the novel's negotiation of this topos have also given rise to two significant critical problems in the twentieth-century reception of *Emma:* the debate over the treatment of sexual love between women in the text, and the canonical question of Austen's ironic tone, both in general and in the particular rendering of such relationships. These questions are at least partially produced by the way in which the novel's admirably achieved realism works to reconcile the contradictions at work in the discourse of female friendship with which it is centrally concerned. But these problems also merit scrutiny because of the work they themselves do, the way in which readings of a canonical English novel shape current ideas about female sexuality and sexual identity, the very ideas in whose early production the novel played such a central role. The point of view from which Emma's female friendships constitute either a failure or a consolidation of Austen's careful verbal control allows us to see how the imbrication of modern notions of identity with the vexed category of female sexuality inflects not just thematic considerations (such as what Emma's friendships mean) but formal ones as well. These critical contests exemplify the contemporary inheritance of those eighteenth-century struggles over identity that lie at the heart of modern culture. As such, they provide an implicit argument for the necessity of understanding identity's history, its violent "naturalization" within the literary genre of the novel and the novel's formal investment in a particular kind of realist representation, the realism that was to dominate the nineteenth-century English novel.

After delineating the provenance of these problems in *Emma*'s twentieth-century critical history, I turn to the novel itself, offering a reading of its plot so as to address the problems of authority and sexuality raised by the premise of a powerful heroine committed to her friendships with other women and at odds with the institution of marriage. Emma is positioned by the other characters in the novel as "masculine" both sexually and socially because she tries to take up the position of lover or husband with regard to her female friends. Emma's "masculine" assumption of power also threatens the carefully calibrated class hierarchy on which the novel's social world depends. The novel's closure—Emma's marriage—requires the loss of Emma's authority and, with it, her female friends, a loss the novel codes as a gain because it results in Emma's acquisition of a husband and a proper sense of the scope of appropriate power for bourgeois women.[7] This realignment establishes not only appropriate gender and sexual norms but proper class alliances as well, both hierarchies negotiated and contested through the issue of female friendship in the novel. As Emma's power fades, the novel demonstrates what kinds of moral, verbal, and bodily reformations are required to produce bourgeois female virtue as the definitional property of the novelistic heroine.

## *Emma*'s Critical Problems

First, let's examine the curious critical history of the novel's treatment of female sexuality. The mid-twentieth-century criticism that established Austen's current reputation as a great novelist takes for granted the existence of a sexual dynamic between Emma and Harriet; yet recent feminist and political criticism either overlooks this reading of their relationship or denies it defensively. In the first vein, Marvin Mudrick, for example, notes how "unexpected" is the spectacle of "the clever and sophisticated Emma, transported by the presence of the most insipid girl imaginable. Moreover, Emma's attention never falls so warmly upon a man; against this feeling for Harriet, her good words for Mr. Knightley's appearance seem pale indeed." Mudrick continues: "Emma's interest in Harriet is not merely mistress-and-pupil, but quite emotional and particular: for a time at least . . . Emma is in love with her: a love unphysical and inadmissible, even perhaps undefinable in such a society; and therefore safe. And in all this web of relations . . . we return always to Emma's overpowering motive: her fear of commitment."[8] And Edmund Wilson claims that while he does "not want to suggest for *Emma* any specific Freudian formula," it is nonetheless clear that "Emma, who was relatively indifferent to men, was inclined to infatuations with women." Wilson worries that Knightley "would be lucky if he did not presently find himself saddled, along with the other awkward features of the [marriage] arrangement, with one of Emma's young protégées as an actual member of the household."[9] Writing decades later but relying on the same psychological and critical vocabulary, Laura Mooneyham chastises Emma for her "emotional coldness" and the "frigid world" she makes for herself before marriage.[10] Emma's "misdirected love" for Miss Taylor, Jane Fairfax, and Harriet Smith, according to Mooneyham, stands "in implicit contrast to the love of Mr. Knightley for which Emma unconsciously searches."[11] In directing Emma's erotic energies away from her friendships with women, Mooneyham concludes, "Emma's marriage to Mr. Knightley is among the most mature and satisfying matches in Austen's work."[12]

Such critical psychologizing is best understood in the context of the "homosexual panic" of the mid–twentieth century. As John D'Emilio notes, the publication of the Kinsey reports on male and female sexual behavior in 1948 and 1953 revealed that homosexual behavior was much more widespread among "ordinary" white Americans than had been previously thought. "At the time, however," D'Emilio argues, "the information provided by Kinsey served not to ameliorate hostility toward gay men and women, but to magnify suddenly the proportions of the danger they allegedly posed."[13] As information about the ubiquity of homosexual desire "seeped into popular consciousness," D'Emilio suggests, it became the province of an ever greater field of "experts," from State Department officials to literary critics, to identify the presence of such dangerous tendencies. The prevalent interpretive frame for such information, of course, was the American psychoanalytic model based on "the assumption that the homosexual man or woman lived in isolation, as a maladjusted pathological personality."[14] Mudrick's, Wilson's, and Mooneyham's readiness to read Emma's relationship to Harriet in sexual terms, then, stems from their assumption that female homosexuality is Emma's "problem," to be identified and anatomized by the critic to explain the necessity of her "mature" acceptance of Knightley's love at the end of the novel. This position of expertise allows these critics to take excessively hostile (and surprisingly characterological) views of Emma the character and *Emma* the novel.

Feminist and revisionist accounts of Emma's friendship with Harriet, then, have had to contend with a formidable legacy of homophobia in accounting for the relationship.[15] Unfortunately, many writers have countered the hostility of critics such as Mudrick, Wilson, and Mooneyham with an equally misplaced defensiveness that denies, rather than addressing differently, the sexual reverberations of intimacy between women in Austen's novel. Tony Tanner suggests cautiously:

> Without wishing to get involved with irrelevant and extraneous speculations about the relationship between Emma and Harriet, I think it can be

justifiably (and not salaciously) suggested that Harriet *is* used by Emma in various ways as a fantasy sexual object. . . . Harriet can be persuaded/ forced into a surrogate figure, a substitute of Emma's making, who will engage in all the potentially dangerous male-female (i.e. sexual—we can say it even if Jane Austen does not think it necessary to spell it out) relationships which might amuse or distract Emma (*something* has to distract her) and which she can enjoy vicariously.[16]

The homosexual aspect of the relationship is dismissed as "irrelevant," "extraneous," and (especially telling) "salacious" here; "male-female" relations are the only possible sexual ones in such an account. In defending *Emma* from the vague charge of representing a homoerotic relationship between women, Tanner shuts down the field of interpretation presented as much more "potentially dangerous" than Emma's relationships with her would-be suitors.

Claudia Johnson critiques the "salacious" school of *Emma* criticism more explicitly when she identifies midcentury criticism of Emma as "transparently misogynist, sometimes even homophobic."[17] In a later discussion, Johnson goes further, identifying Emma as "an effeminate man" in the novel's universe.[18] Noticing that in the history of *Emma* criticism, the character Emma "was commonly charged with lesbianism," Johnson argues instead that the novel is relatively unconcerned with female sexuality.[19] Rather, she contends, the novel explores the definition and promulgation of appropriate heterosexual manhood,[20] and according to this standard, Emma herself is to be applauded because she does not submit to the "degradation" of proper femininity, defined in ridiculous terms by such characters as Mrs. Elton and Isabella. As Johnson herself notes, however, this compelling argument looks only at the novel's "gender-based censure" of the masculine characters.[21] The question of feminine sexuality appears unimportant in such an argument precisely because its reliance on the explanatory power of gender subsumes sexual representations and phenomena into an inaccurate and inadequate category. Johnson's argument would seem to provide further evidence for the merit of a sexuality-based scrutiny of the novel.

Despite their hostility to the representation of female sexuality in the novel, then, Mudrick, Wilson, and Mooneyham, writing in a climate in which the importance of homosexuality was particularly heightened, are able to identify an aspect of the novel in general and Emma's relationship with

Harriet in particular that later, more politically progressive critics ironically work to obscure. In what follows I would like to sketch an account of Emma's sexual agency in the novel that profits both from feminist revisions of Jane Austen criticism and from a willingness to take female homosexuality seriously as a category at play in *Emma*. In the words Emma uses to describe another confusing sexual marker in the book (Jane Fairfax's piano), her attentions to Harriet might be seen not as merely "the tribute of warm female friendship" but "in no other light than as an offering of love" (147).

Feminist critics have also become involved, if less explicitly so, in the production of a particular formal reading of Austen's fiction, a reading that insists on the characteristic ironic tone of her novels as the product of careful authorial control. This critical commonplace has been useful to feminists in that it provides one of the few examples of a woman writer being taken seriously by mid-twentieth-century critics as an artist making conscious choices about her material. But it has given rise, I would argue, to an overly intentionalist reading of Austen's politics. Most feminist critics of Austen's fiction, for example, argue that Austen herself was a feminist or (to use a less anachronistic term) a champion for the "rights of woman." Mary Evans, for example, claims that "Austen can be interpreted as a feminist" because of her insistence that women and men must act according to the same moral values, because she values "the part that women play in domestic and family life," and because "she portrays women acting independently of men and patriarchal interests."[22] Although Evans wants to attach these claims to an assumption about Austen's will and intentions, they seem most useful to me as statements about what kinds of representation we find in Austen's novels. Evans correctly directs the attention of feminists to women's actions, roles, and agency in the novels; none of these matters require an assessment of Austen's psychology or politics in contemporary terms. The problems inherent in such an assessment become clear when Evans argues:

> If feminism is construed to be about the defence and articulation of values that are non-material, that place importance on individual happiness and the mutual support and comfort that people can offer to one another, then Austen stands firmly within a feminist camp, for her novels are—as much as they are concerned with the affirmation of a socially valid moral code—

powerful statements on the importance of the domestic world, mutuality and respect between the sexes, and the rights of women to self-determination.[23]

Feminism, of course, need not be "construed" in this way at all. The striking absence from this definition of any consideration of gender or sexuality as specific terms or concepts—and Evans's insistence on a utopian vision of individual relations—places her firmly within a particular liberal-feminist paradigm that by no means provides a universal definition of feminism. Evans's implication that such a definition works not only for our time, but for Jane Austen's as well makes the mistakes in this assumption all the more extensive in their effects on her analysis.

Other critics have argued for Austen's feminism in more careful and interesting terms, however. In *Jane Austen, Feminism, and Fiction,* Margaret Kirkham seeks to establish Austen's "declared position as a feminist moralist" in the context of eighteenth-century debates over the "rights of woman" and women's education.[24] Explicitly refuting Marilyn Butler's argument that Austen was a committed anti-Jacobin conservative,[25] Kirkham argues: "Austen's subject-matter is the central subject-matter of rational, or Enlightenment, feminism and . . . her viewpoint on the moral nature and status of women, female education, marriage, authority and the family, and the representation of women in literature is strikingly similar to that shown by Mary Wollstonecraft in *A Vindication of the Rights of Woman.*"[26] By linking Austen with her most radical contemporary in women's writing, Kirkham makes the polemical case that Austen's novels are encoded but clearly readable arguments for the "rationalist eighteenth-century argument about ethics . . . the idea that women are accountable beings of the same kind as men."[27] By demonstrating that the representation of women as rational members of society was an already politicized position in the turn-of-the-century debate over women's nature and status, Kirkham clarifies the discontinuity between the politics of class and state and those of gender. In other words, even if Austen's heroines and their worlds work against Jacobin radicalism and political revolution, they may work for an extension of the power of middle-class women, which Kirkham identifies with feminism. In Kirkham's account, Austen self-consciously argues for a revolution in gender relations in her novels.

Claudia Johnson also contests Butler's axiomatic account of Austen's conservatism, claiming that "Butler's account actually denies Austen the dignity of being a warrior of ideas. Far from having wielded any herself, she purportedly imbibed the tendentious and intrinsically conservative propaganda she is imagined to have been indoctrinated with since childhood, without being able or inclined to consider the interests served by its representations."[28] Johnson, then, argues even more explicitly than Kirkham for authorial agency, seeking to establish Austen's "distinctively flexible, rather than ferociously partisan" position in turn-of-the-century political debates.[29] Like Kirkham, Johnson identifies the figure and writings of Mary Wollstonecraft as the sexually scandalous and politically dangerous figure against which Austen's representations of women were written and read. She contends that no explicit allusions to Wollstonecraft "were necessary to remind audiences that female characterization, such as Emma's or Fanny's, was already a politicized issue in and of itself."[30] Indeed, she charges, Wollstonecraft's ghostly presence on the literary scene after her death in 1797 rendered female authorship a much more problematic enterprise than it had been at any point during the eighteenth century. Johnson argues that "for a woman novelist writing at the end of the eighteenth century, the issue of gender affected more than choices of characterization, and indeed it eventually called into question the act of authorship itself. No woman novelist, even the most progressive, wished to be discredited by association with Mary Wollstonecraft, particularly after Godwin's widely attacked *Memoirs* disclosed details about her sexual improprieties and suicide attempts."[31] Kirkham seeks to establish the continuity between Wollstonecraft's concerns and Austen's; Johnson argues that Austen worked carefully to distance herself from the scandal of her predecessor's life and reputation while maintaining some of the space that Wollstonecraft's writings carved out for the representation of women as rational beings. Both accounts stress Austen's authorial control over her characterizations of women and their political consequences.

In emphasizing Austen's control over her material, these revisionist feminist critics remain well within a dominant strain in modern Austen criticism. Austen's twentieth-century reputation for literary greatness rests largely on the skill and control her works are seen to manifest, especially in their use of irony. Mudrick praises "the relaxation of achieved technique" in Austen's depiction of Emma, "the ironic portrait of a girl who falls into mild self-deception and whose trustworthy friend always and finally helps her out."[32]

For Mudrick, the aesthetic pleasure available in Austen's novels derives from the author's sure control over the dynamics of their irony: "The ironic reverberations . . . reinforce one another in a structure whose apparent lightness is less remarkable only than its compact and powerful density."[33] Ian Watt also stresses Austen's self-conscious use of irony "as a means of moral and social judgement [that] . . . enlarges the reader's understanding of experience through making him [*sic*] realize how limited is that of her fictional characters."[34] These critics point to the limited social scope of the novels as a necessary precondition for the artful, highly polished verbal form of Austen's fiction.

Wilson, however, shifts the ground for such ironic judgments from author to reader, arguing that in *Emma*, "there is something outside the picture which is never made explicit in the story but which has to be recognized by the reader before it is possible for him [*sic*] to appreciate the book. Many women readers feel instinctively the psychological rightness of the behavior attributed to Emma, and they are the ones who admire the novel."[35] For Wilson, then, this "something outside the picture" that qualifies the "story" also qualifies the grounds on which the reader might "admire" Austen's fiction. And, significantly, this (ironic) distance between the "story" and "something outside" it also marks the space between male and female readers. Women are the ones who admire this reverberation between text and reader; for Wilson, women's admiration is "instinctive" rather than critical, raising the question of unconscious or uncontrolled elements of ironic representation—and raising them in specifically gendered terms.

Like the homophobic observations of midcentury critics that can alert us to the eroticism overlooked by recent feminist accounts of Austen's fiction, Wilson's palpably misogynist comment provides an occasion for rethinking the relation between feminism, gender, and textual control. The homophobic and misogynist anxieties of these critics point to the elements of Austen's fiction that trouble their attempts to position Austen as the exemplary novelist of the heterosexist literary tradition they seek to establish. Given the preoccupation of sexist and heterosexist critics such as Mudrick, Wilson, and Mooneyham with the nexus of female homosexuality and ironic control, the problems it poses for patriarchal critical hegemony surely make this intersection a fruitful one for feminism. Rather than avoiding these issues in an attempt to forestall reproducing the misogyny and homophobia with which they have been treated by previous critics, feminist criticism would do well to attend to exactly how such issues threaten the patriarchal codes of fiction and criticism.

To explore that "something outside the picture," I wish to shift the definition of Austen's irony away from an insistence on her skillful control over ironic representation in her fiction. Instead, I offer an observation of Paul de Man's: "Irony comes into being precisely when self-consciousness loses control over itself. . . . For me, at least, the way I think of it now, irony is not a figure of self-consciousness. It's a break, an interruption, a disruption. It is a moment of loss of control, and not just for the author but for the reader as well."[36] By considering the ironic possibilities of "moment[s] of loss of control" in *Emma*, we can account for the intersection between representations of female homoeroticism, women's sexual agency, and gendered power relations in the novel and their representation across the complex and contradictory discourse surrounding women's friendship in the period. This intersection is precisely that element of the text that falls outside intentional authorial control. In the interests of a feminist emphasis on the agency of women authors, Kirkham and Johnson argue convincingly for the extent to which Austen was aware of and participated in political debates over issues of gender and sexuality in her time. But to make such an argument is to limit our notion of "feminism" to the parameters established by Enlightenment feminism itself—to take the object of study too much in its own terms. Those terms, based firmly in the doctrine of the "rights of man," focus necessarily on extending the power of "woman" defined in the terms most useful to bourgeois culture: white, middle-class, heterosexual, and "virtuous." Such an exclusionary gesture precludes the possibility of a specifically feminist critical analysis of the limitations of such a representation of "woman," an analysis that examines bourgeois ideology's careful and brutal construction of such a figure out of a matrix of resistant possibilities. What do such resistances, at play in the representations of female friendship in the novel, have to offer a feminist genealogy of sapphic sexual identities and practices?

Female Friendship and Sexual Authority

The conflicts this question solicits are raised on the first page of the novel, which opens by sketching some of the unfortunate consequences of unregulated female friendship. We are introduced to the title character through a description of the shortcomings of her intimacy with her governess, Miss Taylor, which sets up problems that will resonate throughout the novel: "Even before Miss Taylor had ceased to hold the nominal office of governess, the mildness of her temper had hardly allowed her to impose any restraint; and the shadow of authority being now long passed away, they had been living together as friend and friend very mutually attached, and Emma doing just what she liked; highly esteeming Miss Taylor's judgement, but directed chiefly by her own" (1). The heterosexual plot of the novel requires that to marry, Emma must submit her own "judgement," allowed full play in her friendship with Miss Taylor, to that of Mr. Knightley and the institutions of family and estate that he represents. Female friendship is the central issue over which this conflict between Emma's antimarital female autonomy and Mr. Knightley's institutionalized, patriarchal power is played out. The heterosexual plot can be resolved, Emma can be married, only when she finally gives up the friend of her own choice, the inappropriately lower-class and sensual Harriet Smith, and makes overtures instead toward the cold and "deserving" Jane Fairfax, toward whom Mr. Knightley and her whole community have been urging Emma throughout her life.

These three friendships anchor the novel's construction of female desire and hence of the heterosexual love that results in her choice of Mr. Knightley as husband; yet female friendship is represented in the novel as the significant threat to Emma's virtue and marriageability. The intimacy with which Emma and Miss Taylor lived together is ending as the novel opens and Miss Taylor becomes Mrs. Weston; the critique of this relationship clarifies the necessity of breaking up that intimacy to begin the story of Emma's schooling in heterosexual heroineship. Emma's friendship with Harriet raises the possibilities of autonomous female desire and class transgression; for a heroine to pursue these autonomous possibilities would make marriage, in the novel's terms, impossible. Of course, such conflicts produce the narrative tension that makes *Emma* an exciting novel for its readers, both in the early nineteenth century and later, but I will go on to argue that this narrative excitement does not always work to support and consolidate the heterosexual plot. Rather, the sexual possibilities raised by Emma's inappropriate friendships, particularly with Harriet and Miss Taylor/Mrs. Weston, reverberate with one another in ways that produce anxiety and disruption, both for the characters and for the narrative itself, because the novel's plot depends on the closure conventionally imposed on the domestic novel by the marriage of the heroine. Of course, the "danger" of unregulated female friendship is explicitly posed in the novel as the site of the sexual and social lessons that Emma must learn so as to marry; but here I sketch a relationship between the three friendships in the novel that produces effects beyond what Eve Kosofsky Sedgwick calls "the spectacle of a Girl Being Taught a Lesson."[37] Given the compelling narrative pleasure offered by the "punishing, girl-centered moral pedagogy and erotics of Austen's novels,"[38] such a spectacle cannot be contained by its suturing within the text itself; the effects of such "erotics" continue, even when the novel ends, in the ways that Austen's representation of female desire speaks to other such representations being consolidated into an ideological category by their interaction in the social world beyond the novel.

Significantly, the single appropriate female friendship allowed the heroine is one that disappears: Emma and Jane Fairfax become friends just as Jane's own marriage is about to remove her from the neighborhood. "Appropriate" female friendship thus turns out to be the absence of female friends. Emma's progressive isolation through the novel provides a typically Austenian account of the limitations of female domestic power, even in this, the novel in which such power seems to be celebrated most straightforwardly. By placing a rather optimistic account of the novel's production of female homosexual desire alongside an exploration of the dynamic of diminution that characterizes its construction of female heterosexuality, I intend to expose the gaps between the novel's implicit and explicit stories, its unintended effects and intentional social observation. Such an interrogation allows us to identify two different movements emerging from the depiction of female sexuality in *Emma:* First, female homosexuality is firmly installed in the definition of the nineteenth-century novelistic heroine, consolidating some of the conflicts over female sexuality that I have analyzed in previous chapters and setting in motion new ones. Second, the very smoothness with which Emma's potentially sexual relationships with other women is made part of Austen's story of domestic female power, in moving that portrait away from eighteenth-century "virtue," produces an irreducibly sexualized notion of female identity that relies for its development on the intensity of same-sex bonds. The representation of female heterosexuality, then, is made dependent on its disavowed and implicit sapphic "other."

The novel's attention to the construction of female bodies via a female gaze motivates the category of female homosexual agency from the beginning. Emma's interest in Harriet Smith is first marked out as an interest in Harriet's body: "Miss Smith was a girl of seventeen whom Emma knew very well by sight and had long felt an interest in, on account of her beauty. . . . She was a very pretty girl, and her beauty happened to be of a sort which Emma particularly admired. She was short, plump and fair, with a fine bloom, blue eyes, light hair, regular features, and a look of great sweetness" (13). This wealth of physical detail follows full descriptions of Mrs. Bates, Miss Bates, and Mrs. Goddard, none of which included any concrete bodily description. In contrast to the three other women, who are identified by marital, family, and occupational status, respectively, Harriet is identified with and by both her physical beauty and Emma's interest in it.

Female friendship is also the mechanism through which Emma's beauty, crucial to her status as a heroine, is established. Once again, the relationship between women (Mrs. Weston's regard for Emma), rather than a heterosexual relationship, establishes a space in which qualities of physical attractiveness are explicated and commented on. The desiring gaze directed toward female bodies in the novel is the gaze of a woman. In contrast to Mr. Knightley's cautious admission that Emma is "pretty," Mrs. Weston's praise is enthusiastic and detailed: " 'Pretty! Say beautiful rather. Can you imagine any thing nearer perfect beauty than Emma altogether—face and figure? . . . Such an eye!—the true hazle eye—and so brilliant! regular features, open countenance, with a complexion! oh! what a bloom of full health, and such a pretty height and size; such a firm and upright figure' " (24–25). Mr. Knightley responds to this emphatic catalogue with "I think her all you describe," throwing the agency for noticing Emma's body on Mrs. Weston. It is female friendship, then, rather than heterosexual relations, that allows for the acknowledgment and admiration of the heroine's body as attractive, as sexual.

However, the deployment of female friendship for the production of female desire in the novel is not without problematic consequences. Women's admiration of one another can become dangerously sexualized because of its structural resemblance to conventions of heterosexual marital love. For while the novel must imagine affection between women as a virtuous site for the production of female desire, the concentration of female desire and female beauty into relationships the novel must also undermine creates a paradox. The contradictory functions demanded of female friendship in the novel mean that the effects of its representation inevitably exceed the requirements of the functions themselves. Thus, from the beginning, depictions of female friendship produce representations of anxiety as well as of desire for the text.

Such anxiety is particularly evident in the ways in which the language of friendship is sexualized at certain moments in *Emma*. For example, Emma's notice of Harriet is described in the conventional language of courtship, with Harriet's effect on Emma cast in terms most often used in the period to describe a woman's effect on a man: "[Emma] was so busy in admiring those soft blue eyes, in talking and listening, and forming all these schemes [for 'improving' Harriet] in the in-betweens, that the evening flew away at a very unusual rate" (14). "Soft" eyes are often attributed to heroines as they gaze at heroes. Harriet also manifests an "early attachment" to Emma that the latter finds "very amiable" (15). A novelistic convention of the period (inaugurated, perhaps, with Richardson's *Pamela*) held that men often finally fell in love with women whom they knew to admire them, out of "gratitude" for such admiration. Indeed, Harriet exhibits all the pliability Emma must learn to become a heroine herself, rather than simply to admire one: she must replace her desire for "soft blue eyes" looking into hers with the desire Harriet feels, a sole "desir[e] to be guided by any one she looked up to" (15). Later, in justifying her encouragement of Harriet's refusal of Robert Martin, Emma again speaks from the position of the desiring hero. Such a gesture manifests the stance of desire that Emma takes toward her friend. She asserts, "I know that such a girl as Harriet is exactly what every man delights in—what at once bewitches his senses and satisfies his judgement" (42). Emma's claim to knowledge based on desire scandalizes Mr. Knightley, who calls their intimacy "foolish" and "unfortunate." Emma's insertion into this "male" position, however, is not merely a reversal of gender roles that leaves the binary codes of gender intact, making Emma a "man" because she speaks the language of the novelistic hero. As Teresa de Lauretis notes, such an appropriation of male sexual privilege can produce a representation of an erotic charge between women based on the difference (a difference of sexuality) between them. Such a cross-gender representation, then, rather than reinforcing the agency of the position previously coded "male," produces "an assertion of sexual agency and feelings, but autonomous from men, a reclaiming of erotic drives directed toward women, of a desire for women that is not to be confused with woman identification."[39] Such an assertion of different sexual positions, desires, and practices among women interrupts one of the cardinal tenets of the ideology of virtuous romantic friendship: that women's sexual desires always flow in the same direction (toward men), rendering the all-female space of female friendship innocent of sexuality. On the level of the text's conscious didacticism, then, Harriet is an inappropriate object of friendship for Emma, because Emma's assertion of her own desires and preferences in the friendship inserts sexuality into the very domestic scene that is supposed to preclude sexual desire. With Harriet, Emma takes on too much the role of the lover; to learn to be a heroine, she must learn to be beloved. Beyond this conventional eruption of narrative tension, however, the narrative places Emma in a relationship with Harriet that does more than simply block the marriage plot. That relationship, developed to its logical conclusion in the early-nineteenth-century cultural imagination, evokes a dimension of homosexual desire and female autonomy that goes well beyond simply impeding marriage to offering women other sexual possibilities besides marriage. In that sense, Emma's friendship with Harriet represents forces outside the narrative's, or the culture's, complete control.

Mr. Knightley's criticism of Emma's friendship with Mrs. Weston before her marriage brings some reference to the social consequences of female sexual intimacy into the novel: he claims that the relationship made Emma a husband and Miss Taylor a wife. Mrs. Weston alludes explicitly to Mr. Knightley's disapproval of her relationship with Emma:

> "I should have been sorry, Mr. Knightley, to be dependent on *your* recommendation, had I quitted Mr. Woodhouse's family and wanted another situation; I do not think you would have spoken a good word for me to any body. I am sure you always thought me unfit for the office I held."
>
> "Yes," said he, smiling. "You are better placed *here;* very fit for a wife, but not at all for a governess. But you were preparing yourself to be an excellent wife all the time you were at Hartfield. You might not give Emma such a complete education as your powers would seem to promise; but you were

receiving a very good education from *her*, on the very material matrimonial point of submitting your own will, and doing as you were bid; and if Weston had asked me to recommend him a wife, I should certainly have named Miss Taylor." (23–24)

The hostility of this exchange (the strangely interposed adverb "smiling" serves only to emphasize its sinister aspects) brings together several different levels of relationship between the speakers. The explicit conflict between them is economic: Mrs. Weston makes clear that before her marriage it lay in Mr. Knightley's power to deprive her of her living on the basis of his disapproval of her friendship with Emma. Significantly, his disapproval has nothing to do with Miss Taylor's accomplishments or abilities as a teacher; her "powers" meet with his oblique approbation. His claim is rather that their relationship was a topsy-turvy inversion of what it ought to have been, a specter of misplaced authority in which the student becomes the teacher and the teacher is "very fit for a wife, but not at all for a governess." And, crucially, because Emma usurps the position of teacher, her role in the relationship becomes sexualized: she educates her governess not in the lessons of the schoolroom but "on the very material matrimonial point of submitting" her will to a husband's. Mrs. Weston's awareness that Mr. Knightley would not have given her a "recommendation" for another place thus refers not to a professional but to a character reference. Mr. Knightley's judgment of her inadequacies as a governess for Emma is a moral one. When fears about the immorality of female teachers become explicit in the period, they were most often fears about sexuality and even, as in the Woods-Pirie case, fears about sexual relations between women involved in intimate friendships. Such fears could ruin a teacher's career, as it did for Marianne Woods and Jane Pirie, whose case I discussed in Chapter 3. Mr. Knightley's disapproval of Miss Taylor's intimacy with Emma and his refusal to countenance the relationship with his "recommendation" invokes the potential indecency of the intimacy itself. Knightley's ironic "recommendation" of the governess to Mr. Weston as a wife sets up Miss Taylor as sexual in relation to Emma as well.

The sexual import of the irony here derives not from authorial intention, however, but precisely from Austen's inability to control the already sexualized web of references that spins out from the representation of relations between assertive middle-class girls and their governesses. At one level, most likely that of the author's didactic intention, the comparison of Emma's friendship with Miss Taylor to a proper marriage ironically demonstrates the limitations of the relationship, limitations that can be transcended only when Emma finds someone to make a wife of her as she made a wife of Miss Taylor. But in the context of turn-of-the-century fears about the all-female school-room as a sexual scene, the image of the teacher-student relationship as a marital one spills over the bounds of a controlled, didactic irony and reverber-ates back against its grounding assumption: that a sexual relationship between women is impossible, and thus a situation in which women turn wives for one another must be supplanted by heterosexual romance. Fanny Hill's sexual apprenticeship with Phoebe, the freakish, cross-dressing feminist of Edge-worth's *Belinda,* the scandalous sexuality of colonial women as it disrupts the female boarding school, the Byronic self-construction of Anne Lister's sap-phic identity: such social and textual possibilities hover "outside the picture" the novel paints of the dangers of female friendship. To allude (ironically) to the sexual impossibility of Emma's relation to Miss Taylor creates (ironically) a representation of its possibility.

The discussion of female friendship between Mr. Knightley and Mrs. Weston also raises the question of female authority in the novel. It sketches out the implicit bargain of the heterosexual plot for heroines and their women read-ers: if they submit to marriage and the patriarchal will, they will be granted a position from which to speak and a field of knowledge particular to them within that institution. When Mr. Knightley objects to "this great intimacy between Emma and Harriet Smith" (22), Mrs. Weston attempts to defend not just their specific relationship but women's friendship in general. And she defends such friendship in terms of the specificity of the experience of women—in gendered terms. Mrs. Weston challenges Mr. Knightley's compe-tence as a man in judging this matter, saying, "Mr. Knightley, I shall not allow you to be a fair judge in this case . . . perhaps no man can be a good judge of the comfort a woman feels in the society of one of her own sex, after being used to it all her life" (23). By establishing her own authority in gendered terms, Mrs. Weston is able to contend with Mr. Knightley's arguments with-out compromising her own position in the slightest. She contradicts Mr. Knightley point by point and ends by asserting, in the face of his wish to see Emma "in love, and in some doubt of a return," that she does "not recom-

mend matrimony at present to Emma" (26). Female friendship is thus constructed as explicitly opposed to heterosexual marriage. While he claims he
"is not to be talked out of my dislike of her intimacy with Harriet Smith," she
asserts, "And I, Mr. Knightley, am equally stout in my confidence of its not
doing them any harm" (25). Such a claim to equality ("equally stout") is a
move distinct from Mrs. Weston's invocation of her disempowered position
with regard to Mr. Knightley at the beginning of the conversation. Her refusal
to submit to his opinion on this matter demonstrates the authority she
has gained through her marriage. She need no longer tremble without Mr.
Knightley's recommendation. Her gender endows Mrs. Weston with a particular kind of authority in this discussion; to return to Nancy Armstrong's
formulation, this is the power of the domestic woman. As we have seen,
Armstrong convincingly argues that this figure played a crucial role in legit-
imizing the spread of middle-class cultural authority during the eighteenth
century, reaching its recognizably modern form in late-eighteenth- and early-
nineteenth-century domestic fiction such as Austen's. The domestic woman
"was inscribed with values that addressed a whole range of competing interest
groups and, through her, these groups gained authority over domestic relations and personal life."[40] As such a figure, Mrs. Weston is allowed to invoke
her gender as the basis for her authority on questions of desire: crucially, here,
both female friendship and marriage involve such questions. Both, then, have
an implicitly sexualized social meaning.

Emma's attempts to argue from the same authority are ironized by the
narrative because unlike Mrs. Weston, she does not display the traits of domestic marital virtue that shore up such authority. When Mr. Knightley ac-
cuses her of encouraging Harriet to refuse Robert Martin, she manifests silent
discomfort rather than Mrs. Weston's "stout . . . confidence": "She did not
repent what she had done; she still thought herself a better judge of such a
point of female right and refinement than he could be; but yet she had a sort
of habitual respect for his judgement in general, which made her dislike
having it so loudly against her; and to have him sitting just opposite to her in
an angry state, was very disagreeable" (43). Paradoxically, Emma must be
schooled as she herself schooled Mrs. Weston, in "the very material matrimonial point of submitting" her will to another's, before she can claim the
authority of the domestic woman over matters of desire and affect. This is the
contradiction at the heart of the period's solidifying ideology of domestic

female power: the domestic woman must give up her material autonomy to her husband in marriage to achieve some limited authority within the sphere of family life. What she loses, in the limited terms of domestic fiction, is the power to choose her female friends; what she gains is the equivocal opportunity to become an agent in the institution that defines the limitations of her desire. As Armstrong notes, this agency was "a form of power that appeared to have no political force at all because it seemed forceful only when it was desired. It was the power of domestic surveillance. [Representations of the domestic woman] established the need for the kind of surveillance upon which modern institutions are based."[41] My analysis of *Emma* differs from Armstrong's, however, in reading scenes such as the one just cited in terms of its revelation of the limitations of domestic female power. Armstrong wants to emphasize the extent and stature of this form of power, its crucial role in the formation of modern institutions, in order to stress "the ways in which modern culture has empowered middle-class women."[42] In *Emma*, however, the constraints and conditions of that power, not just its enablements, are laid bare. We see the careful construction of the domestic woman who solidifies her class privilege and assumes authority over certain aspects of her social world; but we also see what that world must be constructed without, the impossible desires and relationships whose denial forms its foundations. The authority of the domestic woman thus depends on the limitations of its sphere. As Armstrong's argument implies, however, these limitations were masked by the trajectory of domestic fiction, which rendered the assumption of this kind of authority both natural and desirable.

To read *Emma* only in terms of the power of Emma's "female narrative" (which emphasizes emotion and affective ties) as Armstrong does is to take the novel too much in its own terms. Armstrong's description of Emma's position ventriloquizes the explicit story the novel tells about itself, glossing over moments of conflict and anxiety such as the scene above between Emma and Mr. Knightley. Echoing Austen's language, Armstrong argues that "Emma is already too much in charge of the house when the novel opens" and that "the power Emma inherits as the woman of the house proves disruptive" to social relations in the novel.[43] The trajectory of Armstrong's critical work imitates that of Austen's novel: Emma's "female narrative" of emotion and affect must learn to accommodate Mr. Knightley's "male narrative," which reads characters for the external marks of social status they bear, so as to create what Armstrong calls "genuinely monogamous desire."[44] Armstrong presents the two narratives as equally powerful in both social and linguistic terms. Rather than taking place in a hierarchy, "male" and "female" narratives (and characters) balance each other in a relationship of hetero-sexual complementarity; the transformation by which Emma's marriage to Knightley can be effected is "a double one whereby he acknowledges the value of an unextraordinary woman such as Harriet and she understands the uncommon value of a common man [Robert Martin]."[45] Within such an emphatically gendered framework, "desire" is only ever heterosexual desire. The role of sexuality in Emma's interactions with women remains as implicit for Armstrong's analysis as it is for the novel itself. Indeed, Armstrong argues that "to fill the model Mr. Knightley sketches out for her, Emma must not only learn that she desires, but must also suppress the aggravation she feels towards women she cannot absolutely control."[46] Loss of control in Emma's relationships with women, in Armstrong's analysis, gives rise not to desire (which Emma must acquire later from a male "model") but to "aggravation," a much less serious or interesting response. By reducing the intensity of Emma's unions and conflicts with Mrs. Weston, Harriet, and Jane Fairfax to the level of a minor annoyance, Armstrong renders unreadable some of the most anxious and tension-filled moments of the novel. She presents Austen's fiction as the seamless triumph of a moment in literary history at which novels "do not have to launch elaborate self-defenses anymore, for they have appropriated the strategies of conduct books to such a degree that fiction—instead of conduct books—can claim the authority to regulate reading."[47] According to Armstrong, conflict over gender and sexuality had disappeared "on the fictional front, where the battle for representing the woman had already been won."[48] Such a conclusion takes the verbal polish of the novel at face value, producing a mystified reproduction of the novel's own strategies for suppressing ideological contradiction. By pressing the question of what Emma must give up, unlearn, and cease to desire in order to enable the conclusion of the novel's heterosexual plot, some of the workings of those contradictions shed their mystery and become visible to analysis.

The dissolution of Emma's friendship with Harriet is the most prolonged example in the novel of such a diminution of Emma's inappropriately gen-dered "hero's" power. One of the central strategies in *Emma* for masking this loss as a gain is to provide another, "appropriate" friendship for Emma, ostensibly to replace her interest in Harriet. Significantly, Emma's struggle to like Jane Fairfax is introduced as a struggle to find her attractive, her reconciliation to the idea of befriending Jane a discovery of the latter's beauty. The implicit possibility of female friendship resting on the question of desire is obliquely raised as Emma reviews her reasons for not liking Jane. "Why she did not like Jane Fairfax might be a difficult question to answer" (111), and the novel never does answer it directly, which suggests that this relationship is not entirely representable in its terms. The narrative casts the problem of Emma's dislike as a moral one: "there were moments of self-examination in which her conscience could not quite acquit her" (111) of thinking or behaving as she ought with regard to Jane. The most concrete of her reasons almost all cluster around issues of desire and intimacy: "she did not know how it was, but there was such coldness and reserve—such apparent indifference whether she pleased or not . . . and it had been always imagined that they were to be so intimate—because their ages were the same, every body had supposed they must be so fond of each other" (111). Jane's "coldness and reserve" contrast markedly with Harriet's "soft blue eyes" and "early attachment" to Emma. Clearly, too, Emma is repelled by Jane's unwillingness to take up the flirtatious, "pleasing" role at which Harriet had excelled. Anne Lister complains in similarly equivocal terms about the failure of her friend, Miss Pickford, to take pains to charm her: "I wish she would care a little more about dress. At least not wear such an old-fashioned, short-waisted, fright of a brown habit with yellow metal buttons as she had on this morning. . . . I would rather have a pretty girl to flirt with. . . . She is not lovable. . . . I do not greatly admire Miss Pickford."[49] Like Anne Lister, Emma places a high value on the willingness of other women to please her through their appearance and attention. Such a sense of entitlement emanates from their class positions, for both Anne Lister and Emma are firmly ensconced within the leading families of their own community. Lister's words clarify the implicit but controlling assumption in *Emma* that for a woman to seek such attention from other women could be coded in the period as a desire for the sexualized attention a man would conventionally expect in a similar relationship: the submission of will and opinions, the desire to please and appear attractive. But instead of Lister's bold assertion of such desires, domestic fiction can present them only as implicit and troubling assumptions behind codes of narrative authority. Thus,

Emma chastises herself for harboring "a dislike so little just [in which] every imputed fault [is] . . . so magnified by fancy" (111). The goal of overcoming these unsatisfactory reasons—"These were her reasons—she had no better" (111)—is to present her renovated desires to Mr. Knightley in "a recantation of past prejudices and errors" (112). Clearly, then, the function of this friendship in the narrative is to offer Emma the opportunity to "submit" her will and desires to patriarchal scrutiny rather than to explore or satisfy those desires on her own behalf.

At this early stage in the narrative, however, Emma's coerced approval of Jane Fairfax still takes the inappropriate form of interest in her powers of pleasing and her beauty—interest, that is, in her ability to fulfill the same role with regard to Emma that Harriet does. Hence, we get another detailed catalogue of a woman's physical attributes, which culminates in Emma's acknowledgment of "a very pleasing beauty" hitherto overlooked: "Her eyes, a deep grey, with dark eye-lashes and eye-brows, had never been denied their praise; but the skin, which she had been used to cavil at, as wanting colour, had a clearness and delicacy which really needed no fuller bloom" (111–112). Such language places Jane firmly in the category of heroine, with Emma once again usurping the right of the hero to observe, judge, and desire. This kind of intimacy, then, still poses a narrative problem: Emma must learn not simply to like Jane Fairfax but also to like her in the proper way. Thus, her new appreciation for Jane's loveliness and her interest in Jane's body "were charming feelings—but not lasting" (112). Jane's function in the narrative is to resist becoming the object of such desires on Emma's part; Emma continues, then, to find her "so cold, so cautious! There was no getting at her real opinion" (113). Like Anne Lister, Emma assumes that the women in whom she is interested should render themselves transparent to her, while she herself remains opaque. After probing Miss Pickford on the state of her affection for Miss Threlfall, Lister muses, "I am now let into her secret & she forever barred from mine."[50] The privilege of access to other people is one denied the heroine. Because Emma still insists on it here, she is not yet the kind of female friend a novel of heterosexual romantic love can endorse.

Emma's friendships and the desire they engender threaten not just heterosexual relations but also class hierarchies. The possibility of class transgression arising from inappropriate female friendship becomes clear early in the novel, when Emma encourages Harriet to refuse an offer of marriage from a local yeoman, Robert Martin. Mr. Knightley takes her to task specifically for displacing Harriet (and her expectations) from her proper class position. His critique clarifies patriarchal definitions of marriage and female friendship in the novel. Emma establishes the conflict between her position and Mr. Knightley's in class terms from the outset: "Mr. Martin is a very respectable young man, but I cannot admit him to be Harriet's equal" (40). Mr. Knightley, "red with surprize and displeasure," moves immediately to the assumption that Harriet's refusal is rooted in her friendship with Emma: " 'Emma, this is your doing. You persuaded her to refuse him. . . . Emma, your infatuation about that girl blinds you' " (40). He follows with a catalogue of strikes against Harriet's claim to a better match, beginning with the damning assertion, "She is the natural daughter of nobody knows whom." Emma's response appeals directly to the power of her own friendship to raise Harriet's class status.

> "What! think a farmer (and with all his sense and all his merit Mr. Martin is nothing more) a good match for my intimate friend! Not regret her leaving Highbury for the sake of marrying a man whom I could never admit as an acquaintance of my own! . . . I must think your statement by no means fair. You are not just to Harriet's claims. . . . Mr. Martin may be the richest of the two, but he is undoubtedly her inferior as to rank in society.—The sphere in which she moves is much above his.—It would be a degradation." (41)

The most striking feature of this passage which purportedly establishes Harriet's claims is that it is all about Emma. "*My* intimate friend," "a man whom *I* could never admit," "*I* must think your statement"—Emma's outrage rests securely on the assumption that, like a husband, she can raise the woman she loves to her own rank by her countenance alone. Even the final reference to "the sphere in which she moves" is an oblique reminder of Harriet's association with Emma rather than a description of Harriet's own claims to equality. Mr. Knightley challenges Emma's implicit faith in her own social power by undermining the friendship itself: " 'Till you chose to turn her into a friend, her mind had no distaste for her own set, nor any ambition beyond it. She was as happy as possible with the Martins in the summer. She had no sense of superiority then. If she has it now, you have given it. You have been no friend to Harriet Smith, Emma' " (41). Mr. Knightley first ridicules the friendship by ironically placing it in the realm of Emma's arbitrary whims ("till you chose to turn her into a friend"). Even more radical, he then denies the existence of the friendship at all, claiming that Emma is "no friend to Harriet." Paradoxically, however, he must admit Emma's power to change Harriet's expectations even as he challenges the basis of that power in their friendship. He admits that if Harriet has a "sense of superiority" (as she clearly does, based on the material evidence of her refusal of Robert Martin), Emma has "given it." Even in his most direct attack on the friendship, then, there is some anxiety about its power. Emma clearly *has* changed the "sphere" in which Harriet moves, so already their friendship has shifted class relations in Highbury. Mr. Knightley's direct attack is on Emma's attempt to raise Harriet's status by providing her with a gentleman to marry; implicitly, however, his "tall indignation" (40) is leveled at an intimacy whose power is already revealing its material effects.

Emma's explicit intention in breaking down the class barriers between herself and Harriet is to secure their intimacy through Harriet's marriage: "I only want to keep Harriet to myself" (44). She cannot have Harriet marry Robert Martin because she herself "could never admit [him] as an acquaintance." Her interest in raising Harriet's status, however, stems not from a democratic interest in erasing class distinctions but from her own sense of bourgeois entitlement, the sense that she should get what she wants because she wants it. Unlike Richardson's Mr. B. or even Austen's Fitzwilliam Darcy, Emma cannot incorporate her desire for a woman into existing class hierarchies. She does not yet understand the limitations of bourgeois ideology for women but acts out of an assumption of privilege that the novel codes as masculine.

Significantly, she has no interest in marrying a man outside her own class; she is "insulted" (92) by Mr. Elton's proposal, for example. Her indignation over his assumption that she would be willing to marry him takes the form of exactly the critique of class transgression Mr. Knightley had mounted in their discussion of Robert Martin: "[That he] should suppose himself her equal in connection or mind!—look down upon her friend, so well understanding the gradations of rank below him, and be so blind to what rose above, as to fancy himself shewing no presumption in addressing her!—It was most provoking" (92). Here Emma concedes the point she had argued so strenuously with Mr. Knightley: that of Harriet's social inferiority to her. For if Harriet's rank is "below" Mr. Elton's and Emma's is "above" Mr. Elton's, then Harriet's place is indeed the "obscurity" (43) to which Mr. Knightley consigns her. Clearly, Emma's attempts to assert her own power are not consistent in terms of class interests. She critiques or defends class boundaries in a series of shifting strategies to make space for her desires: to authorize her intimacy with Harriet, for example, or to distance herself from Mr. Elton.

The success of such strategies is clearly crosscut by ideologies of gender in the novel, ideologies that at this point determine Emma's actions only imperfectly. The narrative offers two gendered models of power: an active, formative, pedagogical, "masculine" model and a complaisant and indirect feminine authority over the sphere of affect and desire, no small field in the scope of domestic fiction. Crucially, however, while women may have some authority over domestic relations, based on their supposed knowledge about emotions and relationships, what they cannot have is agency over those relations. Thus, "female domestic power," as we saw in the analysis of *Millenium Hall* in Chapter 1, is the power to interpret existing conditions only, never the power to change or create those conditions. As the first model proves inaccessible to Emma over and over again, the representations of its incorrectness become increasingly internalized and consistent with her character. After the discussion of Robert Martin, for example, Emma continues to assert her own position to herself during and after her conversation with Mr. Knightley. Her assertions rest on assumptions about gendered authority that are ironized and undercut by the narrative context: "Let Mr. Knightley think or say what he would, she had done nothing which woman's friendship and woman's feelings would not justify. He had frightened her a little about Mr. Elton . . . [but] she was able to believe, that he had rather said what he wished resentfully to be true, than what he knew anything about" (45). Her confidence in her own judgment is qualified by such language in these passages as "frightened" and "was able to believe." Her attempt in the last passage to convince herself that Mr. Knightley is wrong when he says that Mr. Elton will never marry Harriet anticipates Elton's resentful revelation when he proposes to Emma that he thinks himself far above her friend socially. This anticipation further undercuts the basis of Emma's authority here in "woman's friendship and woman's feelings." She has clearly presumed too much on these bases.

Later in the narrative, after Mr. Elton's proposal, her internal critique is much more stringent and explicitly alludes to the impropriety of her assumptions about her own power: "The first error and the worst lay at her door. It was foolish, it was wrong, to take so active a part in bringing any two people together. It was adventuring too far, assuming too much, making light of what

ought to be serious, a trick of what ought to be simple. She was quite concerned and ashamed, and resolved to do such things no more" (93). Instead
of exerting passive influence within the feminine space demarcated by the
hierarchies of class and gender, Emma has been too "active," has been "adventuring too far" beyond the proper location of female power. The use of
the term "adventure" in the period implies both a journey, such as a "colonial
adventure," and a scandal involving a risk to reputation, in which no lady
should ever be involved. Emma has indeed been "assuming too much"—she
has been assuming the masculine power of sexual choice and initiation. It is
not for the domestic woman to determine sexual relations—to decide, for
example, who will marry whom—but to manage the ones in which she finds
herself enmeshed.

As Emma comes to assume more and more of the qualities of the heroine, the
representations of her own desire fade. Instead, we see her conducting her
female friendships in an exemplary manner, as if to turn them into spectacles
of appropriate behavior for the consumption of Mr. Knightley and the education of the female reader. When Jane Fairfax's appointment as a governess is
announced, for example, instead of "forming . . . schemes" for her own
unspoken pleasure, as she had with Harriet, Emma produces a flurry of
material artifacts in an almost mercantile display of right feeling. Her motiva-
tions are represented in terms that require the presence of an audience: "She
wanted to *show* a value for [Jane's] society, and *testify* respect and consideration" (267; emphasis added). In the face of Jane's escalating refusals to accept
Emma's penitential services, Emma writes a note, calls for the apothecary's
opinion, writes another note "in the most feeling language she could command" (268), drives to Miss Bates's, questions Miss Bates on the street since
Jane refuses to let her in the house, and finally, in a gesture whose humor
derives only from its ultimate place in this list of excessive gestures of display,
sends Jane "some arrow-root of very superior quality" (268). The arrowroot
is, of course, returned. Emma's response to this litany of rejection is again cast
in terms of how it appears: she is "mortified . . . that she was *given so little credit*
for proper feeling" (269; emphasis added). The conjunction of credit and
proper feeling here (like Pamela's distribution of money after her marriage)
attests to Emma's increasing insertion into the bourgeois order of domestic
female power, whose economic underpinning is money and whose ideologi-

cal guarantee is propriety. Her acceptance of the limitations of her own desires in such an order is demonstrably completed when the chapter ends with Emma's internalization of the value of her actions as a spectacle for patriarchal consumption: "She had the consolation of . . . being able to say to herself, that could Mr. Knightley have been privy to all her attempts of assisting Jane Fairfax, could he even have seen into her heart, he would not, on this occasion, have found anything to reprove" (269). Of course, the function of the notes, drives, and arrowroot exchanges of the previous passage was precisely to allow Mr. Knightley to be "privy" to her motives, to make her "heart" fit to be "seen." Emma has at last given up the masculine privilege she felt was her right when Jane withheld it from her earlier in the narrative: the right to see and have access to the behavior of others, to be an arbiter of behavior, to "reprove." She becomes the heroine whose heart is open for the hero's inspection.

The specific narrative condition of such a change is that Emma must give up her intimacy with Harriet. This renunciation of autonomy, desire, and transgression is accomplished in two stages. The first is the heightened drama and urgency of Jane Fairfax's situation; as her fate trembles between marriage and governessing, Jane's ambivalent class position replaces Harriet's as the site of narrative interest. Thus, for Emma it becomes "a more pressing concern to show attention to Jane Fairfax, whose prospects were closing, while Harriet's opened" (267). The second stage involves the situation of Emma and Harriet as rivals rather than intimates, which requires the sudden transformation of Mr. Knightley from a patriarchal father to a lover. The language through which Emma's marital interest in Mr. Knightley is established is uncharacteristically violent for this novel: "It darted through her, with the speed of an arrow, that Mr. Knightley must marry no one but herself!" (280). Nowhere else in the novel does Austen use either a metaphor of weaponry or a clichéd allusion to Cupid, the symbol of sexual love in the classical pantheon. The oddity of the language here testifies to the speed with which the narrative must now change direction. The desires and relationships on which the plot has rested until now must quickly be renovated in the service of heterosexual closure.

One of the first consequences of this shift, of course, is the cleaving of the intimacy between Harriet and Emma. Instead of thinking of each other, they now begin to think only "of Mr. Knightley and themselves" (281). Emma's pleasure in looking at Harriet becomes an equally intense aversion to the sight of her: "Oh God! that I had never seen her!" (283). To complete Emma's interpellation by the ideology of bourgeois marriage, she now precisely reproduces Mr. Knightley's original evaluation of Harriet's social claims, in a passage that reenacts much of the emotional intensity of the earlier conversation between the enraged patriarch and the then recalcitrant Emma:

> Oh! had she never brought Harriet forward! Had she left her where she ought, and where he had told her she ought!—Had she not . . . prevented her marrying [Robert Martin] . . . all would have been safe; none of this dreadful sequel would have been. . . . Who had been at pains to give Harriet notions of her own self-consequence but herself?—Who but herself had taught her, that she was to elevate herself if possible, and that her claims were great to a high worldly establishment?—If Harriet, from being humble, were grown vain, it was her doing too. (285)

Emma has come to identify with Mr. Knightley's notions of "safety"—social stability buttressed by appropriate heterosexual pairings within class boundaries. In this passage, Emma concedes almost point by point Mr. Knightley's charges against her early in the novel, revealing her successful internalization of the standards motivating his critique of her friendship with Harriet. The emotional intensity of this passage represents how seamlessly Mr. Knightley's arguments, which Emma had strenuously resisted on the basis of "woman's friendship and woman's feelings," have meshed with Emma's character by the end of the novel. Crucially, Mr. Knightley's anger and reproof need not be explicitly represented here; Emma's desires and those of her future husband have become continuous.

Emma's internalization of Mr. Knightley's desires becomes even more explicit when he proposes to her. In fact, the scene is oddly wordless; his proposal and her acceptance are rather a matter of assumptions and hints than of speeches. In contrast to the earlier, failed proposal by Mr. Elton, in which his desires and Emma's were spelled out in conversation, here both parties are rendered nearly mute by the narrative. In this scene, crucial to the heterosexual closure of the domestic novel, desire is strangely unrepresented. The spirited conversation and explicit self-interrogation of Emma's earlier encounters with sexuality—her first meetings with sexually available young women, matchmaking conversations with Harriet, proposals to herself and her friend—are replaced with guarded references to absence and loss. Having invested so much desire in relationships now judged inappropriate, the narrative seems unable to force that desire into the new form required by the heterosexual plot. Desire itself, the legitimating basis for the bourgeois companionate marriage with its rhetoric of choice, seems to have been banished from the narrative with the exit of Emma's female friendships.

This banishment is only apparent, however; a sapphic agency remains present in this scene. Such agency is a form of desire that the heterosexual plot cannot accommodate, yet female sexuality is paradoxically also the very figure for desire itself. This paradox, in which the narrative loses control over a central figure in its own resolution, accounts for the heavily ironic and truncated ending of the novel. Indeed, whatever charge exists in the scene of the disclosure of heterosexual desire that closes this plot derives almost entirely from the extent to which those relationships linger here, to which issues and emotions sketched out in the narrative in terms of female friendship still operate through the language appropriated by it. Mr. Knightley is not able to propose, for example, until Emma calls herself his friend. Assuming that he is about to declare his love for Harriet, she says, "If you have any wish to speak openly to me as a friend, or to ask my opinion of any thing that you may have in contemplation—as a friend, indeed, you may command me" (295). The repetition of this loaded word, which has been the site of such fierce conflict between Mr. Knightley and Emma throughout the novel, suggests that whatever charge exists in their relationship derives mainly from this conflict—that the issue of friendship, over which their desires have met and mingled throughout the novel, remains the only avenue for desire between them. Mr. Knightley signals the weird displacement of this mechanism when he responds, "Extraordinary as it may seem, I accept it, and refer myself to you as a friend" (296). Clearly, this proposal cannot easily accede to the demands of "ordinary" novelistic convention. Harriet herself must be represented as part of the scene, at the same time as the narrative insists that she is *not* part of it. Keeping the secret of Harriet's love for Mr. Knightley, Emma reflects,

> was all the service she could now render her poor friend; for as to any of that heroism of sentiment which might have prompted her to entreat him to transfer his affection from herself to Harriet, as infinitely the most

worthy of the two . . . Emma had it not. . . . She had led her friend astray, and it would be a reproach to her for ever; but her judgement was as strong as her feelings, and as strong as it had ever been before, in reprobating any such alliance for him, as most unequal and degrading. (296–297)

At the moment when Emma is most clearly abandoning her friendship with Harriet in the service of heterosexuality, the narrative cannot completely dismiss it. Unlike Edgeworth's Harriot Freke, Austen's Harriet Smith is too naturalized a part of the heroine's sexual identity to be explicitly excoriated. Emma's desires are still excessive, almost formless, ricocheting uncontainably between Mr. Knightley, herself, and Harriet. She still fantasizes about having the power to determine the shape of the desires around her, still arrogates the right to determine whether matches should be made or broken. Invoking her friendship with Harriet allows the possibility of such desire, such power, in a scene that is otherwise tentative and abstractly represented. This invocation of female friendship is the most concrete passage in the scene, which is described as a "dream" (296).

Mr. Knightley's attempt to propose to Emma takes the form not of the conventional declaration but of a series of negations: " 'Tell me, then, have I no chance of ever succeeding? . . . I cannot make speeches, Emma. . . . God knows, I have been a very indifferent lover' " (296). Emma's response is even more radically negative; she is at first silent, which delights Mr. Knightley: " 'You are silent,' he cried, with great animation; 'absolutely silent! at present I ask no more' " (296). When she finally does speak, her words are not represented, which keeps her still silent for all intents and purposes: "What did she say?—Just what she ought, of course. A lady always does" (297). Emma is one of the most voluble of Austen's female leads; her silence at the moment when she finally assumes the mantle of heroine, when she finally accedes to her role in the heterosexual narrative she has been represented as resisting all along, is a telling indicator of the compromise she makes to achieve the authority of the domestic woman. Perhaps because so much narrative energy has been invested in Emma's resistance to this compromise, the proposal scene is qualified rather than climactic. Emma is not only silent but physically weak as well, "ready to sink under the agitation of this moment" (296). Instead of revealing the truth of relations between the hero and heroine, their engagement is founded on the suppression of truth, the strange dislocation of the desires generated by the rest of the narrative: "The change had perhaps been somewhat sudden.... She felt its inconsistency.... Seldom, very seldom, does complete truth belong to any human disclosure; seldom can it happen that something is not a little disguised, or a little mistaken; but where, as in this case, though the conduct is mistaken, the feelings are not, it may not be very material" (297). The narrative cannot seamlessly endorse Emma's conversion to an obedient domestic woman willingly taking her place in the social machinery of her oppression. The site of her conversion is not the happy ending of heterosexual convention but a moment "untrue," "sudden," "inconsistent," and "disguised."

The novel runs down then, tidily taking care to marry Harriet Smith and Jane Fairfax off to men appropriate to their original class positions. The possible threat of social mobility opened up by female friendship is efficiently closed down by marriage. Both women effectively disappear from Emma's life. Her friendship with Harriet had been "declining" (319) since they took up the position of rivals, and the latter's marriage to Robert Martin effectively removes her from the kind of intimacy they had shared throughout the novel. Jane Fairfax, whom Mr. Knightley's "known wishes" had marked out for Emma to "find a friend there instead of in Harriet Smith" (289), has "already quitted Highbury" (334) by the time Emma marries. And even Mrs. Weston has been further removed from Emma's life by the birth of her daughter. The last line of the novel seems to allude to the bareness of the space around Emma, once crowded with female intimates: "But, in spite of these deficiencies, the wishes, the hopes, the confidence, the predictions of the small band of true friends who witnessed the ceremony, were fully answered in the perfect happiness of the union" (335). The "deficiencies" explicitly alluded to, of course, are the absences noted by Mrs. Elton of "white satin" and "lace veils"; but the reference to the "small band" witnessing Emma's marriage also points to just how the numbers around Emma have been diminished and who in particular must necessarily be absent for the novel to end as it does.

This ending has a sense of diminution—what Claudia Johnson calls "exclusion and decrescendo"[51]—because of the disavowal of the excitement generated by Emma's sapphic intensities throughout the rest of the novel. Homosexuality has become necessary to heterosexual desire here in a way that was to become characteristic not only of nineteenth-century novelistic heroineship but also of the now consolidated notion of identity as sexual truth for which the heroine of the domestic novel stood as an emblem and a guarantee. Austen's punished heroine, stripped of her most emphatically sexualized relationships, is yet paradoxically a figure for the triumph of bourgeois virtue over the temptations of class and sexual transgression. This figure, produced by the sexual temptations she has overcome and defined by the sexual secrets her "triumph" silences, was to become the paradigm of legal, medical, and fictional discourses on identity that characterized the nineteenth-century notions of subjectivity identified by Foucault as the "dissemination and implantation of polymorphous sexualities."[52] The effects of Austen's text, then, exceed its didactic and moral intentions because it marks a moment in a much larger cultural change, one in which the representation of female sexuality, via female friendship, was developing and producing meanings that determined how English bourgeois culture saw itself. With sexuality and its discontents positioned so firmly at the center of bourgeois notions of personal agency, the careful unpacking of the various sexual secrets embedded in representations of the heterosexuality valorized as "true" and "natural" will come to occupy cultural attention as never before. Sapphism will thus have a role to play in defining the truth and naturalness of heterosexuality, no longer from a position of complete alterity, as in the *Millenium Hall* world, but as the site of the heroine's closest shave with sexual vice and narrative failure.[53]

It is one of my arguments in this book that such representations of relations between women were uniquely effective in domesticating and making disappear the violent hierarchies of race and nation produced by England's colonial program, consolidating the fears of difference produced by these forces into the differences of sex and gender that fall under the purview of the domestic novel and its virtuous heroine. This claim can perhaps be epigrammatically illustrated by a return to the "gipsies," briefly glimpsed at the beginning of this chapter as they almost as briefly appear in *Emma*'s plot. We noted then that the terror inspired by the threatening ethnic Other, the danger posed to the unmarried woman by her contact with such a threat, is recruited into the service of the novel's sexual story. But ultimately the figure of the racial Other is to be even more emphatically dematerialized. We learn that the gypsies are soon forgotten, that "the whole history dwindled" for most residents of Highbury. But for Emma's two nephews, the incident becomes the material for a favorite story: "Henry and John were still asking every day for the story of Harriet and the gipsies, and still tenaciously setting [Emma] right if she varied in the slightest particular from the original recital" (229). The chapter in which the gypsies make their appearance ends here, with a symptomatic assertion of the role they have played in generating a narrative that is bound by convention (for its tenets must not be "varied in the slightest particular"), that is fictional ("the story of Harriet and the gipsies" eliminates the other participant, Miss Bickerton, in the service of satisfying narrative coherence), and that is domestic, a story told by a doting woman to entertain children by the fireside. It is perhaps this quality about Jane Austen's fiction that has led critics to credit it as the inaugural moment of novelistic realism and the high-water mark of the fiction of courtship: its ability to produce the kinds of "characteristic amnesias," in Benedict Anderson's words, that allow for the construction of the modern subject.[54]

# "Separated Only by a Wall": Sapphism and
# Romantic Friendship in the Discourse of Identity

The implications of my argument in this book are threefold. First, I hope I have demonstrated the importance of sexual intimacy between women as both a possibility imagined in English culture and as a context for understanding novelistic female friendship. Second, the preceding readings have made it clear that to find something like "lesbians" or "lesbianism" in eighteenth-century British literature is not necessarily to find feminist or progressive heroines or texts. Representations of intimacy between women formed a much more flexible category, one that could be recruited in the service of arguments from across the political spectrum precisely because of its unspoken centrality to bourgeois culture's imagining of itself. And, finally, the varied and uneven relations between images of sapphism and female friendship, on the one hand, and images of Turks, French, Africans, and Indians, on the other, suggest that ideas of race and nation must be investigated to provide an accurate history of novelistic representations of female friendship.

The French Revolution and the English controversy it engendered bisect the period covered in this book. The ferment of the early 1790s comes about thirty years after the publication of *Millenium Hall* in 1762 and about thirty years before the publication of *Emma* in 1816. Although none of the foregoing chapters has treated the revolutionary debate directly, this debate must be seen as a turning point in the English understanding of the political consequences of intimacy between women. The comparatively explicit and open assertion of women's bonds in *Memoirs of a Woman of Pleasure* and *Millenium Hall* gives way, in the work of "reactionary," post-Revolution novelists Edgeworth and Austen, to a notion of female friendship as a psychological rather than physical phenomenon, one that has the capacity to test the heroine's moral stature and fitness for domestic leadership rather than the power to organize her living space and bodily contacts. At the same time, however, it would be a mistake to see this, as might some readers of Foucault, as a victory for the homophobic forces of repression. The very recruitment of sapphic characters and stories into the bourgeois narrative of self-legitimation shifted those characters and stories from specific and limited cultural locations (a brothel or a strange, unaccountable "byass"; a secluded genteel manor and a scarred but virtuous heroine) to a diffuse, imprecise, and for those reasons ubiquitous cultural resource. The distinction I make here is not unlike Eve Kosofsky Sedgwick's famous analysis of the twin "minoritizing" and "universalizing" discourses of homosexuality in twentieth-century, Anglo-American culture.[1] Of course, just as the "minoritizing" and "universalizing" ways of understanding homosexuality in twentieth-century America contradict yet nonetheless coexist with one another, so the local and physical manifestations of love between women that characterize the mid-eighteenth-century texts persist in and inform the psychologized and transcendent forms privileged in the domestic novel. That is, a shift does occur, but it is precisely a shift in emphasis and priority rather than a complete displacement. Although—and, in fact, because—the sapphist and the romantic friend are mutually contradictory ways of understanding intimacy between women, both remain crucial to the narrative of identity. The newly hegemonic notion of sovereign subjectivity—of the truth of the self as interior and psychic—is an attempt to master the unmasterable irrationality of living in a body, an experience that the midcentury discourse of embodied and located female intimacy makes central to its understanding of the self. The "triumph" of sovereign subjectivity, after all, cannot successfully banish the physical and the irrational from human experience. Indeed, we might speculate that this inevitable failure is the origin of the demise of bourgeois psychologism with the dawn of postmodern deconstructions of the self at the end of the nineteenth century in the hands of Freud and Nietzsche; this "failure at the origins" might also be called a return of the repressed.[2]

This book may offer a prehistory of such postmodern discourses, one that helps establish the continued importance of ideas of female homosexuality to modernity itself. But the shift I describe can also be understood in more historically specific terms as one aspect of the insistent "psychologizing" of the bourgeois subject, a process identified by Nancy Armstrong. The status of female sexuality in the revolutionary debates helps us understand the political valence of this repositioning of female friendship and sapphic love.

Many have noted the importance of the debate on female sexuality to English Jacobin sexual politics.[3] Indeed, Katherine Binhammer calls the debates over sexuality in the period a "sex panic" and compares them with the late-nineteenth-century crackdown on prostitution and the current AIDS panic.[4] Significantly, Binhammer argues against reading these debates as an opposition between "conservative and radical—support of versus opposition to the French Revolution," because such a simplification "masks the intricate and important ways in which this very opposition manufactured a consensus around female sexuality and gender."[5] This consensus included the assumption that "female sexuality—since it influenced the political state of a nation—was a matter of national security."[6] But the consensus also rested on a crucial contradiction in domestic ideology: "The discursive production of women's sexual passivity is made possible by the prior assumption that female sexuality is active and potentially threatening. . . . The ideal of domesticity requires some version of *furor uterinus* in order to legitimate the need to restrict women's movements; the new female subject was only virtuous because she also had the potential to corrupt."[7] Binhammer's persuasive analysis usefully underlines the complex and contradictory status, as well as the cultural centrality, of notions of female sexuality in the period. As an element in the "sex panic" of the 1790s, female friendship offered to both Jacobins and anti-Jacobins a discursive resource for their own legitimation, because both revolution and reaction were crucial components in the emergence of a bourgeois democracy centered on the importance of the individual and the successful incorporation of dissent and difference. Divisions within the domestic—between vice and virtue as ways of understanding sexual acts, between force and coerced consent as forms of power—as well as divisions within the self—conscious efforts toward virtue, however defined, and unconscious or irrational or instinctual eruptions of vice—are both telling figures and effective producers of such an incorporation.

As Binhammer demonstrates, many debates about the sexual licentiousness of French revolutionary and English Jacobin sentiment centered around the figure and writings of Mary Wollstonecraft.[8] Many critics have noted the impact of the publication of William Godwin's 1798 *Memoirs,* in which he recounted Wollstonecraft's life, including her extramarital liaisons and suicide attempt, on the status of women writers and on arguments for sexual freedom, both of which Wollstonecraft was taken to represent.[9] Indeed, Wollstonecraft was the main target of a long satiric poem, Richard Polwhele's "The Unsex'd Females" (1798), in which she is called "the Arch-priestess of female Libertinism."[10] Despite her advanced views about the institution of marriage and her willingness to engage in cohabitation without it, however, Wollstonecraft was not, as Polwhele insinuates and as contemporary scholars have often assumed, an advocate of the free and frequent expression of sexual desire. Indeed, she held pleasure of every kind in rationalist contempt and suspected a fondness for what she called "sensuality" to be at the root of women's oppression. Rather than advocating what Polwhele called "unhallow'd lust,"[11] Wollstonecraft argued that "chastity must more universally prevail" if women were to achieve their rightful place in society.[12] *A Vindication* is animated by a critique of, even a disgust with, the body and its pleasures that accords surprisingly well with the anti-Jacobin sentiments of a Polwhele. Even within marriage, Wollstonecraft argues, "a master and mistress of a family ought not to continue to love each other with passion" (114) but rather ought to cultivate disinterested friendship, "the most holy bond of society" (113).

But Wollstonecraft is particularly suspicious of the bodily intimacies that prevail among women. She contends: "That decent personal reserve, which is the foundation of dignity of character, must be kept up between woman and woman, or their minds will never gain strength or modesty. . . . On this account also, I object to many females being shut up together in nurseries, schools, or convents" (236). The image of women together calls up one of Wollstonecraft's favorite terms of opprobrium, the "seraglio" (see, for example, 83): as we learned in Chapter 2, one of the prevalent associations of the harem for the English imagination was that of the sexual licentiousness that might occur between women "shut up together" in circumstances of luxury and pleasure.

What is most remarkable about Wollstonecraft's discussion of physical intimacy between women here is not, in fact, about women at all. In the middle of this discussion, she digresses into a vivid description of the sexual conditions prevailing at boys' boarding schools:

> The little respect paid to chastity in the male world is, I am persuaded, the grand source of many of the physical and moral evils that torment mankind, as well as of the vices and follies that degrade and destroy women; yet, at school, boys infallibly lose that decent bashfulness, which might have ripened into modesty, at home.
>
> And what nasty indecent tricks do they not also learn from each other, when a number of them pig together in the same bedchamber, not to speak of vices, which render the body weak, whilst they effectually prevent the acquisition of any delicacy of mind. . . . In what an unnatural manner is innocence often violated; and what serious consequences ensue to render private vices a public pest. (282)

The exact character of the "nasty indecent tricks" alluded to here must be inferred. Although the "vices" that "render the body weak" could equally refer to masturbation or to sex between boys, the passage's concern for the "violation" of "innocence" suggests two parties, a violator and an erstwhile innocent. As well, for "private vices" to become a "public pest," it would seem that more parties than the vicious (that is, the masturbator) must be involved, again suggesting that the threat here is not "the solitary vice" but sex *between* boys or men. Struck by the descent from Wollstonecraft's usually Latinate diction to the pungent vernacular phrase "pig together," the reader is then reminded of the actual subject of this part of *A Vindication:* "the bad habits which females acquire when they are shut up together" (283). So while Wollstonecraft does not literally represent sapphism in this passage, her sudden swerve toward considerations of sex among schoolboys suggests that this may indeed be the "bad habit" that animates much of Wollstonecraft's disgust for female sexuality and women's bodies in *A Vindication.*

Such sensual habits are linked, for Wollstonecraft, to a particular kind of writing and reading: "I exclaim against novels!" (306). Wollstonecraft distrusts novels because they lead women to value their grossly "sensual" desires above the virtues of rational work and friendship. It is women "subjected by ignorance to their sensations" and those who "plump into actual vice," according to Wollstonecraft, who are most subject to the novelist's blandishments. "These are the women who are amused by the reveries of the stupid novelists, who, knowing little of human nature, work up stale tales, and describe meretricious scenes, all retained in a sentimental jargon, which equally tend to corrupt the taste, and draw the heart aside from its daily duties" (306). These "flimsy works" (308) are dangerous, Wollstonecraft believes, because "the reading of novels makes women" use "the language of passion" (309): not "the legitimate passion" for intellect or justice, but "strong expressions and superlatives . . . which only mimic in the dark the flame of passion" (309).

The seeming paradox of Wollstonecraft's own fictional production can be understood only if we resist the temptation to cast the Jacobins as the proponents of free love, in the sense of sexual liberty and experimentation, and their opponents as puritanical and sexually repressive. Fiction escapes the epithet of "novel," for Wollstonecraft, if it is used to critique rather than encourage romantic love based on sexual desire. Both her novels, *Mary* (1788) and *The Wrongs of Woman; or Maria* (1798), concern female friendship, and both betray a deep skepticism about sexual love. *Mary* is a particularly significant case, animated by what the novel explicitly calls a "romantic friendship" between the titular heroine and her friend Ann.[13] Unhappily married, Mary's only experience of love is with Ann: "Her friendship for Ann occupied her heart, and resembled a passion" (19). Despite the fact that "Mary always slept with Ann" (23) and exclaims, "I cannot live without her!" (26), the novel offers a stringent critique of any passion, be it religious, sexual, or emotional, in which "the mere body worships" (30). Indeed, it is this tendency toward sensual enthusiasm, the result of an unsupervised childhood with an immoderate, novel-reading mother, that makes Mary less than Wollstonecraft's ideal because she is constrained by her circumstances from developing and using her rational capacities for happiness. After Ann's death, Mary falls in love with the virtuous but sickly Henry, and the novel explicitly equates the two relationships in the interests of its argument that "love and friendship are very distinct" (36), with the latter to be preferred. Mary's relationship with Ann would certainly have been sufficient: "Had Ann lived, it is probable [Mary] would never have loved Henry so fondly" (49). Indeed, it "was an advantage to Mary that friendship first possessed her heart; it opened it to all the softer sentiments of humanity:—and when this first affection was torn away, a similar one sprung up, with a still tenderer sentiment added to it" (60). The novel ends after Henry's death, leaving Mary longing for literal disembodiment in the form of her own demise. She joyfully contemplates death as the place in which, significantly, "there is neither marrying, nor giving in marriage" (68). This vision echoes her earlier moments of greatest happiness, in which "when her understanding or affections had an object, she almost forgot she had a body which required nourishment" (12). Although Wollstonecraft is critical of Mary's untutored enthusiasms in general, it is at these moments of disavowal of the body that Mary most closely resembles the Wollstonecraftian ideal, in which reason rises above sensual passion to produce true virtue.

Indeed, acquiring this psychic rather than physical "sensibility" was crucial, in Wollstonecraft's view, to the progressive project. In *A Vindication of the Rights of Men* (1790), the famous rebuttal to Edmund Burke's *Reflections on the Revolution in France,* Wollstonecraft actually compares Burke's vivid and impassioned scene-painting to the strategies of one of those sentimental novelists who distract slave-owning ladies from their distress after viewing a flagellation.[14] Wollstonecraft argues for the virtues of "rational satisfactions" as against the "*melting* feelings" produced by the contemplation of mere physical phenomena such as suffering or beauty.[15] The "sensual prejudices" of those enslaved by love or cruelty are the natural enemies of "reason" and the "enlarged views" it promotes.[16] The "mechanical instinctive sensations" promoted by an "affecting narrative" such as Burke's are merely the "vague declamation of sensibility"; Wollstonecraft prizes, in both literary and political terms, "the active exertions of virtue" instead.[17] Indeed, in "The Cave of Fancy," a posthumously published work, Wollstonecraft's sage defines the proper form of virtuous sensibility precisely in terms of its ability to convert physical sensations into psychic ones: "To give the shortest definition of sensibility, replied the sage, I should say that it is the result of acute senses, finely fashioned nerves, which vibrate at the slightest touch, and convey such clear intelligence to the brain, that it does not require to be arranged by the judgment."[18] To rewrite "vibrat[ing] at the slightest touch" as "convey[ing] . . . clear intelligence to the brain" is nothing if not a rationalization, a sublimation from which the body will have to be expelled.[19] Here we see the rationalist and Dissenting roots of Wollstonecraft's Jacobinism, with its otherworldly and intellectual emphasis, providing a springboard for the emergence of the same bourgeois psychologism that anti-Jacobin novelists such as Edgeworth and Austen helped produce.

So although Wollstonecraft was accused by such anti-Jacobins as Polwhele of endorsing a French-style libertinism also symbolized by Marie-

Antoinette's supposed sapphism, Wollstonecraft's feminist critique of such libertinism linked it instead with the literary and political sensuality of aristocratic apologists such as Burke. Ironically, however, the friendship Wollstonecraft prefers to sexual love could also be the target of anti-Jacobin critique because of its idealism. Romantic friendship, with its potential associations with excessive, exalted feeling and unworldly attachment, could be considered by reactionaries to be as symptomatic of dangerous revolutionary immorality as sapphism itself. In a 1798 number of the inflammatory periodical the *Anti-Jacobin,* the satirists parody a German drama in which romantic friendship plays a role. The following dialogue means to imply the shallow and impractical bonds advocated by "innovators" such as Wollstonecraft:

> CECILIA I had long been looking out for a congenial Spirit!—my heart was withered—but the beams of your's have re-kindled it.
> MATILDA A sudden thought strikes me—Let us swear an eternal friendship.
> CECILIA Let us agree to live together!
> MATILDA Willingly—(With rapidity and earnestness.)
> CECILIA Let us embrace.—(They embrace).[20]

Continuing in this vein in a later number, the editors report that "the meeting between Matilda and Cecilia . . . and their sudden intimacy, has been censured as unnatural." They claim that the scene is taken, "*almost word for word,*" from a German drama "now much in vogue."[21] The implication is clearly to censure the "vogue" for Germanic emotionalism in literature and life, which the editors contrast with good old English common sense. Yet Wollstonecraft's rejection of the exaggerated language and romantic sentiment of Burke and the novelists shares this distaste for superficial "passion." Despite their polemics, then, both Wollstonecraft and the *Anti-Jacobin* are on the same side, at least as far as female friendship goes. Both reject excess, emotionalism, and the body in favor of elevated moral distinctions and a psychologized notion of self.

The *Anti-Jacobin*'s parody of romantic friendship urges us to resist the conclusion that virtuous romantic friendship was championed by reactionaries as against French aristocratic or English Jacobinic sapphism. Both anti-Jacobin and revolutionary writers could draw on the range of representations of intimacy between women to excoriate the other side—because both sides

were really on the same side, pushed by history inexorably toward an investment in the psychology of the individual that would become the hallmark of
bourgeois culture, of which the radicalism of Godwin and Wollstonecraft was
itself a part. Sapphism and romantic friendship, rather than identifying mutually exclusive and separate spheres of female intimacy, continued to exhibit a
dangerous intimacy in such representations.

The shift in emphasis to a universalized notion of subjectivity predicated on disembodied notions of female friendship, however, occurs alongside and may be an important contributor to the canonization of the novel.
Nineteenth-century novelistic realism, with its emphasis on the moral drama
of individual psychic development, replaced the empirical conventions of
eighteenth-century prose, which could survey and describe the gross as well
as the subtle, the possible as well as the probable, the sapphist as well as the
romantic friend. The rational heroines of Austen and Edgeworth were much
closer to Wollstonecraft's ideal than their conservative political investments
would seem to indicate. Unmoved by heterosexual passion and governed by a
healthy self-interest, characters such as Belinda and Emma represent the
extent to which Wollstonecraft's ideas exemplified rather than resisted the
new bourgeois consensus about the virtuous self. This elevation in the novel's
status was "progress" in the typical sense of bourgeois positivism: the incorporation of complexity into a simple form taken to be universal. In the
success of this form lies the success of the novel as a genre.

Let me close with a return to the very rich diaries of Anne Lister, the
aristocratic sexual adventurer we encountered in Chapter 3. When European
travel once again became available to the English after the close of the Napo-
leonic Wars in 1815, Lister became interested in seeing the world. After a
short visit to France in 1819, Lister returned there to live for a while in 1824.
In Paris, Lister made the acquaintance of Maria Barlow, an English widow
with whom she soon became sexually intimate. Among their many Parisian
pleasures, Lister records an early conversation in which they gingerly sound
each other out about their relation to the sexual as well as political revolutions
of the 1790s: "Went to Mrs Barlow & sat with her an hour. Somehow she
began talking of that one of the things of which Marie Antoinette was accused
of was being too fond of women. I, with perfect mastery of countenance, said
I had never heard of it before and could not understand or believe it."[22] This
was in October 1824. In March 1825, the pair made a pilgrimage to one of the

premier sites in the sapphic history of the French Revolution: "Mrs Barlow & I set off at 11-35 to see the Prison of the Conciergerie at the Palais de Justice. . . . The chapel, behind which is made the entrance to the formerly dark, damp cells where Marie Antoinette & the Princess Elizabeth were confined, separated only by a wall (tho' they did not know it), is therefore interesting & the cells themselves, now turned into an Expiatory Chapel, are particularly so. . . . What must it have been during the Revolution?"[23] "Separated only by a wall" in the English sapphist's novel-fed imagination, the French friends (or were they fiends?) inspire narrative speculation. Whether sapphists or romantic friends, the story of the two women has already become part of a passionately felt personal history.

⏎⏎6  NOTES

Introduction

1  *Thraliana: The Diary of Mrs. Hester Lynch Thrale (Later Mrs. Piozzi), 1776–1809,* 2d ed., ed. Katherine C. Balderston (Oxford: Clarendon, 1951), 749, 949.

2  Marie Antoinette's biographers have differed on the issue of whether the queen was actually the lover of her two intimate female friends, first the princesse de Lamballe and later the comtesse de Polignac. But as Terry Castle demonstrates in *The Apparitional Lesbian: Female Homosexuality and Modern Culture* (New York: Columbia University Press, 1993), "rumours about Marie Antoinette's homosexuality had begun to spread across France—even to England—well before the French Revolution" (128), fueling the publication (in France) of a host of pornographic antiroyalist pamphlets throughout the 1780s. And Castle notes that the queen's supposed homosexuality was "made part of the Revolutionary Tribunal's death-dealing case against her" (131) before her execution in October 1793.

3  *Thraliana,* 957.

4  Ibid., 487.

5  Terry Castle believes the representation of Marie Antoinette as a sapphist played a crucial role in the development of modern lesbian identity, arguing that the queen "functioned as a kind of lesbian Oscar Wilde" in the early twentieth century, giving "those who idolized her a way of thinking about themselves. And out of such reflection—peculiar as its manifestations may often look to us now—something of the modern lesbian identity was born" (*Apparitional Lesbian,* 149).

6  Michel Foucault, *The History of Sexuality,* vol. 1, *An Introduction,* trans. Robert Hurley (New York: Vintage, 1980). Foucault asserts that the modern period is characterized by "a certain inclination . . . to direct the question of what we are, to sex" (78), an inclination that his work has, of course, been central in challenging.

⏎⏎155

7 Nancy Armstrong, *Desire and Domestic Fiction: A Political History of the Novel* (New York: Oxford University Press, 1987), 8. Armstrong's hypothesis has become something of an axiom in feminist criticism of eighteenth- and nineteenth-century literature. For example, Gary Kelly in *Women, Writing, and Revolution, 1790–1827* (Oxford: Clarendon, 1993) repeats much of Armstrong's language when he claims that in the discursive conflicts of the 1790s, "a certain figure of 'woman' was constructed to represent a professional middle-class discourse of subjectivity as opposed to communal or courtly sociability, 'nature' rather than decadent 'civilization,' domesticity as opposed to the public and political spheres, and the 'national' culture, identity and destiny rather than local, temporary, narrow interests of rank or region" (4). Kelly's observations about the relations between the domestic woman and narratives of class and nation, in particular, represent an attempt, like mine, to test Armstrong's hypothesis in a more precise historical and discursive frame than did she in her groundbreaking survey of the novel from the eighteenth to the twentieth century.

8 Thomas Laqueur's fascinating history of the sexed body, *Making Sex: Body and Gender from the Greeks to Freud* (Cambridge: Harvard University Press, 1990), carefully documents one reason for the increasing importance of the female body as a signifier in modern culture. Laqueur argues that the rise of empirical science saw the waning of an account of women's bodies as inferior versions of men's, in favor of a notion of Woman as "an altogether different creature [from Man] along a horizontal axis whose middle ground was largely empty" (148). One consequence of this shift, according to Laqueur, was that "as the natural body itself became the gold standard of social discourse, the bodies of women—the perennial other . . . became the battleground for redefining the ancient, intimate, fundamental social relation: that of woman to man. Women's bodies . . . came to bear an enormous new weight of meaning" (150).

9 See my article " 'She Was Too Fond of Her Mistaken Bargain': The Scandalous Relations of Gender and Sexuality in Feminist Theory," *diacritics* 21, 2–3 (Summer–Fall 1991): 89–101.

10 An early, important response is Irene Diamond and Lee Quinby, *Feminism and Foucault: Reflections on Resistance* (Boston: Northeastern University Press, 1988). More recent feminist readings of Foucault include Ann Cvetkovich, *Mixed Feelings: Feminism, Mass Culture, and Victorian Sensationalism* (New Jersey: Rutgers University Press, 1992), especially chapter 2, "Theorizing Affect: Twentieth-Century Mass Culture Criticism"; and Lora Romero, "Bio-Political Resistance in Domestic Ideology and *Uncle Tom's Cabin*," *American Literary History* 1, 4 (Winter 1989): 715–734.

11 In particular, see the excellent collection by Margo Hendricks and Patricia Parker, eds., *Women, "Race," and Writing in the Early Modern Period* (New York: Routledge, 1993). See also Firdous Azim, *The Colonial Rise of the Novel* (New York: Routledge, 1993), a feminist and anticolonialist account of eighteenth- and nineteenth-

century uses of the novel for British imperialism. The collection edited by Andrew Parker et al., *Nationalisms and Sexualities* (New York: Routledge, 1991), provided a pathbreaking entry into the field, but the volume does not include a single essay considering the relation of female homosexuality to nationalism. Some of the most valuable work on the literary history of Africans in Britain in the period is currently being done by Helena Woodard; see "The Production of an African-British Text and the Formation of a Black Literary Discourse in Late Eighteenth-Century England" (Ph.D. diss., University of North Carolina, 1992).

12 Louis Crompton, *Byron and Greek Love: Homophobia in Nineteenth-Century England* (Berkeley: University of California Press, 1985), 1.

13 See, for example, Robert Purks Maccubbin, ed., *'Tis Nature's Fault: Unauthorized Sexuality during the Enlightenment* (Cambridge: Cambridge University Press, 1987), which contains five articles on sodomy and male homosexuality but none on female homosexuality. G. S. Rousseau, one of the foremost historians of eighteenth-century sexuality, remarks in his contribution to Maccubbin's volume, "The Pursuit of Homosexuality in the Eighteenth Century: 'Utterly Confused Category' and/or Rich Repository?" that "it is apparent at once how interesting it would be to compare" his own account of male homosexuality "with the varieties of female homoeroticism in the eighteenth century" (138), but beyond this sketchy allusion he is silent.

14 Peter Wagner, *Eros Revived: Erotica of the Enlightenment in England and America* (London: Secker and Warburg, 1987), 224.

15 Felicity Nussbaum's *Torrid Zones: Modernity, Sexuality, and Empire in Eighteenth-Century English Narratives* (Baltimore: Johns Hopkins University Press, 1995) is of great interest to the feminist historian of sexuality who would be attentive to the ways in which sexuality is shaped by its colonial context. See especially chapter 6, "Feminotopias: The Seraglio, the Homoerotic, and the Pleasures of Deformity," which will be discussed in more detail in my first chapter.

16 Randolph Trumbach, "London's Sapphists: From Three Sexes to Four Genders in the Making of Modern Culture," in *Body Guards: The Cultural Politics of Gender Ambiguity*, ed. Julia Epstein and Kristina Straub (New York: Routledge, 1991), 112. Martha Vicinus, "'They Wonder to Which Sex I Belong': The Historical Roots of the Modern Lesbian Identity," *Feminist Studies* 18, 3 (Fall 1992): 473.

17 Betty Rizzo, in her fascinating and meticulously researched study *Companions without Vows: Relationships between Eighteenth-Century British Women* (Athens: University of Georgia Press, 1994), focuses on a particular economic and domestic relationship: "the companionate relationship, that of the employer and the humble companion" (1). Rizzo's work represents an important revision of the term "companionate marriage," demonstrating that for British women, "the companionate relationship of the eighteenth century mirrored the marriage relationship and was often identified with it" (1). Thus, "the term *companionate marriage,* referring to a companion in the sense of the woman's or humble companion—not an

equal at all—acquires an ironical inflection" (3). Rizzo does not pursue the sexual implications of the equation between women's companionate relationships and marriage, choosing instead to investigate the power relations of the domestic household and the ways in which critiques of the companionate relationship could function as veiled critiques of the institution of marriage. Indeed, Rizzo argues, "the ease with which Burney and others drew the parallel between marriage and close relationships between two women suggests that to their minds sexuality was far from the most important aspect of marriage" (8). The implications of the present study suggest, I think, that, like romantic friendship, the companionate relationship existed on a continuum with more overtly sexualized representations of love between women and that managing this distinction was part of the cultural work performed by such emphatically desexualized representations.

18 Castle, *The Apparitional Lesbian*, 28. Carolyn Woodward, "'My Heart So Wrapt': Lesbian Disruptions in Eighteenth-Century British Fiction," *Signs* 18, 4 (Summer 1993): 838–865.

19 Woodward, "'My Heart So Wrapt,'" 844.

20 Ibid., 839.

21 Ibid.

22 Vicinus, "'They Wonder to Which Sex I Belong,'" 473.

23 Lillian Faderman, *Surpassing the Love of Men: Romantic Friendship and Love between Women from the Renaissance to the Present* (New York: William Morrow, 1981), 16.

24 Ibid.

25 Carroll Smith-Rosenberg, "The Female World of Love and Ritual: Relations between Women in Nineteenth-Century America," in *The Signs Reader: Women, Gender, and Scholarship*, ed. Elizabeth Abel and Emily K. Abel (Chicago: University of Chicago Press, 1983). Although Smith-Rosenberg focuses on nineteenth-century American women, her account is useful for a study of the earlier British discourse of romantic friendship for both empirical and theoretical reasons. First, Smith-Rosenberg uses several eighteenth-century examples, and several of the women whose letters and diaries she cites traveled or lived in England. Second, she uses these case histories to support more general claims about "the long-lived, intimate, loving friendship between women" and its relation to female sexuality more generally (27, 54).

26 Drawing on the tradition of anthropological studies of human sexuality (following Mary McIntosh) rather than feminist theory, Randolph Trumbach, in "The Origin and Development of the Modern Lesbian Role in the Western Gender System: Northwestern Europe and the United States, 1750–1994," *Historical Reflections / Réflexions Historiques* 20, 2 (Summer 1994), also seeks to understand lesbianism in terms of gender rather than sexuality. He argues that the social organization of sexual relations in the late eighteenth century is best understood as a system of four genders—masculine, feminine, sodomitical, and sapphist—rather than as two genders with differing "sexual orientations" (289). Like Faderman's

and Smith-Rosenberg's, however, Trumbach's strategy of giving priority to gender involves him in some logical contradictions. How, for example, can he simultaneously argue that sapphism needs to be understood as a gender and also that "the behavior of sapphists . . . was not attributed to the physical structure of their bodies, but was supposed to arise from the moral corruption of their minds" (289)? The latter statement certainly seems to argue for the status of sapphism as a psychic category—an identity—part of the emerging discourse of sexual identity. "Femininity," on the other hand, was certainly understood as a function of the female sexed body in the period. Gender and sexuality have differing relations to the privileging of the body: gender is thought to be readable from the body (for example, by Cleland when Fanny Hill observes two men having sex and wonders how both can be men), whereas sexuality is considered—for example, by Hester Thrale—to be a moral (or what we might call psychic) trait.

27 Faderman, *Surpassing the Love of Men,* 19.

28 Ibid., 20.

29 Smith-Rosenberg, "Female World of Love," 35.

30 Ibid., 41, 39, 32.

31 Ibid., 28.

32 In *Women, Writing, and Revolution,* Gary Kelly makes a similar point when he argues, "By the late 1790s there was a growing insistence by many cultural revolutionaries in Britain that professional middle-class culture alone could save the country from the incompetence of its aristocratic rulers, the disaffection of the 'lower orders,' and the military threat from Revolutionary France" (27).

33 Ian Watt observes, in *The Rise of the Novel: Studies in Defoe, Richardson, and Fielding* (Berkeley: University of California Press, 1957), that it is "very evident that the eighteenth century witnessed a tremendous narrowing of the ethical scale, a redefinition of virtue in primarily sexual terms. . . . The same tendency can be seen at work on the ethical vocabulary itself: words such as virtue, propriety, decency, modesty, delicacy, purity, came to have the almost exclusively sexual connotation which they have since very largely retained" (157). Enlarging on these remarks, Michael McKeon, in *The Origins of the English Novel* (Baltimore: Johns Hopkins University Press, 1987), notes "the detachment of 'honor as virtue' from male aristocratic honor" over the course of the eighteenth century and virtue's "relocation within not only commoners but women, who increasingly come to be viewed not just as a conduit but as the repository of an honor" now equated with chastity as virtue (158).

34 In *Torrid Zones,* her fascinating study of maternity and sexuality in eighteenth-century writing, Felicity Nussbaum points specifically to attempts "to define and legislate racial purity through such policies as natal alienation and antimiscegenation laws" as ways in which the regulation of sexuality and "the domestic virtue demanded of Englishwomen" (2) helped shape English ideas of both sexuality and race. Nussbaum contends that "because the women in both torrid and frigid

regions possess bodily torrid zones, women of all regions threaten to inject sexuality into the most temperate geographical domains even as imperial discourse strains to confine it to certain areas. Androgynous, transgressive, 'monstrous,' lesbian, and working-class women—indigenous *and* colonizing women—are all linked metaphorically to bawdy women and are located on the fringes of respectability akin to brute savagery" (10). I would argue that these associations are best understood not as equivalencies in a list but rather as differently mobilized signifiers whose relation to one another varies with the context, intention, and effect of any colonialist representation. Rather than equating, for example, "lesbians" and "working-class women," we can learn more about the eighteenth-century sexual imaginary by attending to variations in the ways these categories are made to resemble (or differ from) each other.

35 Here I am using the categories "bourgeois" and "middle class" in the classic terms enumerated by Engels. The bourgeoisie, as the propertied class "almost exclusively in possession of all the means of consumption, and of the raw materials and instruments (machines, factories) necessary for their production" as Engels observed in 1847, was also in possession of the ideological state apparatuses necessary for the promulgation of the bourgeoisie's own account of itself as a cultural norm. Between the bourgeoisie and the working class existed "intermediate and transitional strata," which Marx also referred to as the middle class (*A Dictionary of Marxist Thought,* ed. Tom Bottomore [Cambridge: Harvard University Press, 1983], 54). It is this group, Marxists have argued, that can numerically and demographically be said to be "emerging" in the period under discussion in this study. However, as Barbara Ehrenreich notes, the middle class is always in the process of disappearing, characterized by a desire for upward mobility that encourages it to adopt bourgeois cultural values as its own. In this sense, then, it is bourgeois values that are "emerging" as the story the middle class tells about itself. Bourgeois ideology is the rationale for the rise to power of the new middle class. Thus, the "rise of the middle class" as understood in this study is less a demographic or economic phenomenon (in fact, the distribution of wealth changed very little over the course of the eighteenth century) than an ideological one: certain attributes, associated in representation with the "middle class"— virtue, individuality, hard work—were state sanctioned and culturally valued and were considered to be the proper aspirations of everyone from peasant to aristocrat. Thus the "rise of the middle class" was a triumph of *representation* in which the novel played an important role. Barbara Ehrenreich, *Fear of Falling: The Inner Life of the Middle Class* (New York: Pantheon, 1989).

36 Margo Hendricks and Patricia Parker, introduction to *Women, "Race," and Writing,* 1. For another helpful discussion of eighteenth-century usage of "race" and several related terms, see Nicholas Hudson, "From 'Nation' to 'Race': The Origin of Racial Classification in Eighteenth-Century Thought," *Eighteenth-Century Studies* 29, 3 (Spring 1996): 247–264.

37 Linguist Keith Walters, an authority on both Tunisian Arabic and African American English, points out that the term "African" "always refers to Sub-Saharans ('Blacks')—North African Arabs are erased by this term as used by Europeans *and* Sub-Saharans." Personal communication with Keith Walters, 2 September 1994.

38 As Theodore W. Allen documents in *The Invention of the White Race,* vol. 1, *Racial Oppression and Social Control* (London: Verso, 1994), this link between racial inferiority and particular bodily characteristics such as skin color was a historically new phenomenon, emerging in the late seventeenth century. Allen persuasively argues that the construction of the white Irish as an inferior "race" destined for English subjugation was a crucial early tool of English colonialism. For Allen, the crucial "hallmark of racial oppression" is not skin color but the assignation of "all members of the oppressed group to one undifferentiated social status, a status beneath that of any member of any social class within the colonizing population" (32). But a definition of "race" that began as a marker of status was transformed by the nascent nineteenth-century discourses of evolution and eugenics into a description of bodies, bodies distinct from and inferior to the bodies of the colonizers. See Noel Ignatiev, *How the Irish Became White* (New York: Routledge, 1995).

39 Benedict Anderson, *Imagined Communities: Reflections on the Origin and Spread of Nationalism,* rev. ed. (London: Verso, 1991), 141.

40 Ibid., 154.

41 For excellent discussions of the emergence of the category "race" in early modern Europe, see Hendricks and Parker, *Women, "Race," and Writing,* especially the editors' introduction (1) and essays by Linda E. Boose (36), Kim F. Hall (179), and Verena Stolcke (276).

42 Peter Hulme, in *Colonial Encounters: Europe and the Native Caribbean, 1492–1797* (London: Methuen, 1986), names this explosion "colonial discourse," delineating its basis in "the presumption that during the colonial period large parts of the non-European world were *produced* for Europe through a discourse that imbricated sets of questions and assumptions, methods of procedure and analysis, and kinds of writing and imagery, normally separated out into the discrete areas of military strategy, political order, social reform, imaginative literature, personal memoir and so on" (2). Mary Louise Pratt, in *Imperial Eyes: Travel Writing and Transculturation* (New York: Routledge, 1992), also argues forcefully for the notion of a colonial space "*produced* for Europe": travel writing in particular "produced other parts of the world for the imaginations of Europeans," 18.

43 Pratt, *Imperial Eyes,* 74.

44 McKeon, in *Origins of the English Novel,* calls the two organizing principles of the novel's development "questions of truth" (epistemological questions) and "questions of virtue" (social ones), the titles of his book's two main sections.

45 Suvendrini Perera, *Reaches of Empire: The English Novel from Edgeworth to Dickens* (New York: Columbia University Press, 1991), 7.

46   McKeon, *Origins of the English Novel,* 4.

47   Edward Said, *Culture and Imperialism* (New York: Knopf, 1993), xii–xiii. Said is using the term "imperialism" to denote relations between advanced capitalist countries and "client" or "dependent" ones, rather than in the sense of an "imperialist epoch" (roughly speaking, the twentieth century) ushered in by the creation of world markets because of the export of capital from metropole to colony. For a discussion of this debate over the term in Marxist theory, see the entry "imperialism and world market" in Marx, *A Dictionary of Marxist Thought,* 223. Azim (*Colonial Rise of the Novel*), whose critique of the novel is discussed below, also uses "imperialism" in this general way, as virtually a synonym for "colonialism." See note 49, this chapter.

48   Said, *Culture and Imperialism,* xii.

49   Firdous Azim, *Colonial Rise of the Novel,* suggests a connection between Watt's bourgeois individual and questions of imperialism in her examination of the history of subjectivity in eighteenth-century English culture. She concludes that "the novel is an imperial genre, not in theme merely, not only by virtue of the historical moment of its birth, but in its formal structure—in the construction of that narrative voice which holds the narrative structure together" (30). Azim argues that eighteenth-century intellectual culture, especially the widely read work of Locke and Descartes, came to some consensus around the "attempt to define the subject as homogenous and consistent, and to delineate the constituents of the citizen-subjects brought into being by the Western Enlightenment discourse" (10). The consistent narrative point of view that the domestic novel came to privilege, then, was a politically efficacious construct, defining certain cultural styles as universally human and certain forms of identity as appropriate to full citizenship in metropolitan nation-states. Work such as Said's and Azim's breaks with the assumptions of Watt's and McKeon's class-based analyses because it exposes the implication of the novel in giving new credence, in a specifically modern form, not only to national, class-based hierarchies but to international ones based on racial and national status as well, as all these belief systems faced the particular pressures of the eighteenth century's distinctively rapid pace of social change.

O N E   Resisting Reform: *Millenium Hall*

1   It is to these assumptions, I argue below, that *Memoirs of a Woman of Pleasure* is in part responding. I discuss these novels achronologically because *Millenium Hall* expresses the normalized public discourse about female friendship that *Memoirs* satirizes and sexualizes, so that although Cleland could not have been responding to Scott's text, Scott's text offers the clearest example of the available counterdiscourse which surrounded intimacy between women and which shaped Cleland's satire.

2 According to Lillian Faderman, "By the second half of the eighteenth century in England, romantic friendships became a popular theme in fiction." This popularity apparently bore some relation to actual practices among women, for Faderman argues that "all serious female friends were familiar with Sarah Scott's novel. . . . [*Millenium Hall*] was the *vade mecum* of romantic friendship . . . the most complete fictional blueprint for romantic friendship in the eighteenth century." See Faderman, *Surpassing the Love of Men*, 103–104.

3 George E. Haggerty, " 'Romantic Friendship' and Patriarchal Narrative in Sarah Scott's *Millenium Hall*," *Genders* 13 (Spring 1992): 109; further page references will be given parenthetically in the text. Haggerty, as do I, critiques Faderman's *Surpassing the Love of Men*, arguing that "lesbian relations were by no means unimaginable in the eighteenth century and were, moreover, assumed to be practiced even among [gentlewomen and royalty]" (111). Aside from Haggerty and Faderman, the most prominent commentator on *Millenium Hall* has been Jane Spencer, who edited the Virago edition of the novel which appeared in 1986 and which marked the first reissue of Scott's text since the eighteenth century. Spencer discusses the novel briefly in her book *The Rise of the Woman Novelist: From Aphra Behn to Jane Austen* (Oxford: Blackwell, 1986) but comments on it more fully in the introduction to the Virago edition. There, she praises the novel's "utopian vision of female community" and its "clever contrast" of the "plight" of women in the outside world with "the delights of the female community," noting with satisfaction that "unmarried life at Millenium Hall is evidently Scott's ideal" (introduction to *A Description of Millenium Hall*, by Sarah Scott [1762; reprint New York: Penguin, Virago, 1986] 1986), xii, xiv.

4 Michel Foucault, *Discipline and Punish: The Birth of the Prison*, trans. Alan Sheridan (New York: Vintage, 1979), 195.

5 Ibid., 203.

6 In *Torrid Zones*, Felicity Nussbaum makes the interesting argument that it is specifically the ladies' "domain over the disabled" (156) that makes this a novel that "replicates class differences and engages in the benevolence that can be exercised only through privilege" (160). About the sexual status of the characters' relationships, Nussbaum argues that although the novel makes "an obdurate affirmation of nonsexual attachments . . . an undercurrent of homoerotic bonding unsettles the narrative" (153). By contrast, I contend that it is precisely the definition of sexuality as outside the purview of Millenium Hall that gives its proprietors their peculiar form of power.

7 Armstrong, *Desire and Domestic Fiction*, 19.

8 Ibid.

9 Ibid., 251, 19.

10 Ibid., 251.

11 Ibid., 19.

12 Ibid., 255.

13  For a fascinating discussion of women's participation in abolitionist boycotts, see Charlotte Sussman, "Women and the Politics of Sugar, 1792," *Representations* 48 (Fall 1994): 48–69. For a fuller analysis of the relation between ideologies of femininity and British capitalism and consumerism, see Sussman, *Consuming Anxieties* (Stanford: Stanford University Press, 1998).

14  Moira Ferguson, *Subject to Others: British Women Writers and Colonial Slavery, 1670–1834* (New York: Routledge, 1992), 19.

15  Sarah Scott, *A Description of Millenium Hall*, ed. Jane Spencer (1762; reprint, New York: Penguin, Virago, 1986), 117. All further citations will be given parenthetically in the text.

16  One of the reasons the Millenium Hall "household" is a site of such struggle is that it lacks husbands and children, the furniture of the bourgeois household that was to emerge as a norm over the next fifty years. Instead, the Millenium Hall ladies run an establishment similar to the feudal "household" the bourgeois family was to displace—one in which the term "family" is understood to include servants and dependents and in which men were much less visible, concerning themselves instead with the farmwork and trade of the estate. The novel represents an attempt imaginatively to bridge the two forms of "household."

17  Melinda Alliker Rabb, "Making and Rethinking the Canon: General Introduction and the Case of *Millenium Hall*," *Modern Language Studies* 18, 1 (Winter 1988): 13.

18  By presenting such a spectacle for female readers, of course, Scott inadvertently solicits the very questions of female pleasure that are marginalized within her novel. Indeed, I am arguing that the representation of domestic female power in the novel might offer the pleasure of fantasy to female readers.

19  Foucault, *Discipline and Punish*, 209.

20  This distinction echoes the language of the passage quoted above, in which the ladies of Millenium Hall claim only to "influence," never to "enforce" the acceptance of bourgeois norms. Once again, in Foucauldian terms the distinction is one between a visual, disciplinary mode associated with progress and modernity in the novel and an older mode marked by physical coercion.

21  Foucault, *Discipline and Punish*, 202.

22  Jane Spencer reports that "most contemporary comments on the estrangement blame George Scott, and there was even a rumour that he had tried to poison his wife" (introduction to *Millenium Hall*, vi).

23  Such presents, like the "valuable marks of distinction" the Millenium Hall ladies bestow on the poor, work both to construct and to represent the power relations in this relationship. Miss Melvyn is several years older than Louisa, and this (power) difference makes her hesitate to accept gifts from the younger girl: "Had Louisa been the same age as herself, she would have felt a kind of property in all she possessed; friendship, the tenure by which she held it" (41). After much wrangling, Louisa finally convinces Miss Melvyn to accept her gifts and thereby allow her to feel the "joy of giving" (42). "Miss Melvyn felt her little friend's

reproach, and saw that she had done her injustice in thinking her youth rendered her incapable of that perfection of friendship, which might justify the accepting of her offer" (42). Once again, we see in the novel's representation of affection and benevolence a contradictory double economy of material inducement and ideal example. Relationships of intimacy or "influence" (to echo the "We do not set up for reformers" speech) are always underwritten by material need or force. The novel's construction of bourgeois affect thus bridges the transition between an older, disciplinary society and the emerging hegemonic codes of middle-class subjectivity.

24 This is the phrase that Maria Edgeworth uses to describe the convictions of the chastened Lady Delacour, rescued from the excesses of Methodism by a reconciliation with her husband. See Chapter 3.

25 Spencer, introduction to *Millenium Hall,* vi.

26 In *Companions without Vows,* Betty Rizzo argues for another, more conscious, and active strategy by which the novel displaces its critique of marriage. She contends that "Sarah Scott had no intention of taking on the patriarchs in regard to marriage, and she used the institution of humble companionship in the place of marriage in this book, attacking it vigorously, claiming that the Hall was founded to provide women with a better alternative" (22). In Rizzo's reading, the novel is not conservative but strategic, framing its critique of marriage in terms of a more widely acceptable attack on the abuses possible in relations between a powerful woman and her female dependent. In either reading, however, the importance of the Millenium Hall women's disclaimer of active public and political engagement is crucial to the novel's construction or appropriate forms of female power.

27 Rabb, "Making and Rethinking the Canon," 11.

28 Sancho praises Sterne and "the humane author of Sir George Ellison" for their portrayals of the evils of slavery; see *Letters of Ignatius Sancho,* ed. Paul Edwards and Polly Rewt (Edinburgh: Edinburgh University Press, 1994), 86. See also Helena Woodard's discussion of the cultural impact of the writing of Ignatius Sancho, Ottobah Cugoano, and Olaudah Equiano in "The Production of an African-British Text and the Formation of a Black Literary Discourse in Late Eighteenth-Century England" (Ph.D. diss., University of North Carolina, 1992), and her manuscript "The Politics of Race and Reason: The Eighteenth Century and the African-British Writer."

29 Sarah Scott, *The History of Sir George Ellison,* ed. Betty Rizzo (1766; reprint, Lexington: University of Kentucky Press, 1996), 10. Ellison became the "man of real sensibility" when the novel was abridged and retitled *The Man of Real Sensibility, or, The History of Sir George Ellison* (Philadelphia: Humphreys, 1774) for publication in Scotland and the thirteen colonies. Further references will be to the Rizzo edition, using the abbreviation *Ellison,* and will be given parenthetically in the text.

30 Ferguson, *Subject to Others,* 101.

31 Olaudah Equiano, *Interesting Narrative of the Life of Olaudah Equiano, or Gustavus*

*Vassa, the African,* in *The Classic Slave Narratives,* ed. Henry Louis Gates Jr. (New York: Mentor, 1987), 78.

32   Ibid., 80.

33   Sharpe cited in David Brion Davis, *The Problem of Slavery in the Age of Revolution, 1770–1823* (Ithaca: Cornell University Press, 1975), 396. Measures to abolish, limit, or hinder the importation of slaves were proposed by colonial legislatures in Massachusetts (1771) and Virginia (1772) but were ultimately defeated by the governor and the Crown, respectively (23).

34   Ibid., 350, 358, 362.

35   Ibid., 455.

T W O   Domesticating Homosexuality: *Memoirs of a Woman of Pleasure*

1   In fact, in *Imagined Communities* in his most extended remarks about the sexual status of national identification, its potential for fantasy, and the erotic opportunities such bonds both construct and constrain, Benedict Anderson identifies sexual relations between men as characteristic of a national consciousness conditioned by Protestantism. Commenting on Leslie Fiedler's analysis of homosocial bonds in the American novel, Anderson says: "Rather than national eroticism it is, I suspect, an eroticized nationalism that is at work. Male-male bondings in a Protestant society which from the start rigidly prohibited miscegenation are paralleled by male-female 'holy loves' in the nationalist fiction of Latin America, where Catholicism permitted the growth of a large mestizo population" (202 n. 32). Although the racialized conditions Anderson argues for here differ between England and the American colonies, the shaping force of Protestantism in the development of both English and American national identities suggests that same-sex love may be a crucial and hitherto unexplored aspect of the ideology of Englishness.

2   *Satan's Harvest Home: Or the Present State of Whorecraft, Adultery, Fornication, Procuring, Pimping, Sodomy, and the Game at Flatts . . . and Other Satanic Works, Daily Propagated in This Good Protestant Kingdom* (London, 1749). Future references will appear parenthetically in the text and will be to this edition.

3   Both George Haggerty and Felicity Nussbaum cite Eric Partridge's *Dictionary of Slang and Unconventional English,* 7th ed. (New York: Macmillan, 1984), as the source of the following definition for "flat-fuck," which also suggests an etymology for "the game at Flatts": "Simulated copulation by a pair of women: lesbian colloquially." See Haggerty, " 'Romantic Friendship,' " 120, and Nussbaum, *Torrid Zones,* 240.

4   John Cleland, *Memoirs of a Woman of Pleasure,* ed. Peter Sabor (1748–49; reprint, Oxford: Oxford University Press, 1985), 159. All future references will be to this edition and will appear parenthetically in the text.

5   Nussbaum, *Torrid Zones,* 17.

6 For an exception, see Carol Houlihan Flynn, "What Fanny Felt: The Pains of Compliance in *Memoirs of a Woman of Pleasure," Studies in the Novel* 19, 3 (Fall 1987). Flynn argues that Cleland's "ironic exploration of [the] 'irksome sensations' [of sexual pleasure] makes him not a feminist, but a spur to feminism, as diligent as Fanny Hill herself, one who confounds didactic principles as he lays bare the pains, pleasures and costs of civilization" (294).

7 The novel provides, according to Janet Todd, "a penis view of women," merely a "fantasy of the female system" (*Women's Friendship in Literature: The Eighteenth-Century Novel in England and France* [New York: Columbia University Press, 1980], 88, 100). Patricia Meyer Spacks, in "Female Changelessness; or, What Do Women Want?" *Studies in the Novel* 19, 3 (Fall 1987), concurs that the novel is the product of "male fantasy" in which "Fanny's gratification inevitably coincides with male gratification" (273, 275). And, in "'I's' in Drag: The Sex of Recollection," *Eighteenth Century: Theory and Interpretation* 22, 1 (Winter 1981), Nancy K. Miller argues that the structure in which a man writes about female sexuality for the pleasure of other men "allows the male bond of privilege and authority to constitute itself within the laws of proper circulation"; the rhetorical structure in which one woman addresses another is a "female impersonation" that "translates into structures of masculine dominance and authority" (49, 54).

8 As Terry Castle notes in "Matters Not Fit to Be Mentioned: Fielding's *The Female Husband," ELH* 49, 3 (Fall 1982), "Lesbianism has a long history as a *topos* in pornographic literature, and was never more popular perhaps than in the eighteenth century" (612). Of course, the explicit intention of such representations is heterosexual male titillation; it is my argument in this chapter, however, that the discursive tension linking romantic friendship and sapphism, as well as the sodomitical context of reader reception in the 1750s, complicates and at times even contradicts this intended effect.

9 For an important discussion of the narratological consequences of the convention of male-authored novels written in a first-person, female voice, see Madeleine Kahn, *Narrative Transvestism: Rhetoric and Gender in the Eighteenth-Century English Novel* (Ithaca: Cornell University Press, 1991). Kahn argues that feminist approaches such as Nancy Miller's, which emphasize the appropriativeness of the male writer's adoption of a female persona, are "correct" but not "ultimately true." Instead, she contends, the "dynamic structure of transvestism reveals transvestism's inability to be fixed in either category despite its attempts to reaffirm once and for all the hegemony of the masculine" (7). I attempt here to chart one consequence of precisely this instability.

10 Miller, "'I's' in Drag," 51.

11 Ibid., 49.

12 Philip E. Simmons, "John Cleland's *Memoirs of a Woman of Pleasure:* Literary Voyeurism and the Technique of Novelistic Transgression," *Eighteenth-Century Fiction* 3, 1 (October 1990): 47.

13  Ibid., 50.

14  Ibid., 53.

15  Eve Kosofsky Sedgwick, *Between Men: English Literature and Male Homosocial Desire* (New York: Columbia University Press, 1985), 1, 2.

16  Felicity Nussbaum argues, as do I, that "the *Memoirs* makes available to its heroine, author, and readers heterosexual, homosexual, bisexual and omnisexual erotic responses" (*Torrid Zones,* 105), but Nussbaum concludes by reasserting the convention that in the novel, "sexual desire for the same sex is necessary but must be rechannelled toward men in order to be fully satisfying" (106). I suggest instead that the proliferation of nonheterosexual bodies and gazes in the novel works against the notion that heterosexuality is "fully satisfying" either as a sexual practice or as a strategy for narrative closure.

17  Donald H. Mengay, "The Sodomitical Muse: *Fanny Hill* and the Rhetoric of Cross-Dressing," in *Homosexuality in Renaissance and Enlightenment England,* ed. Claude J. Summers (New York: Harrington Park, 1992), 188.

18  Kevin Kopelson, "Seeing Sodomy: *Fanny Hill*'s Blinding Vision," in *Homosexuality in Renaissance and Enlightenment England,* ed. Summers, 175.

19  Peter Sabor, "The Censor Censured: Expurgating *Memoirs of a Woman of Pleasure,*" in *'Tis Nature's Fault,* ed. Maccubbin, points out that *Memoirs of Fanny Hill,* the abridged version of the novel prepared by Cleland in 1750 in order to avert suppression, omits both the male homosexual incident and the lesbian scenes with Phoebe at the beginning of the novel (195).

20  Peter Sabor, "Note on the Text," in Cleland, *Memoirs,* xxvii.

21  Ibid., xiii. Simmons speculates that the "bit of seemingly gratuitous violence against Fanny" at the end of the homosexual scene, in which she trips and knocks herself out while running to report the men, "raises the possibility that Cleland's sympathies actually lie with the two men" ("John Cleland's *Memoirs,*" 61).

22  Like the prostitute, the author must strive to please his reader, to make of his or her "desires" "indispensable orders" so as to survive. Recall that Cleland wrote the *Memoirs* under severe economic duress and following its suppression served a year in debtor's prison.

23  Todd, *Women's Friendship in Literature,* 73.

24  Ibid., 70.

25  In his discussion of the female reader of the *Memoirs,* however, Simmons argues that to read this text, eighteenth-century women would have to become, in effect, men: "We can go some way towards addressing the questions raised by the possibility of the female reader if we remind ourselves of the social fact that the production and consumption of pornography occur within a male-controlled discourse serving male interests. With the exception of the feminist reader of pornography, to whom my assumptions about reader response may not apply, we

can think of the female reader of Cleland's text as having to some degree internalized the conventions of the male discourse and appropriated for herself the functionality of the male gaze. . . . [W]e should see the 'female reader' and the 'male reader' not as static entities but as zones of conflict. In a male-authored work such as the *Memoirs,* Cleland's imitation of sentimental 'women's' writing, even—indeed, especially—when such imitation becomes parodic, can be seen as one more salvo in the battle for control over representations of female subjectivity" (47–49). In this battle, however, some shots inevitably go astray of the author's intentional effect on readers. The notion that "feminist readers" would operate outside "male-controlled discourse" obliterates the necessity of making any feminist critique from within that discourse—as feminist criticism of Cleland continues to exemplify. Also, the assumption that a feminist reader would resist the "erotic material" made available to women readers via the "male gaze" sets aside the possibility of various feminist readers who might take pleasure in disrupting the heterosexist intentions of pornographic representation. And finally, Simmons fails to imagine a female reader whose homosexual pleasures and desires might be generated or satisfied by the text.

But even within what Simmons calls "a male-controlled discourse serving male interests," ideology does not work seamlessly. Just as female subjectivity and sexuality is contested ground in eighteenth-century fiction, "male interests" are cut across with contradiction and conflict. Not only might the psychic labor through which a woman reader appropriates "for herself the functionality of the male gaze" produce sexual desires and identities that exceed the boundaries of heterosexuality, but the "male gaze" might not always be heterosexual either. If the readerly subjectivities constructed by the novel are "zones of conflict," it would be fruitful not to shut down these contestations by assuming either monolithic male desires and interests, always at work on women, or monolithic female desires whose interests are always successfully subsumed to enable male heterosexuality in and beyond the text.

26 Todd argues that Fanny's repugnance for the male homosexuals she witnesses later in the novel may have an economic base: "For women who are successful in society, like Fanny and [her next madam] Mrs. Cole, sexuality has become an economic commodity, which they buy and sell, trade for money and marriage. A sexual relationship which is neither an economic one nor, like that of Phoebe and Fanny, a preparation for the market throws in question the whole elaborate scheme which successful women have erected and accepted" (*Women's Friendship in Literature,* 96). The novel's representation of female sexuality as public, as a tradable commodity, works against the emerging alignment of sexuality with women and of sexuality and women with the private realm.

27 The medieval assumption of female sexual voraciousness persisted through the eighteenth century, competing with an emerging ideology of female sexual pas-

sivity. The hegemony of the latter view by the nineteenth century does not indicate that the former disappeared, of course. Thomas Laqueur argues in *Making Sex* that "human sexual nature changed" (5) in the late eighteenth century, resulting in the cultural production of a female body no longer conceived as a diminished version of the male but rather as an incommensurably different object. One "of many possible manifestations of this newly created sex," according to Laqueur, was "the assertion that women were passionless; or alternatively the proposition that, as biologically defined beings, they possessed to an extraordinary degree, far more than men, the capacity to control the bestial, irrational, and potentially destructive fury of sexual pleasure" (150). However, the one-sex model has a "continued life," according to Laqueur; here he explicitly differs from Foucault, "who would see one *episteme* decisively, once and for all, replacing another" (21). Thus, the doctrine of female sexual passivity became more prominent and naturalized, but the notion of female sexual voraciousness remained available for use against women when useful. The older form of misogyny was typically used to define workingwomen, nonwhite women, and women who had sex with one another in the nineteenth century; on this point, see Sander Gilman, *Difference and Pathology: Stereotypes of Sexuality, Race, and Madness* (Ithaca: Cornell University Press, 1986).

28   Crompton, *Byron and Greek Love*, 1.

29   Sabor, "Note on the Text," xix.

THREE   Colonizing Virtue: *Belinda*

1   I'm using the metaphor of "specters" and "haunting" here under the influence of Terry Castle, who in *The Apparitional Lesbian* offers a seductive history of the relation between images of ghosts and the literary representation of lesbians. See especially chapter 5, "The Diaries of Anne Lister," in which Castle treats much more completely the same diarist I discuss below. Like the present argument, Castle's analysis of Lister's diaries challenges "the conventional notion that most women remained blissfully ignorant about sex before Freud" (105).

2   This is the term used by Rachel Jennings in her Ph.D. dissertation, "The Union and Its Limits: Histories, Regions, and Empires in the Nineteenth-Century British Novel" (University of Texas, Austin, 1995). In this important study of Edgeworth's political vision, Jennings argues that "Edgeworth envisions a global economic community in which individual entrepreneurs interact on a rational, familiar, and equal basis. . . . [H]er conception of a hegemonic global community does not acknowledge either cultural difference or geographical distance as natural limits to English capitalistic activity" (102). My own understanding of the role of colonialism in Edgeworth's fiction is crucially shaped by Jennings, who argues convincingly for Edgeworth's status as a nineteenth-century theorist of imperialism whose complexity and importance rival those of Marx. Jennings also provides

the most comprehensive available discussion of Edgeworth's tales and stories that feature colonial settings.

3 Maria Edgeworth, *Belinda* (1801), ed. Kathryn Kirkpatrick (Oxford: Oxford University Press, 1994), 219. All further references to *Belinda* are to this edition and will be given parenthetically in the text. Kirkpatrick's edition, like Eiléan Ni Chuilleanain's admirable Everyman edition of the novel (London: J. M. Dent, 1993), follows the 1801 first edition. The Pandora edition (London: Routledge, 1986), on the other hand, silently incorporates the changes made by Edgeworth when the novel was reprinted for Anna Laetitia Barbauld's "British Novelists" series in 1810. The 1810 edition eliminates the scene in which Belinda actually agrees to marry Vincent (apparently considered a promise too grave to breach); furthermore, the "exchanges in the debate on passion and custom between Belinda and Lady Delacour" (Ni Chuilleanain, introduction, xxv) are toned down and less potentially radical; and perhaps most important, the black slave Juba does not marry an English servant girl, as he does in the original version. These changes, according to Ni Chuilleanain, make the Belinda of Edgeworth's revised 1810 edition "a more conventional heroine" (xxv). Although I am following the first edition the very existence of the somewhat bowdlerized 1810 edition (which was the version of the novel read throughout the nineteenth century), underscores my argument about the way in which colonial and sapphic representations of sexuality impact the conventions of heroine description. For a thorough discussion of the history of *Belinda*'s publication, see Kathryn J. Kirkpatrick, "'Gentlemen Have Horrors upon This Subject': West Indian Suitors in Maria Edgeworth's *Belinda*," *Eighteenth-Century Fiction* 5, 4 (July 1993): 331–348.

4 Lillian Faderman prepared a volume based on the transcripts of this case and entitled *Scotch Verdict: Miss Pirie and Miss Woods v. Dame Cumming Gordon* (New York: William Morrow, 1983). Most of this volume consists of excerpts from the trial transcripts, which Faderman claims are "edited . . . considerably, but always with a concern for the accuracy of the ideas expressed in the original documents" (iii), rendering its utility for scholars problematic. According to Faderman, this is the case on which Lillian Hellman based her 1934 play *The Children's Hour*.

5 *Miss Marianne Woods and Miss Jane Pirie against Dame Helen Cumming Gordon* (New York: Arno, 1975). This edition is an unedited reprint of the original trial materials, in which each portion of the testimony is paginated separately. My references will include section title and page number and will be given parenthetically in the text.

6 Of course, this move could not completely shut down the disturbing possibilities of female agency raised by the judges' desire to find the "truth" of the trial in bourgeois female purity and passionlessness. Another strategy was employed to relocate the possibility of female homosexuality within the British national space but still outside the realm of middle-class female virtue: in the school's servants, Mary Brown and Charlotte. These women were suspected by Lord Meadowbank

of implanting the "unnatural" idea of the teachers' sexual relationship in the minds of the young ladies. See Chapter 2 above for a further discussion of strategies for representing female homosexuality as interior to Britain.

7 Elizabeth Mavor, ed., *A Year with the Ladies of Llangollen* (London: Penguin, 1984), 136. This edition too attests to the frustrating informality of much of the scholarship on romantic friendship. Claiming that the life of the "Ladies of Llangollen" "was not so much a linear progression from point to point as a kind of dignified *eddying*," Mavor presents excerpts from Eleanor Butler's diaries from 1784 to 1819 not in chronological order but by grouping "together all the thrawn Januaries of their lives, their ecstatic Mays, limpid Septembers and beloved candlelit Decembers" (13). This editing decision flattens and obscures the relation of Butler's account to history, rendering it a static portrait of "their quiet and enviable life together" (13) rather than an attempt at an accurate account of this eighteenth-century woman's self-representation.

8 Faderman, *Surpassing the Love of Men*, 122.

9 Mavor, *Ladies of Llangollen*, 135.

10 Ibid., 136.

11 Ibid., 178.

12 Anne Lister, *I Know My Own Heart: The Diaries of Anne Lister, 1791–1840,* ed. Helena Whitbread (London: Virago, 1988), 210. All further references to Lister's diaries will be to this edition and will be cited parenthetically in the text. This volume was reprinted by New York University Press in 1992 with a brief introduction by Helena Whitbread. A second volume of Lister's diaries, entitled *No Priest but Love: Excerpts from the Diaries of Anne Lister, 1824–26* was also published by New York University Press in 1992 with some scholarly notes and a brief, descriptive introduction to each section by Helena Whitbread.

13 Lister, *I Know My Own Heart*, 234.

14 Ibid., 235–236.

15 Ibid., 145.

16 Lister records having "said [to Miss Pickford] she was very agreeable. I just felt towards her as if she were a gentleman, & treated her as such. This seemed to suit very well" (ibid., 271). Lister also often refers to herself as a "gentleman" in comments on her own dress and activities.

17 Ibid., 273.

18 Ibid., 237, 256.

19 Ibid., 145, 179.

20 Ibid., 297.

21 Ibid., 270–271.

22 The Sixth Satire of Juvenal, "On Getting Married," describes the vices of women, particularly their lustfulness and inchastity. Lister may be referring specifically to the following passage:

> Foul longings burn inside each girlish breast,
> and cries are uttered as the passion mounts.
>
> .   .   .   .   .   .   .   .   .   .   .   .
>
> Saufeia whips these slave-girls into contest
> and beats them, too, with her agility
> till Medullina wrests the crown from her.

Some translators render the "wrestling" here more explicitly sexual. Lister may also recall the passage about "manly girls" who "court that strength that will negate their sex," wear armor, and fight in wars and arenas. And she may be recalling several references to male homosexuals who "teach our wives to move their pelvises and whatever else they know." Juvenal, *Satires*, trans. Jerome Mazzaro (Ann Arbor: University of Michigan Press, 1965), 73–74, 71, 75. Interestingly, an eighteenth-century "imitation" of this satire adds female friends to the list of threats to a wife's virtue:

> The fiercest storms, the nuptial peace offend,
> Rise from th'intrusion of the BOSOM FRIEND.
> This bosom friend, deny it if you can,
> Displays her love by hatred to the man

See Edward Burnaby Greene, *The Satires of Juvenal Paraphrastically Imitated, and Adapted to the Times* (London: J. Ridley, 1763), 72. Although Lister and Miss Pickford would have read the satires in Latin, they may have been familiar with this translation.

23  Lister, *I Know My Own Heart*, 273.

24  Lister's reliance on literary allusion to construct a story about her own sexuality provides an early and formative example of what Eve Kosofsky Sedgwick calls "the reign of the telling secret" in modern epistemologies of the self. Lister's delicate and literary probing of Miss Pickford demonstrates how "resilient and productive a structure of narrative" is "the love that is famous for daring not to speak its name." Sedgwick, "Epistemology of the Closet I," *Raritan* 7, 4 (Spring 1988): 39.

25  Lister, *I Know My Own Heart*, 273.

26  Ibid., 296, 146.

27  See my conclusion for a fuller discussion of the 1790s debate over the "unsexed" status of educated women and women writers.

28  See the discussion of slavery as a metaphor for English women's oppression in Chapter 1 above.

29  See, for example, the anti-Jacobin novels *Sense and Sensibility* (1811) by Jane Austen and *Adeline Mowbray* (1804) by Amelia Opie. In *Letters for Literary Ladies* (1795), Edgeworth, though an advocate for women's education, distances herself from the Wollstonecraftian "literary ladies" whose accomplishments were associated

with radical sexual politics. In the first letter, a sensible father who wishes to educate his daughter fends off charges of being "a champion for the rights of woman" (2). He reassures his anti-Jacobite and antifeminist friend and correspondent, who advocates little or no formal education for women, by saying: "You dislike in the female sex that daring spirit which despises the common forms of society, and which breaks through the delicacy and reserve of female manners. So do I" (37). He suggests such reading as the classics in translation. Such appropriate texts, he argues, are the best safeguards of virtue. "No woman can be happy in society who does not preserve the peculiar virtues of her sex. When this is demonstrated to the understanding, must not those virtues, and the means of preserving them, become objects of the first and most interesting importance to the sensible woman?" (36). "Letter from a Gentleman to His Friend upon the Birth of a Daughter," in *Letters for Literary Ladies: To Which Is Added, an Essay on the Noble Science of Self-Justification* (Georgetown: Joseph Milligan, 1810).

30 The crowd shifts its attention from the duel to the race because Clarence plays on their Francophobia, exhorting them to help on his pigs "for the love of Old England" (59). Significantly, Harriot Freke had explained their predicament to him in French, presumably so that the crowd wouldn't understand that she was appealing for help. Mrs. Freke is linked to things French at other points during the novel as well—for example, when she declares herself a champion for the "rights of woman" with the slogan "*Vive la liberté!*" (229). And the Frenchness of Lady Delacour's name and her position at the head of a salon of wit and fashion and her independence from her husband underline the novel's equation between the inappropriate agency these women wield and their aristocratic, "Frenchified" notions of social relations. Such a rejection of French ideas, always a strain in English popular thinking, was particularly acute for the bourgeois English in the period following the French Revolution. The middle class distanced itself from both the popular violence of the French lower classes and the luxurious excesses of the aristocracy in an attempt to reassure itself that such an event would not happen in England. As historian Louis Crompton notes, "Nowhere did English Francophobia find more impassioned expression than in attitudes toward sex" (*Byron and Greek Love,* 4).

31 Janet Todd notes that "the corrupting power of books was a commonplace of eighteenth-century thought," in *Women's Friendship in Literature,* 210 n. 16. Nancy Armstrong discusses how, in their moral and educational writings, Maria Edgeworth and her father "accept the view that prevailed during the eighteenth-century, which said fiction behaved subversively and misled female desire" (*Desire and Domestic Fiction,* 15). The danger not just of reading but also of reading novels had become so conventional by midcentury that satirizing it could form the major narrative structure of Charlotte Lennox's *The Female Quixote* (1752) as well as Jane Austen's better-known *Northanger Abbey* (1818), written in the 1790s.

32  Armstrong, *Desire and Domestic Fiction,* 20.

33  The presence in this scene of Mr. Vincent, a member of the planter class, also raises the question of the implications for English class relations of the very different structures of authority that governed English society in the Caribbean than in the metropolis. In a way, of course, Mr. Vincent also represents a kind of decadence—the luxurious and lazy life of the sugar cane aristocrat, which was being vigorously decried at this time in antislavery literature and which the novel itself criticizes through the Mr. Vincent plot. In this plot, the laziness and luxury of "Creole" men and women comes under the critical eye of Mr. Vincent's guardian, the moral philosopher Mr. Percival.

34  The figure of the witch has been associated with that of the lesbian since at least the time of the medieval witch-hunts, both by clerical and legal authorities and in popular accounts. In a 1705 Northamptonshire journalistic pamphlet, for example, two women are accused of changing themselves into "two little black Things" and crawling into the bed of another woman, where they "sucked her lower Parts" (*An Account of the Tryals, Examination, and Condemnation of Elinor Shaw and Mary Phillip's [Two Notorious Witches]* [London: F. Thorn, 1705; reprint, Northampton-shire: Taylor and Son, 1866], 4).

35  The last incident in which Juba plays a major role has an interesting history. In less than two paragraphs, Edgeworth describes the wedding of Juba to Lucy, Lady Anne Percival's maid, explaining that "Lady Anne . . . was always eager to promote innocent festivity." But as noted above, this incident was read as far from innocent by its early-nineteenth-century audience. This was one of the incidents that resulted in "hostile criticism" of the novel, and Edgeworth omitted it from the 1810 edition because she was told it "gave the gentlemen the horrors." Chuilleanain, introduction to *Belinda,* xxv. See note 3, this chapter.

36  In *Maria Edgeworth: A Literary Biography* (Oxford: Clarendon, 1972), Marilyn Butler argues persuasively that Edgeworth's political views were more conservative than those of her father, the educational reformer Richard Lovell Edgeworth. Butler claims that the novelist "came to identify herself in a way Edgeworth [senior] never had with the landowning classes. . . . By inclination she was the least controversial of Anglo-Irishwomen, and it was only through complex personal circumstances that she became the author of three progressive, at times even radical, studies of the Anglo-Irish in Ireland" (that is, *Ennui, The Absentee,* and *Castle Rackrent*) (124, 125).

   According to Butler, when Edgeworth began her career as a novelist at the turn of the century, "the novel still had a low intellectual reputation, often on the grounds that it depicted silly, sentimental behaviour, a dangerous example to young girls; and even the intellectual novelists of the 1790s had not made the form respectable, since they were associated with radicalism and with sexual promiscuity" (307). See also Nicola J. Watson, *Revolution and the Form of the British Novel,*

*1790–1825: Intercepted Letters, Interrupted Seductions* (Oxford: Clarendon, 1994), who argues that the epistolary form was discredited by association with 1790s feminists and revolutionaries such as Mary Wollstonecraft and hence parodied by writers who wanted to distance themselves from such radicals.

37  Butler, *Maria Edgeworth,* 149.

38  The terms here are those which Butler (*Maria Edgeworth,* 307) associates with the eighteenth-century view of the novel itself.

39  Ibid.

40  Armstrong, *Desire and Domestic Fiction,* 4.

41  Richard Sheridan, *The Critic* ([1771], in *The Plays of Richard Brinsley Sheridan,* ed. Clayton Hamilton [New York: Macmillan, 1926]) parodying Henry Jones, *The Earl of Essex* (1753): *"Enter Southampton.* Southampton (kneeling): Permit me, madam, to approach you thus" (II.ii.225).

42  Peter Stallybrass and Allon White, *The Politics and Poetics of Transgression* (Ithaca: Cornell University Press, 1986), 5 and passim.

FOUR   Desire and Diminution: *Emma*

1  Edward Said, "Jane Austen and Empire," chap. 2, pt. 2 in *Culture and Imperialism* (New York: Knopf, 1993), 80–97.

2  Ibid., 84.

3  Jane Austen, *Emma,* ed. Stephen M. Parrish, Norton Critical Edition (New York: Norton, 1972), 226. All further references from *Emma* are cited parenthetically in the text.

4  After a period of little interest in the first half of the nineteenth century, Austen began to receive critical acclaim among the Victorians. A characteristic plaudit is this comment from George Henry Lewes's 1852 essay "The Lady Novelists": "Of all imaginative writers she is the most *real.* Never does she transcend her own actual experience, never does her pen trace a line that does not touch on the experience of others. We recognise the second and more special quality of womanliness in the tone and point of view: they are novels written by a woman, an Englishwoman, a gentlewoman; no signature could disguise that fact; and because she has so faithfully (although unconsciously) kept to her own womanly point of view, her works are durable" (quoted in ibid., 370). Lewes here inaugurates a cluster of critical assumptions about Austen's limited focus, her femininity, and her unconscious relation to her art, assumptions that were to remain intact until very recently.

5  In *Women, Writing, and Revolution,* Gary Kelly makes a similar point when he argues that "devices of psychological 'realism' developed by Austen and others were designed in part to naturalize the philosophical or theological underpinnings of their novels" (179).

6  Said, "Jane Austen and Empire," 96.

7  As Betty Rizzo puts it in *Companions without Vows,* in *Emma* "Austen seems to have explored the question of what might become of an attractive young woman who assumes all the prerogatives of a man—the right to reason for herself, do and say as she likes, and plan others' lives for them. When the book is read in this way, Emma's acceptance of her own mistaken effrontery and of Knightley as mentor is painful, resulting in the defeat of the heroine of an antimarriage plot" (9).

8  Marvin Mudrick, *Jane Austen: Irony as Defense and Discovery* (1952; reprint, Berkeley and Los Angeles: University of California Press, 1968), 190, 203.

9  Edmund Wilson, "A Long Talk about Jane Austen," in *Jane Austen: A Collection of Critical Essays,* ed. Ian Watt (Englewood Cliffs, N.J.: Prentice-Hall, 1963), 39.

10  Laura G. Mooneyham, *Romance, Language, and Education in Jane Austen's Novels* (New York: St. Martin's, 1988), 108.

11  Ibid., 113.

12  Ibid., 143.

13  John D'Emilio, *Sexual Politics, Sexual Communities: The Making of a Homosexual Minority in the United States, 1940–1970* (Chicago: University of Chicago Press, 1983), 37.

14  Ibid., 140.

15  For a reading of *Emma* in terms of Adrienne Rich's "lesbian continuum," see Tiffany F. Potter, "'A Low but Very Feeling Tone': The Lesbian Continuum and Power Relations in Jane Austen's *Emma,*" *English Studies in Canada* 20, 2 (June 1994): 187–203.

16  Tony Tanner, *Jane Austen* (Cambridge: Harvard University Press, 1986), 181–182.

17  Claudia L. Johnson, *Jane Austen: Women, Politics, and the Novel* (Chicago: University of Chicago Press, 1988), 122.

18  Claudia L. Johnson, *Equivocal Beings: Politics, Gender, and Sentimentality in the 1790s: Wollstonecraft, Radcliffe, Burney, Austen* (Chicago: University of Chicago Press, 1995), 202.

19  Ibid., 193.

20  Ibid., 196.

21  Ibid., 202.

22  Mary Evans, *Jane Austen and the State* (London: Tavistock, 1987), 44.

23  Ibid., 58.

24  Margaret Kirkham, *Jane Austen, Feminism, and Fiction* (Sussex: Harvester, 1983), xvii.

25  Marilyn Butler, *Jane Austen and the War of Ideas* (Oxford: Clarendon, 1975). In this influential work, Butler argues that for Austen's heroines, "moral progress consists in discerning, and submitting to, the claims of the society around them" (1). The reforms that Austen "perceives to be necessary are within the attitudes of individuals; she calls for no general changes in the world of the established lesser landed gentry" (1–2). Butler continues, "Jane Austen's novels belong decisively to one class of partisan novels, the conservative" (3).

26  Kirkham, *Austen, Feminism, and Fiction,* xi.

27  Ibid., 171.

28  Johnson, *Jane Austen,* xviii.

29  Ibid., xix.

30  Ibid., xxiii.

31  Ibid.

32  Mudrick, *Jane Austen: Irony as Defense and Discovery,* 181.

33  Ibid., 203.

34  Ian Watt, introduction to *Jane Austen: A Collection of Critical Essays,* ed. Watt, 2.

35  Wilson, "Talk about Jane Austen," 38.

36  Quoted in Barbara Johnson, "The Surprise of Otherness: A Note on the Wartime Writings of Paul de Man," in *Literary Theory Today,* ed. Peter Collier and Helga Geyer-Ryan (Ithaca: Cornell University Press, 1990), 14.

37  Eve Kosofsky Sedgwick, "Jane Austen and the Masturbating Girl," *Critical Inquiry* 17, 4 (Summer 1991): 833.

38  Ibid.

39  Teresa de Lauretis, "Sexual Indifference and Lesbian Representation," in *Performing Feminisms: Feminist Critical Theory and Theatre,* ed. Sue-Ellen Case (Baltimore: Johns Hopkins University Press, 1990), 24.

40  Armstrong, *Desire and Domestic Fiction,* 19.

41  Ibid.

42  Ibid., 254.

43  Ibid., 151.

44  Ibid., 153.

45  Ibid., 151.

46  Ibid., 154.

47  Ibid., 158.

48  Ibid.

49  Lister, *I Know My Own Heart,* 239–241.

50  Ibid., 273.

51  Claudia Johnson, *Equivocal Beings,* 18.

52  Foucault, *History of Sexuality,* 12.

53  A typically punitive Victorian example might be Jane Eyre's friendship with Helen Burns in Charlotte Brontë's 1847 *Jane Eyre.* Her pious school friend is the first person Jane ever loves, and this friend has valuable things to teach the heroine, but she must die (rather than just marry down, as Austen's Harriet does) to make the point that Jane's salvation does not lie in the direction of union with other women. By the same token, Jane leaves behind Diana and Mary Rivers and ultimately decides that Rochester's daughter, Adele, must repeat Jane's own experience of parentless boarding school life because her presence in the marital home would deprive Rochester of too much of his new wife's attention.

54  Anderson, *Imagined Communities,* 204.

Conclusion

1 Eve Kosofsky Sedgwick, *Epistemology of the Closet* (Berkeley and Los Angeles: University of California Press, 1990), especially 67–90.

2 For an excellent discussion of these inaugural postmodern deconstructions of the subject, see Elizabeth Grosz, *Jacques Lacan: A Feminist Introduction* (London: Routledge, 1990), especially the introduction.

3 As Eleanor Ty observes, Edmund Burke's responses to the Revolution are animated by sexual fears. Not only does he picture the danger to Marie-Antoinette in terms of sexual vulnerability, but he also propounds "the idea that the seduction of a wife or daughter is the first step towards the undermining of authority" that precedes revolution. See Ty, *Unsex'd Revolutionaries: Five Women Novelists of the 1790s* (Toronto: University of Toronto Press, 1993), 5.

Gary Kelly, *Women, Writing, and Revolution,* documents the importance of sexuality to political dispute in the 1790s. "In the late 1790s British 'anti-Jacobins' welcomed revelations of Mary Wollstonecraft's sexual transgressions as proof that Revolutionary feminism was inimical to bourgeois domesticity and femininity" (25). He continues, "In *A Vindication of the Rights of Woman* Wollstonecraft plays down the sexual passions because she here blames them for the exploitation of women in courtly amorous culture" (26). Elsewhere, Kelly claims, Wollstonecraft argued "for women's erotic equality with men and right to sexual pleasure. . . . Wollstonecraft's views were strengthened by her involvement with avantgarde cultural revolutionaries in London and Paris who rejected marriage and sexual chastity as oppressive property institutions and cultivated an apparently egalitarian sexuality informed by an eroticized culture of Sensibility" (26). In distancing herself from Wollstonecraft, Kelly claims, Hannah More "does not reject Revolutionary feminism so much as modify its version of 'domestic woman' for the Revolutionary aftermath and Romantic nationalism" (29). "After the Revolutionary decade domesticity and the domestic affections were represented as even more fragile havens from a social and political domain irretrievably divided and embattled, even more decisively 'feminine' as a refuge and inspiration for the heroized and professionalized man. Women's extended forms of domesticity were expanded further to include preserving and disseminating the 'national' history, culture, and identity and domesticating the racial and cultural 'other' in the empire" (179–180). In *Equivocal Beings,* her important study of the sexual politics of the 1790s, Claudia L. Johnson argues that "the political rupture of the 1790s . . . gave rise to a war of sentiments about sex, a war in which controversialists, each intensely invested in heterosexual feeling as a foundational political virtue, routinely charge their opponents with deviance of the direst possible consequence, for the fate of the nation is understood on all sides to be tied up with the right heterosexual sentiment of its citizens" (11). In "Modern Lesbian Identity," Randolph Trumbach makes a similar point: "The discussion about these women grew more heated in the 1790s both in England and in France" (299). Trumbach continues: "Burke [in *Reflections*] . . . could not allow Marie-Antoinette to become a symbol of sexual corruption. In the ideological wars spawned by the Revolution, the sapphist role associated with the queen also became a stick with which to beat a feminist like Mary Wollstonecraft, who was accused of masculine manners by more conservative women" (300).

4  Katherine Binhammer, "The Sex Panic of the 1790s," *Journal of the History of Sexuality* 6, 3 (January 1996): 409–434.

5  Ibid., 410.

6  Ibid., 418.

7  Ibid., 433.

8  Wollstonecraft was attacked both as a promoter of sexual promiscuity in women and as "frigid and sexually unattractive" (ibid., 409).

9  As Miriam Brody notes, "Wollstonecraft had openly challenged conventional morality by living with a man outside marriage and bearing an illegitimate child. . . . Wollstonecraft's name, in the years following her death [in 1797], years of political repression and fear of French radicalism, became virtually synonymous with free love and Jacobinism." See Brody, introduction to *A Vindication of the Rights of Woman,* by Mary Wollstonecraft (New York: Penguin, 1986), 63.

10  Richard Polwhele, "The Unsex'd Females: A Poem, Addressed to the Author of *The Pursuits of Literature*" (London: Cadell and Davies, 1798), 20.

11  Ibid., 9.

12  Mary Wollstonecraft, *A Vindication of the Rights of Woman,* ed. Miriam Brody (London: Penguin, 1986). Further references to this volume will be cited parenthetically in the text.

13  Mary Wollstonecraft, *Mary, a Fiction,* ed. Gary Kelly (Oxford: Oxford University Press, 1989), 20. Further references to this volume will be cited parenthetically in the text.

14  *The Works of Mary Wollstonecraft,* ed. Janet Todd and Marilyn Butler (London: William Pickering, 1989), 5:45.

15  Ibid., 46.

16  Ibid., 47.

17  Ibid., 53.

18  Ibid., 1:201.

19  I am grateful to Laura Mandell for generously offering me this reading of *A Vindication of the Rights of Men* and "The Cave of Fancy" in extended comments on a draft of this chapter in September 1996.

20  *Selections from "The Anti-Jacobin,"* ed. Lloyd Sanders (London: Methuen, 1904), 140.

21  Ibid., 149.

22  Lister, *No Priest but Love,* 31–32.

23  Ibid., 83.

*An Account of the Tryals, Examination, and Condemnation of Elinor Shaw and Mary Phillip's (Two Notorious Witches).* London: F. Thorn, 1705. Reprint, Northamptonshire: Taylor and Son, 1866.

Allen, Theodore W. *The Invention of the White Race.* Vol. 1, *Racial Oppression and Social Control.* London: Verso, 1994.

Anderson, Benedict. *Imagined Communities: Reflections on the Origin and Spread of Nationalism.* Rev. ed. London: Verso, 1991.

Armstrong, Nancy. *Desire and Domestic Fiction: A Political History of the Novel.* New York: Oxford University Press, 1987.

Austen, Jane. *Emma.* Ed. Stephen M. Parrish. Norton Critical Edition. New York: Norton, 1972.

Azim, Firdous. *The Colonial Rise of the Novel.* New York: Routledge, 1993.

Binhammer, Katherine. "The Sex Panic of the 1790s." *Journal of the History of Sexuality* 6, 3 (January 1996): 409–434.

Boose, Lynda E. " 'The Getting of a Lawful Race': Racial Discourse in Early Modern England and the Unrepresentable Black Woman." In Hendricks and Parker, 35–54.

Brody, Miriam. Introduction to *A Vindication of the Rights of Woman,* by Mary Wollstonecraft. New York: Penguin, 1986.

Brontë, Charlotte. *Jane Eyre.* Ed. Richard J. Dunn. New York: W. W. Norton, 1993.

Butler, Marilyn. *Jane Austen and the War of Ideas.* Oxford: Clarendon, 1975.

———. *Maria Edgeworth: A Literary Biography.* Oxford: Clarendon, 1972.

Castle, Terry. *The Apparitional Lesbian: Female Homosexuality and Modern Culture.* New York: Columbia University Press, 1993.

———. "Matters Not Fit to Be Mentioned: Fielding's *The Female Husband.*" *ELH* 49, 3 (Fall 1982): 602–622.

Cleland, John. *Memoirs of a Woman of Pleasure*. Ed. Peter Sabor. 1748–49. Reprint, Oxford: Oxford University Press, 1985.

Crompton, Louis. *Byron and Greek Love: Homophobia in Nineteenth-Century England*. Berkeley: University of California Press, 1985.

Cvetkovich, Ann. *Mixed Feelings: Feminism, Mass Culture, and Victorian Sensationalism*. New Jersey: Rutgers University Press, 1992.

Davis, David Brion. *The Problem of Slavery in the Age of Revolution, 1770–1823*. Ithaca: Cornell University Press, 1975.

de Lauretis, Teresa. "Sexual Indifference and Lesbian Representation." In *Performing Feminisms: Feminist Critical Theory and Theatre*, ed. Sue-Ellen Case. Baltimore: Johns Hopkins University Press, 1990.

D'Emilio, John. *Sexual Politics, Sexual Communities: The Making of a Homosexual Minority in the United States, 1940–1970*. Chicago: University of Chicago Press, 1983.

Diamond, Irene, and Lee Quinby. *Feminism and Foucault: Reflections on Resistance*. Boston: Northeastern University Press, 1988.

Edgeworth, Maria. *Belinda* (1801). Ed. Kathryn Kirkpatrick. Oxford: Oxford University Press, 1994.

———. "Letter from a Gentleman to His Friend upon the Birth of a Daughter." In *Letters for Literary Ladies: To Which Is Added, an Essay on the Noble Science of Self-Justification*. Georgetown: Joseph Milligan, 1810.

Ehrenreich, Barbara. *Fear of Falling: The Inner Life of the Middle Class*. New York: Pantheon, 1989.

Equiano, Olaudah. *Interesting Narrative of the Life of Olaudah Equiano, or Gustavus Vassa, the African*. In *The Classic Slave Narratives*, ed. Henry Louis Gates Jr. New York: Mentor, 1987.

Evans, Mary. *Jane Austen and the State*. London: Tavistock, 1987.

Faderman, Lillian. *Scotch Verdict: Miss Pirie and Miss Woods v. Dame Cumming Gordon*. New York: William Morrow, 1983.

———. *Surpassing the Love of Men: Romantic Friendship and Love between Women from the Renaissance to the Present*. New York: William Morrow, 1981.

Ferguson, Moira. *Subject to Others: British Women Writers and Colonial Slavery, 1670–1834*. New York: Routledge, 1992.

Flynn, Carol Houlihan. "What Fanny Felt: The Pains of Compliance in *Memoirs of a Woman of Pleasure.*" *Studies in the Novel* 19, 3 (Fall 1987).

Foucault, Michel. *The History of Sexuality*. Vol. 1, *An Introduction*. Trans. Robert Hurley. New York: Vintage, 1980.

———. *Discipline and Punish: The Birth of the Prison*. Trans. Alan Sheridan. New York: Vintage, 1979.

Gilman, Sander. *Difference and Pathology: Stereotypes of Sexuality, Race, and Madness*. Ithaca: Cornell University Press, 1986.

Greene, Edward Burnaby. *The Satires of Juvenal Paraphrastically Imitated, and Adapted to the Times.* London: J. Ridley, 1763.

Grosz, Elizabeth. *Jacques Lacan: A Feminist Introduction.* London: Routledge, 1990.

Haggerty, George E. "'Romantic Friendship' and Patriarchal Narrative in Sarah Scott's *Millenium Hall.*" *Genders* 13 (Spring 1992).

Hendricks, Margo, and Patricia Parker, eds. *Women, "Race," and Writing in the Early Modern Period.* New York: Routledge, 1993.

Hudson, Nicholas. "From 'Nation' to 'Race': The Origin of Racial Classification in Eighteenth-Century Thought." *Eighteenth-Century Studies* 29, 3 (Spring 1996): 247–264.

Hulme, Peter. *Colonial Encounters: Europe and the Native Caribbean, 1492–1797.* London: Methuen, 1986.

Ignatiev, Noel. *How the Irish Became White.* New York: Routledge, 1995.

Jennings, Rachel. "The Union and Its Limits: Histories, Regions, and Empires in the Nineteenth-Century British Novel." Ph.D. diss., University of Texas, Austin, 1995.

Johnson, Barbara. "The Surprise of Otherness: A Note on the Wartime Writings of Paul de Man." In *Literary Theory Today,* ed. Peter Collier and Helga Geyer-Ryan. Ithaca: Cornell University Press, 1990.

Johnson, Claudia L. *Equivocal Beings: Politics, Gender, and Sentimentality in the 1790s: Wollstonecraft, Radcliffe, Burney, Austen.* Chicago: University of Chicago Press, 1995.

——. *Jane Austen: Women, Politics, and the Novel.* Chicago: University of Chicago Press, 1988.

Juvenal. *Satires.* Trans. Jerome Mazzaro. Ann Arbor: University of Michigan Press, 1965.

Kahn, Madeleine. *Narrative Transvestism: Rhetoric and Gender in the Eighteenth-Century English Novel.* Ithaca: Cornell University Press, 1991.

Kelly, Gary. *Women, Writing, and Revolution, 1790–1827.* Oxford: Clarendon, 1993.

Kirkham, Margaret. *Jane Austen, Feminism, and Fiction.* Sussex: Harvester, 1983.

Kirkpatrick, Kathryn J. "'Gentlemen Have Horrors upon This Subject': West Indian Suitors in Maria Edgeworth's *Belinda.*" *Eighteenth-Century Fiction* 5, 4 (July 1993): 331–348.

Kopelson, Kevin. "Seeing Sodomy: *Fanny Hill*'s Blinding Vision." In Summers, *Homosexuality in Renaissance and Enlightenment England,* 175.

Laqueur, Thomas. *Making Sex: Body and Gender from the Greeks to Freud.* Cambridge: Harvard University Press, 1990.

Lewes, George Henry. "The Lady Novelists." In Jane Austen, *Emma.* Ed. Stephen M. Parrish. Norton Critical Edition. New York: Norton, 1972.

Lister, Anne. *I Know My Own Heart: The Diaries of Anne Lister, 1791–1840.* Ed. Helena Whitbread. London: Virago, 1988.

——. *No Priest but Love: Excerpts from the Diaries of Anne Lister, 1824–26.* Ed. Helena Whitbread. New York: New York University Press, 1992.

Maccubbin, Robert Purks, ed. *'Tis Nature's Fault: Unauthorized Sexuality during the Enlightenment.* Cambridge: Cambridge University Press, 1987.

"Marx, Karl Heinrich." In *A Dictionary of Marxist Thought.* Ed. Tom Bottomore, 302–305. Cambridge: Harvard University Press, 1983.

Mavor, Elizabeth, ed. *A Year with the Ladies of Llangollen.* London: Penguin, 1984.

McKeon, Michael. *The Origins of the English Novel.* Baltimore: Johns Hopkins University Press, 1987.

Mengay, Donald H. "The Sodomitical Muse: *Fanny Hill* and the Rhetoric of Cross-Dressing." In *Homosexuality in Renaissance and Enlightenment England,* ed. Claude J. Summers. New York: Harrington Park, 1992.

Miller, Nancy K. " 'I's' in Drag: The Sex of Recollection." *Eighteenth Century: Theory and Interpretation* 22, 1 (Winter 1981).

*Miss Marianne Woods and Miss Jane Pirie against Dame Helen Cumming Gordon.* New York: Arno, 1975.

Mooneyham, Laura G. *Romance, Language, and Education in Jane Austen's Novels.* New York: St. Martin's, 1988.

Moore, Lisa. " 'She Was Too Fond of Her Mistaken Bargain': The Scandalous Relations of Gender and Sexuality in Feminist Theory." *diacritics* 21, 2–3 (Summer–Fall 1991): 89–101.

Mudrick, Marvin. *Jane Austen: Irony as Defense and Discovery.* 1952. Reprint, Berkeley and Los Angeles: University of California Press, 1968.

Ni Chuilleanain, Eiléan. Introduction to *Belinda,* by Maria Edgeworth. London: J. M. Dent, 1993.

Nussbaum, Felicity. *Torrid Zones: Maternity, Sexuality, and Empire in Eighteenth-Century English Narratives.* Baltimore: Johns Hopkins University Press, 1995.

Parker, Andrew, Mary Russo, Doris Sommer, and Patricia Yaeger, eds. *Nationalisms and Sexualities.* New York: Routledge, 1991.

Partridge, Eric. *Dictionary of Slang and Unconventional English.* 7th ed. New York: Macmillan, 1984.

Perera, Suvendrini. *Reaches of Empire: The English Novel from Edgeworth to Dickens.* New York: Columbia University Press, 1991.

Polwhele, Richard. "The Unsex'd Females: A Poem, Addressed to the Author of *The Pursuits of Literature.*" London: Cadell and Davies, 1798.

Pratt, Mary Louise. *Imperial Eyes: Travel Writing and Transculturation.* New York: Routledge, 1992.

Rabb, Melinda Alliker. "Making and Rethinking the Canon: General Introduction and the Case of *Millenium Hall.*" *Modern Language Studies* 18, 1 (Winter 1988): 13.

Rizzo, Betty. *Companions without Vows: Relationships between Eighteenth-Century British Women.* Athens: University of Georgia Press, 1994.

Romero, Lora. "Bio-Political Resistance in Domestic Ideology and *Uncle Tom's Cabin.*" *American Literary History* 1, 4 (Winter 1989): 715–734.

Rousseau, G. S. "The Pursuit of Homosexuality in the Eighteenth Century: 'Utterly

Confused Category' and/or Rich Repository?" In Maccubbin, *'Tis Nature's Fault.*

Sabor, Peter. "The Censor Censured: Expurgating *Memoirs of a Woman of Pleasure.*" In Maccubbin, *'Tis Nature's Fault.*

Said, Edward. *Culture and Imperialism.* New York: Knopf, 1993.

Sancho, Ignatius. Ed. Paul Edwards and Polly Rewt. *Letters of Ignatius Sancho.* Edinburgh: Edinburgh University Press, 1994.

*Satan's Harvest Home: Or the Present State of Whorecraft, Adultery, Fornication, Procuring, Pimping, Sodomy, and the Game at Flatts . . . and Other Satanic Works, Daily Propagated in This Good Protestant Kingdom.* London, 1749.

Scott, Sarah. *A Description of Millenium Hall.* Ed. Jane Spencer. 1762. Reprint, New York: Penguin, Virago, 1986.

———. *The History of Sir George Ellison.* Ed. Betty Rizzo. 1766. Reprint, Lexington: University of Kentucky Press, 1996.

Sedgwick, Eve Kosofsky. *Between Men: English Literature and Male Homosocial Desire.* New York: Columbia University Press, 1985.

———. *Epistemology of the Closet.* Berkeley and Los Angeles: University of California Press, 1990.

———. "Epistemology of the Closet I." *Raritan* 7, 4 (Spring 1988): 39.

———. "Jane Austen and the Masturbating Girl." *Critical Inquiry* 17, 4 (Summer 1991).

*Selections from The Anti-Jacobin.* Ed. Lloyd Sanders. London: Methuen, 1904.

Sheridan, Richard. *The Critic* (1771). In *The Plays of Richard Brinsley Sheridan,* ed. Clayton Hamilton. New York: Macmillan, 1926.

Simmons, Philip E. "John Cleland's *Memoirs of a Woman of Pleasure:* Literary Voyeurism and the Technique of Novelistic Transgression." *Eighteenth-Century Fiction* 3, 1 (October 1990): 43–63.

Smith-Rosenberg, Carroll. "The Female World of Love and Ritual: Relations between Women in Nineteenth-Century America." In *The Signs Reader: Women, Gender, and Scholarship,* ed. Elizabeth Abel and Emily K. Abel. Chicago: University of Chicago Press, 1983.

Spacks, Patricia Meyer. "Female Changelessness; or, What Do Women Want?" *Studies in the Novel* 19, 3 (Fall 1987).

Spencer, Jane. Introduction to *A Description of Millenium Hall,* by Sarah Scott. 1762. Reprint, New York: Penguin, Virago, 1986.

———. *The Rise of the Woman Novelist: From Aphra Behn to Jane Austen.* Oxford: Blackwell, 1986.

Stallybrass, Peter, and Allon White. *The Politics and Poetics of Transgression.* Ithaca: Cornell University Press, 1986.

Summers, Claude J., ed. *Homosexuality in Renaissance and Enlightenment England.* New York: Harrington Park, 1992.

Sussman, Charlotte. *Consuming Anxieties.* Stanford: Stanford University Press, 1998.

———. "Women and the Politics of Sugar, 1792," *Representations* 48 (Fall 1994): 48–69.

Tanner, Tony. *Jane Austen*. Cambridge: Harvard University Press, 1986.

Thrale, Hester Lynch. *Thraliana: The Diary of Mrs. Hester Lynch Thrale (Later Mrs. Piozzi), 1776–1809*. 2d ed. Ed. Katherine C. Balderston. Oxford: Clarendon, 1951.

Todd, Janet. *Women's Friendship in Literature: The Eighteenth-Century Novel in England and France*. New York: Columbia University Press, 1980.

Trumbach, Randolph. "London's Sapphists: From Three Sexes to Four Genders in the Making of Modern Culture." In *Body Guards: The Cultural Politics of Gender Ambiguity*, ed. Julia Epstein and Kristina Straub, 112–141. New York: Routledge, 1991.

——. "The Origin and Development of the Modern Lesbian Role in the Western Gender System: Northwestern Europe and the United States, 1750–1994." *Historical Reflections / Réflexions Historiques* 20, 2 (Summer 1994).

Ty, Eleanor. *Unsex'd Revolutionaries: Five Women Novelists of the 1790s*. Toronto: University of Toronto Press, 1993.

Vicinus, Martha. "'They Wonder to Which Sex I Belong': The Historical Roots of the Modern Lesbian Identity." *Feminist Studies* 18, 3 (Fall 1992).

Wagner, Peter. *Eros Revived: Erotica of the Enlightenment in England and America*. London: Secker and Warburg, 1987.

Walters, Keith. Personal communication. 2 September 1994.

Watson, Nicola J. *Revolution and the Form of the British Novel, 1790–1825: Intercepted Letters, Interrupted Seductions*. Oxford: Clarendon, 1994.

Watt, Ian. Introduction to *Jane Austen: A Collection of Critical Essays*, ed. Ian Watt, 1–14. Englewood Cliffs, N.J.: Prentice-Hall, 1963.

——. *The Rise of the Novel: Studies in Defoe, Richardson, and Fielding*. Berkeley: University of California Press, 1957.

Wilson, Edmund. "A Long Talk about Jane Austen." In *Jane Austen: A Collection of Critical Essays*, ed. Ian Watt, 35–40. Englewood Cliffs, N.J.: Prentice-Hall, 1963.

Wollstonecraft, Mary. *Mary, a Fiction and The Wrongs of a Woman; or Maria, a Fragment*. Ed. Gary Kelly. Oxford: Oxford University Press, 1989.

——. *A Vindication of the Rights of Woman*. Ed. Miriam Brody. London: Penguin, 1986.

——. *The Works of Mary Wollstonecraft*. Ed. Janet Todd and Marilyn Butler. London: William Pickering, 1989.

Woodard, Helena. "The Politics of Race and Reason: The Eighteenth Century and the African-British Writer." Unpublished manuscript.

——. "The Production of an African-British Text and the Formation of a Black Literary Discourse in Late Eighteenth-Century England." Ph.D. diss., University of North Carolina, 1992.

Woodward, Carolyn. "'My Heart So Wrapt': Lesbian Disruptions in Eighteenth-Century British Fiction." *Signs* 18, 4 (Summer 1993): 838–865.

Lisa L. Moore is Associate Professor of English at the University of Texas at Austin.

Library of Congress Cataloging-in-Publication Data
Moore, Lisa L.
Dangerous intimacies : toward a sapphic history of the British novel / by Lisa L. Moore.
  p.   cm.
Includes bibliographical references (p.      ) and index.
ISBN 0-8223-2036-3 (alk. paper). — ISBN 0-8223-2049-5 (pbk. : alk. paper)
1. English fiction—18th century—History and criticism. 2. Lesbianism—Great Britain—History—18th century—Historiography. 3. Homosexuality and literature—Great Britain—History—18th century. 4. Homosexuality and literature—Great Britain—History—19th century. 5. Lesbianism—Great Britain—History—19th century—Historiography. 6. Women and literature—Great Britain—History—18th century. 7. Women and literature—Great Britain—History—19th century. 8. English fiction—19th century—History and criticism. 9. Femininity (Psychology) in literature. 10. Identity (Psychology) in literature. 11. Women—Sexual behavior—History. 12. Lesbianism in literature. 13. Lesbians in literature. I. Title.
PR858.L46M66 1997
823'.6093538'086643—dc21                                    97-7609